CONCORDIA
UNIVERSITY

This book is a gift
to the Concordia University Libraries
from

Dr. Burton W. Onstine

Alan Brownjohn

Collected Poems

1952–2006

ENITHARMON PRESS

First published in 2006
by the Enitharmon Press
26B Caversham Road
London NW5 2DU

www.enitharmon.co.uk

Distributed in the UK by
Central Books
99 Wallis Road
London E9 5LN

Distributed in the USA and Canada
by Dufour Editions Inc.
PO Box 7, Chester Springs
PA 19425, USA

ISBN 1 904634 21 4 (hardback)
ISBN 1 904634 54 0 (de luxe slipcased
edition of 55 signed and
numbered copies, each one
containing a handwritten poem
from the collection)

Enitharmon Press gratefully acknowledges the financial support of
Arts Council England, London.

British Library Cataloguing-in-Publication Data.
A catalogue record for this book is available
from the British Library.

Typeset in Caslon by Servis Filmsetting Ltd
and printed in England by
Antony Rowe Ltd

Bibliography

Poetry

Travellers Alone, Heron Press, 1954
The Railings, Digby Press, 1961
The Lions' Mouths, Macmillan, 1967
Sandgrains on a Tray, Macmillan, 1969
Warrior's Career, Macmillan, 1972
A Song of Good Life, Secker and Warburg, 1975
A Night in the Gazebo, Secker and Warburg, 1980
Collected Poems 1952–83, Secker and Warburg, 1983
The Old Flea-Pit, Hutchinson, 1987
Collected Poems 1952–1988, Hutchinson, 1988
The Observation Car, Hutchinson, 1990
In the Cruel Arcade, Sinclair-Stevenson, 1994
The Cat Without E-Mail, Enitharmon Press, 2001
The Men Around Her Bed, Enitharmon Press, 2004
Collected Poems 1952–2006, Enitharmon Press, 2006

Novels

The Way You Tell Them, Secker and Warburg, 1990
The Long Shadows, Dewi Lewis, 1997
A Funny Old Year, Dewi Lewis, 2001
Reading by the Moon (in preparation)

For Children

To Clear the River, Heinemann, 1964; Penguin, 1966
    (as John Berrington)
Brownjohn's Beasts, Macmillan, 1971

Educational

Meet and Write 1, 2 and 3, Hodder and Stoughton, 1985–87

As Editor

First I Say This, Hutchinson, 1969

New Poems 1970–71 (with Seamus Heaney and Jon Stallworthy), Hutchinson, 1971

New Poetry 3 (with Maureen Duffy), Arts Council of Great Britain, 1977

The Gregory Anthology (with K.W. Gransden), Hutchinson, 1990

Criticism

Philip Larkin, Longman, 1975

Translation

Torquato Tasso (from Goethe), Angel Books, 1985

Horace (from Corneille), Angel Books, 1996

Recording

Alan Brownjohn reading from his poems, The Poetry Archive, 2005

Critical Study

Lidia Vianu, *Alan Brownjohn and the Desperado Age*, University of Bucharest, 2003

Contents

1960s

1970s

1980s

1990s

15

2000s

For my family and friends

Introduction

More than forty years ago I was asked by Peter Digby Smith, publisher of my first book-length collection of verse, to describe broadly and briefly what I thought my poems were about. I came up with 'love, politics, culture, time'.

With this third volume of *Collected Poems* appearing now as I reach the age of seventy-five, it's tempting to claim a unity, or at least a consistency, of subject-matter over that many years and in around twelve books. I could go on a bit about those being the enduring themes of my poetry, imply a degree of maturity, serenity and wisdom in the later work, and hope to impress. But I can't do that. It would be a pretence. It would not be true.

Those blurb words of four decades back were more of a manifesto than a description. I wanted to keep to them. But manifestos are habitually distorted, or misapplied, or simply forgotten; and I let them go. With the time and freedom to work with deliberation, and keep what amounted to promises to myself and readers, I might have written poems that stuck to those themes and been different: some poems put together less hastily, other more 'thought-through', or 'fleshed-out'. A few might have been tidier (though I do have a tidying disposition). I haven't been prolific, but certainly everything would have been more slowly produced.

So. As things went, these poems were done in the hours left over from earning a living, and originated not in any organised programme but in an almost daily habit of making observations of things and people (including myself) – then, out of what I recorded, spinning reflections, anecdotes, jokes and moral fantasies, etc., etc. They are the end-products of confused, wild and hopeless drafting on endless sheets of paper and in many large notebooks, each of which has served as a kind of rapid-sketching pad. I have worked somewhat like an artist, scrawling phrases, lines and stanzas in handwriting of all sizes, and decorating the pages with loops and arrows and asterisks and deletions. The 'finished'

19

versions have been transferred to a long succession of typewriters (and latterly one elementary word-processor), then scored over with more emendations until suitable for re-typing – but then perhaps restarted on further notebook pages. The process usually stops when I feel I have knocked a bit of reason into the heads of these drafts, and I have done the best *I* can do with them. At least nothing has been changed after it has appeared in a book, with the exception of a couple of solecisms corrected.

In this *Collected Poems*, as before, a few conceivable excesses and blunders (of youth, or middle-age, or advancing years alike) have been allowed to stand; poets have not always improved their work when revising it later in life. Sometimes the habit of observing and theorising has gone into the production of novels; four have appeared from 1990 onwards, and they display the same preoccupations as the poetry. All of this has been a battle. I am very grateful to readers and critics, and to the two archive collections (but especially to the larger one at Penn State University in the USA) which have acquired books and considerable quantities of working and manuscript material. The big notebooks could present problems for any future scholars; but I sense that researchers, like bibliographers, enjoy their nightmares.

Asking myself what I should say at an international conference of writers on the theme 'I write. Who reads me?' I came up with a notion that the best we can do is write in hope and struggle hard to ensure that there is an atmosphere in which our efforts are published, distributed, and above all *preserved*. In a post-modernist (post-almost anything) world where so many invaluable resources are devoted to cheapening the atmosphere and reducing the dignity of life, respect for great traditions of artistic achievement, and for free creative endeavour in the present, requires to be defended and fostered with increasing determination. Sometimes I think that what I have written, in verse or prose, consists of a series of donations to that particular cause.

1950s

1 *The Animals*

Cutting the different shapes of bush,
He chances suddenly on the animal form:
Each shrub becomes a dog, a cat, a tiger.

Yet he does not stop to think as he crops
That in grief of leaf and branch they lack
The adequate life, that their roots
Bind them too sadly to possessive earth.

So he sleeps as the day declines, does not see
Their shadows yearn and lengthen,
And wistful, stretch in desire to be gone,
Away from the ordered garden, on legs
That cannot carry them, in living game.

And they grow as paradoxes, to be seen
Alive but still, sly, abject, posturing,
On the unmoving lawn – unchanged until
Their outlines fade with the growth of summer's green.

2 *The Train*

The train will come tomorrow year,
The signals clamber into signs,
The gates will open on the track
Where weeds have grown among the lines.

A murmur in the listening air
Besides the heart's emphatic beat
Will rise beyond the junction bridge
Out of the summer's static heat,

And round the distant, anxious bend
Engine and carriages appear.
But on a sultry afternoon
Your waiting hope could turn to fear.

Confronted with achieved desires
You may see nothing more to do
Than shrink from noise and turn away
As every devil thunders through.

3 *Travellers Alone*

Night in the streets we tired of
Hides daylight features in tangible dark,
Seals up, presents as finite, endlessness.
We shall not see the sequel to our journey
That every housetop valley spread for us,
Or suburbs' prospect of our wandering.
We shall forget the arriving trains, bound
For the town's heart from stations not our own.

Night hides it gently, cannot dare
The caught precision of the terraces
Shaped in their light of exposing summer,
Possesses cautious fears that will not trust
The corners to themselves, is guardian now
Of the clear river's dimmed façades,
Soothing with care the sharp path's angle
Into the square another statue marks.

Night is consoling, half-anaesthetic
To the full sense – till we see suddenly
The make of shadows friendly to the touch
Rebuke our confidence, the single lamps
Fade from their source, the windows close
Their watching, yellow eyes; then walls dissolve
Into the dark of any barren night,
Night not our friend, bereaved of human light.

4   *A Garden in Summer*

August is skilful in erasing fear,
And out of the full greenhouse into sunlight
I have now followed mine down the terraces
To find nothing where shore and garden meet.

On a clear sea's day it has no place,
Vanished, or simplified in the slanting light
Or under the mild oaks' shadows that turn
From shade to dusk. No place, that is, until

The absence of dread, pure sense of bondage broken, is itself
The burden feared, the freedom threatened suddenly.
And in a consciousness of joy the fear returns,
Fear that its wholeness must be too complete, its passing

Begin where even now the trees are still,
The air grows cold, a summer's tide drains out,
Horizons approach with the closeness of cloud,
And the slow warm wind through the garden falters, dies.

5   *Fantasy*

Fantasy means a landscape disturbed
By one dissimilar element – a chair
Moved by no hand or reason in your room,
A letter never sent and yet received.

These changes make no sense
In the expected world. There is no adjusting
Them to it – rather the world must change
To fit new features, systems reorganize.

You must now imagine each separate object,
Obvious and logical, set in a different scheme.
Walk backwards in the street, get up at night,
Plant sunflowers in your bedroom, play with bricks,
Until the world is altered, as a lens
That, blurred, comes suddenly clear, shows actual shapes.

And the scene, in the saner, accustomed brain
Sets now for disturbance to begin again.

6   *A Teacher of the Deaf*

(for C.E.)

Her purpose is to mould words for them, wholly
Out of the ordinary sight of things, make meanings
To link and connect with objects, to effect communication.
And from their silent country they stretch out
Their wordless thought to her indicating lips, they grasp
Aspects of movement in her face, and make them
Symbols for things themselves, in their feeling sense.

An object is the easiest. Think of *cat*,
The living animal that is, and moves;
(*Is*, of course, is a difficult word; existence
Is no simple attribute.) Yet, incidentally,
Think can be, surprisingly, quite quickly taught.
Thinking, somehow, can be told, or shown, or mimed –
A hand at the head, an expression, then an action.

But only slowly come the classes of things –
So easily confused with the things themselves.
Three cats will not mean *animal* in kind, but only *cats*.
And numbers, though they grasp them, do not help here;
They do not define, but merely multiply *cat*.
Or adjectives will be mistaken for what they describe:
Black cat seems *cat*, a *heavy* book – just *book*.

Yet these are the foothills of her mountain.
On steeper slopes come *for* and *to* and *the*,
Articles, and prepositions of place. These are confused
With the actions done in teaching them. For example,
I walk to the door: walk and *door* are easily learnt,
But *to* and *the* slip by. Her patient lips
Convey a movement, but no meaning stirs.

Some means must be found and used, by way of signs,
To create the elusive sense of such expressions,
That the climbers might move on from the seen and known, and
Up to the strange, invisible *idea*. She will have to make actions
Seem to possess a meaning beyond the facts
And subtler than the movement. She will have to come
At last to the hardest in the range of word and thought,

The unseen abstract, content of mind alone.
This is an escarpment for her. What is *real? Unreal?*
Or what is *wise?* Or *foolish? Good?* Or *bad?*
But once beyond that, the mountain can be viewed
From its highest point; and her sense can be comprehended.
She has now to begin to point out the extended land,
For they, with this summit reached, can *understand.*

7   *Moles*

Beneath our feet (their silence calm as ours)
The unseen creatures laying waste this land
Wreck all the field we walk on, turning up
Their mounds of sun-bleached earth on every hand.

And yet their limit is the outer road
Which halts their upward progress at the hedge,
And on that lower ground their tunnels cease,
In watery daylight, at the river's edge.

Likewise, I doubt the power of any love
To wreck us further with its burrowing toil;
Now it has worked through our two narrow fields,
It finds no larger acres left to spoil.

Our minor beings are not wide enough
To let great love rear hills on their estate.
Their scope includes the gesture and the sigh,
But not the fire to leave them desolate.

8 *11.30*

If we are still together, it is because
Of the need to weed the garden.

Sustaining and disinterested deeds
(Which you might call love)
Are at a discount, but the house still stands.

Necessity does all this: if we are to eat
We need to wash some plates.

Turn the tap on for me, then (let
The water be hot!)

The hate and the unease will die in time
With the death-rattle of the draining sink.

9 *Scrutiny*

Hard as you scan yourself,
There is something that covers up
The person neglecting work,
The glutton and the bore,
The wholly unsociable half:

Replacing them with all
The qualities you prefer:
To be firm but compassionate,
Intolerant of cant,
Or constructively sceptical.

A self-deception which eases
The pestering shames away
Can be dangerous to have,
Can censor important faults,
Gloss over deserved disgraces

– But is mostly for the best:
What crippling horror would not,
Without it, invade the heart,
What doubt to shake the hand,
What guilt, destroying rest?

10   *By Daytime*

(for K.S.T.)

That one we speak of who would harm the sense
If we lay out in her by night and slept,
Is certainly tamed now; has nothing on
The uncomplicated sun;

Has by day no power
Quite equal to the beam which there
Distinguishes the sharp lake from the trees,
And clearly colours the heather
We do not gather.

She inhabits absentmindedly a sky
Not at all her own, ill-fitted to invoke
Her customary presences, and tides;

Seems almost of not much importance any more,
Though we should be fair
To her drained face,
Should admit that it has not been

A day or a place or a mood to worry out
A just opinion of the moon.

11 *Sin of Omission*

The window somewhere that I did not close,
Far back in the day's large hours,
Stands open still; and now at night
The deep house stirs, the corridors
Cold in the blank draught edging from room to room.
Where was the fault that has so surely let
Chance take its certain vengeance on the lazy;
Made curtains restless, distant doors uneasy?

This mere neglect, by daytime small, achieves
A shaming size by night. I listen
To the night's wind
And worry to decide if gracious sleep
Will intervene among the quartering chimes;
Or if I should get up and search about
And coldly grope to trace it in the dark
(The error I have made so many times)?

12 *Balance*

The ceremonious dispositions of hands
In the hushed air of blessing, in prayer,
In particular moments of love,

Contain the exactest peace. Their calm preserves
A dedicated poise: each holy act
Quietly instinct with deep restraint and tact.

They know they must not falter and betray
What is behind their skill. Their wisdom serves
To hold them back from gestures not in tune.

And so, for a short time, they do not tumble
Down from the ceremonious to the true:
They hover still; just manage not to show

That blessing very often condescends,
And prayer pleads up from self-wrought misery,
And love's hands can reach after loveless ends.

13   *Facing Outwards*

A garden pillar, where a grey stone lion
Stares with intended anger, always forward
Down between two plain lines of sheltering trees;
This I look at, and walk towards it now,
Some family symbol, cracked with rain and age
And tame through summer's branches; keeping but
A small part of the thing it stood to mark,
The mere pretence to a resounding rage.

Sometimes, indeed, the setting helps it out.
The winter sky has seagulls, vagrant-white,
Wheeling and crying over the bare trees.
And then the lion, on snow-lit afternoons,
Gains enough boldness just to look like some
Real beast perhaps, whose tawny dust has long
Vanished, like all the statue's dignity,
Blown about air down which the snow has come.

But most new seasons crown that head and trunk
With abject harmlessness; memorial to
A long-departed power, once making clear
The anger shown to strangers, and the pride;
Suddenly bringing back the period when
The vice inside them could not be made known
Except in terms of fearsome statuary,
Where it seemed virtuous in indignant stone.

14 *Bad Advice*

The path trodden most goes confidently near
To the edge of the cliff; not even tufts of grass
Define a nominal boundary between
This hard mud track (for the easy walkers'
Steady shoes) and the drop.

Safely, some yards away, roams indistinctly
Another path: for the fearful and the cautious,
Running inside a fence put up for sheep.
Longer, but wiser, to go by this,
Though it gives no particular view of the sea.

If it has come to choosing here, then
Caution seems best. But look again, its path
Tangles through hedges and pools, and stops for stiles,
And nothing feels better now than the way
Which follows the dizzying parapet.

Walk that path. Surely no hurling gusts
Of today's bleak wind could unbalance you; no jut
Of risky earth would loosen to betray
Such daring feet; and haven't you nearly
Lost your old fear of heights?

15 *For a Journey*

House Field, Top Field, Oak Field, Third Field:
Though maps conclude their duties, the names trek on
Unseen across every county. Farmers call hillocks
And ponds and streams and lanes and rocks
By the first words to hand; a heavy, whittled-down
Simplicity meets the need, enough to help say
Where has yielded best, or the way they walked from home.

You can travel safely over land so named –
Where there is nowhere that could not somewhere
Be found in a memory which knows, and loves.
So watch then, all the more carefully, for
The point where the pattern ends: where mountains, even,
And swamps and forests and gaping bays acquire
The air of not needing ever to be spoken of.

Who knows what could become of you where
No one has understood the place with names?

16   *Lads*

At the next station climbed in
The Volunteers: 'Housman's Pride',
As the regiment might be called,
So full of 'love' and 'death',
Clean bombs and dirty songs.

The Old Irresponsibles,
With only themselves to keep
In cigarettes, drink and girls,
They scatter the silver paper
And bite the chocolate whole;

Then, shiftlessly sprawled and laughing,
In the uniform which makes
Them a no-man's-land between
Our peace and an actual war
They settle back to sleep.

17   *A Day at Work*

And through the parted curtains these grey cats
Came suddenly to sight. Turning their way,
He watched them while they roamed the floor between,
Then called some word or two, and made to rise;
But they had heard, and ran to meet this voice
With heads inclined and dim, obedient eyes.
Where he leant down they curled about his sleeve,
And still the storm howled on about the house;
Chilled with its lightning rooms where months of dust
Stood on the shelves, found the sure crack
Where hail could enter.
                                    And his forgotten book
Lay open on the grass for rain to glance
Over each flurried page the wind blew back.

18   *Red Ink Bubble*

I watched the duration of the bubble.
Through seconds of my time it lived
Light-years of its own,
With the same reflected room on its luminous globe,
And down inside, a minute crimson world,
Intricately formed; as if to demonstrate how
The beautiful can sometimes be accidental.

Shaken into being from an obstinate pen,
It fell between the torn edge and the words
And stayed on the page (while I continued to write)
Unmoved by earthquakes of fingers and storms of breath;
A tiny dome, remaining propped above
Its floor of paper, stained with a dimmer red,
Until at last some unseen pressure broke

Glass wall, and wry, distended images,
And flattened the surface out.
It was as if it were wanting to repeat
That something will always weigh down upon beauty
Haphazardly built, that attempts to stand without
Foundations laid with thought for what they bear:
Beauty without effect except to mirror

Its creator for a time, then vanish, leaving
Scent or stain, only, of what had been there.

19 *Marginalia*

When it was Munich, I was eight.
Miss Adams made her point like this:
'Without a ruler, no one can
Draw me a line that's truly straight.'
And thus, to make her meaning plain:
'Not even any famous man:
Herr Hitler. Mr Chamberlain.'

And through the years, one might infer,
Miss Adams used such other names
As fitted best the days she came
To teach this truth, beloved of her:
'Not even Mr Stalin, and
Sir Winston Churchill, he's the same,
Could draw me one straight line freehand.'

And I should think that through that door,
In one of those brown passages,
I might still find her echoing room
Somewhere along the lower floor;
And hear again that doctrine taught,
To forty different minds for whom
It would seem just as strange a thought.

'No one who thinks that he can draw
Straight lines without a ruler, will
Ever surprise me if he fails –
What do you think your ruler's *for*?
There isn't anyone at all
Could do it. Not the Prince of Wales!
Not even General de Gaulle!'

20   *Snow in Bromley*

As of some unproved right, the snow
Settles the outer suburbs now,
Laying its claim unhurriedly
On gnome and monkey-puzzle-tree.

Observe its power to shape and build,
Even in this unfruitful world,
Its white informal fantasies,
From roofs and paths and rockeries.

And swayed by such soft moods, I fall
Into forgiving nearly all
The aspirations of the place,
And what it does to save its face:

The calm and dutiful obsession
With what is 'best in our position',
The loyal and realistic views,
The rush-hours with the *Evening News* –

The snow fulfils its pure design
And softens every ugly line,
And for a while will exorcize
These virulent proprieties.

Within one mile of here there is
No lovelier place to walk than this,
On days when these kind flakes decide
That what it boasts of, they shall hide.

21 *If Time's to Work*

Because there is somebody washing below,
This tap rasps in its throat. I say again,
I should not really let my hands expect
Water at any time; yet despair must show
If this unnerving guttural cough has wrecked
My strenuous answer to the morning's rain.

The week has stopped at one cold point of day
By the empty bowl; the mirror holds and keeps,
For longer than it should, its uncombed image;
The razor which I hold must shave away
More parts of night; but at this arid stage,
Night seems to have returned, all action sleeps.

And time, it seems to me, now that I wait
Leaning in one white corner, crouched and still,
Means merely, What contains activity:
Those areas of waking which create
The sense of moving, doing, constantly,
However small the purpose they fulfil.

One unexpected pause in this will cheat
Time of such meaning as it can convey:
Minutes, deprived of their brief purposes,
Pass vacantly, no sign to indicate
You lived in every one of them: there is
No kind of time which these blank wastes obey.

If time's to work, it needs the tap to run,
And with its failure had this thought arrived:
In death, too, there may be no more than this,
No certain state of being lost or won
For world or silence – just some endless pause,
And into it, no message dropped to say,

Move to the next brief act which must be lived.

22   *Inheritance*

At seven in the damp light of morning I awoke
Uncomfortably into the room; to find
The windows then already steamed with heat.

A hand to the glass, I knew, would reveal at least
My nearest acres; and besides, that act
Would pass for something done, as surely as

Pens dipped in ink have nearly written words.
I would therefore wipe a gazing-space, a view,
As the day's beginning, token of tasks to come.

But with that gesture came a thing unguessed
In last night's darkness: quick, habitual weeds
Clustering every path, the trees deformed

By blight, or axes, and the fences left to fall.
I did not think this thrusting mockery
Would start so soon; yet knew I now must ask

How plan wide reason for this wide estate
With such needs close at hand? How think of miles
When each near yard fed such huge enemies?

23 'In this city . . .'

In this city, perhaps a street.
In this street, perhaps a house.
In this house, perhaps a room
And in this room a woman sitting,
Sitting in the darkness, sitting and crying
For someone who has just gone through the door
And who has just switched off the light
Forgetting she was there.

24 'We are going to see the rabbit . . .'

We are going to see the rabbit,
We are going to see the rabbit.
Which rabbit, people say?
Which rabbit, ask the children?
Which rabbit?
The only rabbit,
The only rabbit in England,
Sitting behind a barbed-wire fence
Under the floodlights, neon lights,
Sodium lights,
Nibbling grass
On the only patch of grass
In England, in England
(Except the grass by the hoardings
Which doesn't count.)
We are going to see the rabbit
And we must be there on time.

First we shall go by escalator,
Then we shall go by underground,
And then we shall go by motorway
And then by helicopterway,
And the last ten yards we shall have to go
On foot.

And now we are going
All the way to see the rabbit,
We are nearly there,
We are longing to see it,
And so is the crowd
Which is here in thousands
With mounted policemen
And big loudspeakers
And bands and banners,
And everyone has come a long way.

But soon we shall see it
Sitting and nibbling
The blades of grass
On the only patch of grass
In – but something has gone wrong!
Why is everyone so angry,
Why is everyone jostling
And slanging and complaining?

The rabbit has gone,
Yes, the rabbit has gone.
He has actually burrowed down into the earth
And made himself a warren, under the earth,
Despite all these people.
And what shall we do?
What *can* we do?

It is all a pity, you must be disappointed,
Go home and do something else for today,
Go home again, go home for today.
For you cannot hear the rabbit, under the earth,
Remarking rather sadly to himself, by himself,
As he rests in his warren, under the earth:
'It won't be long, they are bound to come,
They are bound to come and find me, even here.'

25   *William Empson at Aldermaston*

This is our dead sea, once a guidebook heath.
Left and right hands worked busily together
A parliament or two,
And there she stands:

Twelve miles of cooling pipes; concrete and secret
Warrens underground; clean little towers
Clamped with strong ladders; red, brisk vans
Which hurry round

The wide, kerbed avenues with pulsing lights
To signify danger; and all this
Extending still its miles, as seas possessed
Of power or anger

Will – except that here
The tide decrees, with threats in yellow paint,
Its own unquestioned bounds, keeps dogs to catch
Someone who gets

Beyond the fence: it seems that otherwise
We shiver from an unclean nakedness,
And need to clothe our hot emotions cold
With wire, and curs.

But let there be some praise, where that is due:
For paint, of enlivening colours, spent
On all these deathly offices. Where typists sit,
Who do not make the thing,

Or scientists, who do not fire the thing,
Or workers, who obey the scientists,
The rooms are beautiful. And anyone
Who passed by car one day

Not knowing what it was would never guess.
(Perhaps some urgent public undertaking
Set up for health, or water? Or a camp
Where other people went

On holidays?) Such airs of carnival,
With death designed as smiling, to conceal
His proper features – these things justified
Replies in kind:

An absurd fête of life, in one Friday field
For which no pass was needed. The effect:
Two sorts of carnival clashing: on this side
The mud, or grass,

The boots and stoves and caravans; that side,
The trim, discreet pavilions of the State.
And one more contrast marked these gaieties:
This side there seemed

Some thousands, while of death's there wasn't one.
Just the white-braided police returned the stare
Of the boys with haversacks, or the fierce
Empirical gaze

Of the man with the Chinese beard, or the pondering glance
Of the woman with the basket on wheels.
And some thought death's precise executives
Had told or asked

The servants of his will to stay away,
Hinting of jobs they might not like to lose,
And they had houses . . . from whose windows, next,
Many faces looked the way

Of the procession; speaking not a word,
But merely watching. How else, then, explain
If this was not the reason, why their children,
Through all the bands and singing,

All the beards and the guitars, did not come out;
But stood behind held curtains, listlessly,
With tight and puzzled faces, or peered through
Some furtive upstairs sunblind

While it passed? No coloured hat, not one
In all the range of shirts and slogans worn,
Seemed odder than these faces. That deep blankness
Was the real thing strange.

26   *The Monumental Mason*

Except there are no graves or flowers,
He has made a miniature cemetery of his garden,
To advertise his stones. And every name

Hammered in granite in that tidy script
Is a scrupulous fiction: nobody I knew
Lived here with such a name; or ever, with it,

Married this wife he left so young and soon.
The first shock passing, which this skill
Appalled my eyes with, I walk on relieved,

Can almost smile. Yet the words presume a power
To be remembered longer than the names
Of strangers, read in passing, on real graves

At actual funerals. Immortal in
Their lack of true existence, they stand here
On public show to draw our fear, or trade;

And this way, they shall live for evermore.

1960s

27 *The Railings*

Once there would have been the woman standing
Between the trees behind the dancing railings as he walked,
But that is not now so.

And once there would have been
A hope of the woman, a figment of the branches
As they shifted with the light –
That might have been, that might have been,
But neither is this any longer true.

Not even now is the hope what it was,
And will not regain the face:
Two years, three years, the walk could go
While only the principle of the woman

Faintly remained. And that would scarcely be enough.
The principle will drain from out a place.
The hope will have to go to other things.

28 *Retirement*

The middle-afternoon is the worst of the blanks.
Shuffle the four equal armies of the contentious cards
And manoeuvre those. Or failing that, indict for yourself
In a never-to-be-written recollection, your successful
Colleague of some brisk campaign. The minor consolations
Of the manageable evening arrive the faster
For either, or both, of these applications of power.

29 *Path to the Observatory*

Cramped in parentheses and double negatives,
The hesitant, in others, most respect
Whatever goes most squarely to the point,
And tries to gain much by confronting much.

For the permanent grief of time, they might admire
This uncompromising answer, given
By a path going straight across the park
To this famous hub of time:

Hardly nervous, never flinching the effects
Of its bold-faced approach (as dubious lovers might).
But challenging time it goes; and chides
The uneven grass nearby, and the ragged trees.

30 *Interlude*

The extended knee, not covered and perhaps
Two feet away across the garden grass
Is as grained and natural as a hand;
Could even be, as a hand is, touched
Without self-consciousness or much design
In a ceremonious gesture, if such existed.
To such size is the thing brought down
By her informal proximity, poised between
That distance and that closeness which both start
Lust. And the urge of talk
Which yesterday broke out in an unwise heat
And tomorrow may impede itself in the throat,
Can be temperate, easily. The sun is out.
An insect travels the pattern of her dress.
The afternoon is calm, with Latin words.

31 *Go Away*

I have come about the ground, is this your ground?
– Go away, I want to kneel by myself
On this first dry patch of the year, and prepare the soil.

That's a right occupation, but my purpose is to warn you
About the ground – Look, a person like me
Has no time to talk. I've only one evening for the garden.

But please, I think your ground may not be safe!
– Yes, but don't come and bother me now. I have bulbs
Which I want to settle in; and there are pebbles to sift out.

Listen, someone is deliberately undermining your garden
– You are worse than the weeds and the greenfly. Go away.
When shall I get these narcissi planted?

But even if you plant them they won't grow. They won't have
Any time to sprout or flower.
– But I've always grown flowers here. Why say things like that?

Because the ground is undermined, they are going
To blow it up. – What you're saying is ridiculous.
I trust them, I know they would never do such a thing.

Then who are those men bending down at the edge of the garden,
What is this spreading tremor of the ground
That snatches the spade from your hand?

What is wrenching the saplings up? – Why expect me to know?
I suppose they must know what they are doing.
I suppose it's for the best. Why don't you go away!

Perhaps the daring made it
Seem all right. Or
The memory of the daring.
At the time, there were
The midges, was the fidgeting
Of bottles in someone's
Crates; all the mere
Ungainliness of limbs:
There was the wanting
To get it done and over,
And to resume a proper,
Acceptable posture.
Only much afterwards, was there
The having done, was there
That person (think of it),
And that place; all the daring
Shame of it. Only afterwards,
That. There was, really,
Nothing at all of this,
Nothing at all, at the time.

33   *1939*

Where the ball ran into the bushes,
And I was sent to find it, being
Useful for that more than to play their game,
I saw instead
This badge, from someone's brother, in
Some regiment of that war: a trophy
Begged for and polished, coveted certainly,
But lost now, slightly touched with dust already,
Yet shining still, under smooth leaves drab with dust.

I knew that people prized such trophies then,
It was the way of all of us. I might,
For no one looked, have taken it
For mine. I valued it. It shone
For me as much as anyone.
And yet some fear or honesty, some sense
It wasn't to be mine – it wasn't more –
Said No to all of this. Besides,
They shouted in the distance for their ball.
For once quite quickly, I
Made up my mind
And left the thing behind.

34 *Farmer's Point of View*

I own certain acre-scraps of woodland, scattered
On undulating ground; enough to lie hidden in. So,

About three times a year, and usually August,
Pairs of people come to one or another patch. They stray

Around the edges first, plainly wanting some excuse
To go on in; then talking, as if not concerned,

And always of something else, not what they intend,
They find their way, by one or another approach,

To conducting sexual liaisons – on *my* land.
I've tried to be careful. I haven't mentioned 'love'

Or any idea of passion or consummation;
And I won't call them 'lovers' because I can't say

If they come from affection, or lust, or blackmail,
Or if what they do has any particular point

For either or both (and who can say what 'love' means?)
So what am I saying? I'd like to see people pondering

What unalterable acts they might be committing
When they step down, full of plans, from their trains or cars.

I am not just recording their tragic, or comic, emotions,
Or even the subtler hazards of owning land –

I am honestly concerned. I want to say, politely,
That I worry when I think what they're about:

I want them to explain themselves before they use my woods.

35 *No Good*

It is no good if any man dreams
Her love is attainable by schemes:
No one can win these modern wars,
Why squander tactics on this sort of cause?

It is no good if one decides
Love can be bought, extravagance provides:
She will be right to stay unmoved,
Those won those ways may end unloved.

It is no good if, slyly, one defends
Courses her other lover recommends:
Guile with her is out of place,
She can read any hidden face.

It is no good in the rare state
Of abused purity, the discarnate:
She will think stories, and surmise;
Agree, with pity in her eyes.

It is no good pretending your
Passion is an unbreakable law:
She may obey it! You'll be spent
In some obscene predicament.

It is no good any way one takes,
The sin is travel if roads are mistakes,
The plague is feet if it's no good proceeding:
I do not think this is too misleading.

36   *Diana and the Transmitter*

Being below it, well!
There are no words at first.
There is nothing quite like
This bloody great steel tower,

Which won't be a toy,
Or any brick, sensible thing,
But coerces the feeble eye
Up hair-thin ladders

To nominal platforms, thrown
From windy leg to leg
– Where it leaves it, hurt and scared,
To acquire a disturbing thought:

If by any crude, romantic
Ruse of some enemy
I had either to climb that stair
Or never see her again

– To climb to the spiked top,
Or even some lower stage
(And I dread this so much
It's almost probable!) –

I know that I couldn't climb,
Not even for that sake;
And I am so humbled by
Those with heads for heights

Or knowledge of engineering, that
I refuge in defiance,
And uncomfortably strike some right
Attitudes, out of fear; like these:

I rebuke the brisk graduates
Working for this tower
(Reforming, transforming
The medium from inside!)

I reject the proponents of better
Advertising art (those makers
Of terylene haloes for whores)
And the conscience-salvers with Granada.

I will not take the excuses
Of the inexcusables who
Make the animal voices
For cartoons; for whom

This tranquillizing monument
Seems particularly built. And
I question the final moral right
Of this meccano phallus

To landscape, anyway, here.
I'd ask this of Collins,
Orr Stanley, Simms; and would have
Their answers less than smooth.

And look: this is nearly making up
For any earlier lack, out
Of weakness, of any proved love
– If, as I think, these curses

Are gesturing to defend (for want
Of any daring will of mine
To try to climb the thing) her
Every facet of virginity.

37   *Yesterday's Fire*

One lifting tatter of black, burnt paper
Soared up, and stayed, like a raven watching,
On a tree's limb. But I am not deterred
By would-be omens.
      A hand quite over
A hand, but quietly, is the only start,
And to part her fingers wrong. Properly so
I placed my left hand then.
        You must be sure
You don't impose some will that gentleness,
Not wanting to offend, might not resist.
I said, I said this carefully,
        'You may withdraw
Your hand mine holds on if you really wish.'
Just then, a brash wind switching the drifting
Of the smoke our way, we both at once
         Jumped back,
Hands kept together; and she did not quite
Disengage till the thing I said
Could be fully taken in. But she understood.
         'You must take back

The hand yourself. I do not want to give
You back discourtesies.' And nicely smiled,
'Make it your will – please not my petulance.'

                                        And as I brought
My hand away, I glanced into the tree,
Where, as I looked, I saw that tatter fall,
Which may have made an omen after all.

38 *Matutinal*

Strong sleep alone in the house makes all the difference.
It must be a good dull day, though: and no birdsong.
Then sleep enough will set most issues right.

So will the indulgent water of the bath,
Where I lie next, ten reassuring minutes. This
Can render any problem easy, and

I often take a pad in, for jotting solutions,
Putting it with the soap and the torn sponge
On the bath edge; it might be useful.

So it's ten-thirty, and everything is easy
– But now a brash sunlight points out patterns
Of undying dust in air to think about,

Or takes up the steam from the surface of the water
Like rising, drifting smoke. And secondly,
The telephone is arrogantly ringing. There is

Time just for the towel, and to leap downstairs
Past the impending shadow of someone
About to knock at the locked and bolted door.

I have snatched off the receiver of the phone, yet
The thing keeps somehow ringing and ringing.
A fault on the line somewhere? As if I would know!

My sleep was worthless: the caller fidgets and coughs
On the step outside; the phone rings on; the black
Receiver slithers on my sweating ear.

39 *Apology for Blasphemy*

I can formulate two
Excuses in mitigation:
First, blasphemy surely admits
Some firm, good name:

Only the loved names can
Incite to abuse and treasons:
You cannot blaspheme over what
You must despise.

Second it was, of course,
A trick, in assistance of love,
And no truth. This is the plain fact.
To please a spy,

Huge factories are built
With shuddering walls of dark steel
– Shells of deception, all a lie.
My words did that.

Let an amending tongue
Now penitently cast for means
To rebegin flattery, since
I shrink in fear

Of how I have blasphemed
If nothing can be seen to crack
These literal words; unmake
What they imply.

It is with metaphor
We can assuage, abolish and
Create. I will apologize
With metaphors:

Listen: you could not know,
But when the snow dashed your face, it made
Patterns on white, violent glass, stone-
Scattered; and as

Your mouth just opened, now,
In a slight surprise, all the lions'
Mouths on the bronze financial doors
Dropped their gripped rings.

40   *Sunsets*

Suddenly caught by how it seems
Possible and quite credible that,
In this last windless minute at

Sunset, that downspread of fields I watch
(Gazing past, from this vantage hill,
Just visible cows to the town) will

Have darkened a little – even though
You can't measure this, and it may be
Your eyes don't tell it truthfully –

I sense a comparison with
Some points in the progress of love:
Times when each element *has* to move

At just the stage when you would want
It at rest – when, dispassionate
-ly, you would want to define and state

To yourself just where you stand. It may
Be a simple error to believe
That love runs on like that, you can deceive

Yourself quite easily. But
So often love seems to be set
On rushing you past anywhere you get

A chance to arrest it, and talk.
And in this, as with nightfall, you sense
That you cannot make much pretence

Of defying any darkness.
It leaves you no other choice.
It happens in front of your eyes.

41   *By Paul's Kitchen Clock*

He trembles, now, at his spyholes of jealousy. How
Appalling his guessing is! Not even a frost night
And white, hard grass such that their body-spaces would show
As hot, cleared blanks on the indifferent ground where they lay
– This would not have kept them back.
So, knowing what door they must surely re-enter by,
He waits to snatch on any audible step, guessing
Signs on her of hand-marks, in her freed and shaken-hair,
And stands ready to be unable to overhear
Words whose meaning he will watch

On their lips, which smile them out; storing for just himself
All of these facts – as politicians learn to cherish
Each act of slander, planning their rivals' overset
With a decayed, set calmness, like the moon's.

42   *The Wall*

Sunlight goes on making
And making its reappearances on that stained wall
Without alteration. It's getting
More elderly, I would say; goes a mellower course
Over chair-dent and sweat-mark,
Moving a window-square which seems
Not so clear now at the edges. To have
Sat once among such motes and specks
Was to be glad to see dust made quick
By illumination, interruption by liveness.
This dust now is literal dust, shown up
By this changed also sun as wandering in air
As thinking wanders in the aged – with
An unkind pleasantness. Such sun
Used not to calm me near to sleep like this.

43   *Eight Investigations*

a junction

Not to meet, then. But can't we maintain
One concessionary contact: of
Some meeting in theory – for instance,
Making an agreement to retain
A *kind* of connection by a glance
Each day at some same landmark? Or have

An intersection of routes planned out
On journeys we are often making?
This could be a place where we again
– At quite different times! – could no doubt
'Meet'; (I would cross it like a night train
Crossing points – rapid, darkened, trembling.)

Sprogo (in the Great Belt)

In that sea-stretch, one minor island,
It makes a misty scrap of jutting
Land from wide water. A calmer green
Covers, though, all but one nearly hand-
Wise gesture of cliff, where can be seen
A caged, rusted lantern, cautioning.

You could be compared with any slim,
Chill, passing thing, at will. Yet, the same,
Let me let this dwindling seamark make
Another image: as, on a whim,
Such a quick distant shape could quite take
The diminuendo of your name.

her drawing

No, this Snow Queen (or Cordelia)
Lies drawn, for you, quite differently;
Is merely some unthinking release
Of a moment's work. Still, I see her
As a projection from your own face,
And think: not knowing, you let her be

Like some taller screen image of your
Own contained precision (thus that high
Glance, your own, muting the hands' gestures).
But as she is yours, I must feel
She is truth itself, all such features
Thrown that large by some flattering eye.

second drawing

A kind of swirl of bracken where curve,
Though static, somewhat ambiguous
Symbols, as if grown part of that ground
Of black-stressed, intricate roots (these leave
The surface at no point, but twist round
And upwards into the dubious

Branches of the plant, form letters, signs
Which could mean your name: such as now bring
My mind quite out, away from this sheet,
Elsewhere in time; past these pencilled lines
To their sudden, living start: your neat
Intent smile, your tensed fingers moving).

concession

Privileged now to see you, tell me
(Because I can't know whether I stare
On some frank, actual thing, that skin
Utterly real, or if I yet see
Only a surface which locks me in
With protective, invisible care

As when one looks out at things through glass)
– Are you like somewhere known with plain sight,
Just as clear as you seem? Or do you
Screen off real knowledge, so letting pass
Everything but the quickest key to
That country of air, your clean daylight?

distance

Invent two rings of falling light; wide
For you in the south and the sun's rage,
But not my light – obliged on a neat
Metal table surface to refer
Only to the black words on this sheet:
Chilled, northern light, bronze-shaded. One page

Written already, lies just outside,
In the fawn dusk of the table-edge,
A failure. Still; I can't stop. Be sure
A thousand mere dark miles won't divide
Fact from longing, break down this posture
Of vain love to a better knowledge.

cliffs

Merely thinking up your name in this
Hazardous high strip and ledge in air
Works a consolation: simply that,
Repeating you, any daring is
Practically possible – leant flat
On this shuddering wall, I can stare

Down on the mapped rocks, or out to sea
Unfrightened. Yet in some safe room to
Hear those syllables. . . . The difference
Scares and drowns out all talking for me.
There is no quick courage helps with this
Unexpected way of meeting you.

epistemology

My same eyes once jumped through the page-long
Paragraphs, flickering over such
Banks of abstract words! A *physical*
Power those words had, that caught the strong
Breath of the mind away. The real
Equivalent, now, is your face. Much

That same way your eyes glance this as mine
Glanced; which now face to your forehead's small
Shades and meanings, seek to sublime this
Craving in verbal charts, and refine
Its enigma in a healing verse:
Neurotic; and metaphysical.

44   *The Preservation*

It's quite worth keeping your surprise at the untrodden
Snow on the long step that particular winter night
– As if we had been indoors for days –

As in that time your every movement told,
And looked responsible. Never had your feet
Set out their marks on things with such grave care,

Or honour of any place. And all the mocking
Extensions to words in your hands' actions
Drained right away, or were absolved

In one cupped, simple gesture, collecting
(To taste and to smile) some snow in a quick mild heap
From the near top of the street wall.

45   *Incident in Milan*

They are going about it now
In such silence; yes,
In the garden even:
Bringing to its end
By mutual disagreement
Their long, long liaison
– The line-clothed girl
And the Italian, Maurielli.

Such a long drag of
Time were they united,
By their only difference:
Of sex; in all else
Being the same, two
Mere stones of dullness,
Solidly grating
Surfaces in talk, talk.

She would elbow
Past him in the kitchen,
And resent the obtruding
Angle of his chair;
She might push his hair
Accidentally out of
The neatness he once
Contrived for her

And then, from habit, kept (he
Hating her, truly,
For that, and glaring
Back to her trim food
– Insulting in the
Gourmet's care with which
She set it out, between . . .)
The violences of

These inarticulates,
Their moments of hounding truth,
Have no Method dignity,
Really. Are more like
Abandoned sandflats where
No one lives, or ploughs.
Close your own shutters. Read
Or sleep. Let them alone.

46   *God's Creatures*

We all hate the sturdy nobility
Of the horse, we mock at it in cartoons
And carnivals. Such set, single-minded
Devotion we parody most with the
Two halves of the pantomime animal,
At odds which way to lurch.
                    Somewhere I once
Saw a pseudo-horse climb up to the high
Diving board at a big swimming gala,
Hesitate on the edge, unfunnily,
Then slough off to become two boring frogs
Which grossly flopped through the chlorinated
Air into the water while we watched,
And indulged in human play at the deep end.

47   *Warm People*

Where complete light is so
narrow it lasts – for six
weeks – all the twenty-four
hours, it's obvious that
window ledges should fill
with tentacle creepers,
or freak geraniums

should front the Arctic with
some days' brash petals. . . .
                              But
I would need it explained
why, where eight months of
the fecund calendar
flowers crowd the out-of-doors,
people still nurse blooms for
their cramped houses, lodge them
in pots and boxes round
every piled room (while
leaves cram the windows up
outside.) Is there a point
in their insistence on
this claustrophobia
of growth?
              It wouldn't be
their claim to one success?

48   *A Hairdresser's*

Something I remember from six is
Waiting for mother to dry, sat with
Home Chat and knitting books to read while
The warm cage glowed round her settled hair.

That was in a corner up in a
Room above the Gentlemen's Saloon,
Out of the way. But they *exhibit*
Them now, as here, turning magazines

Under the gesturing fingers of
Their talkative priestesses. Tall glass
In the High Street, florid with pot-plants,
Sets the new style: Huge, groomed photographs

And offers of 'Life restored'. It's a
'Fine art', you couldn't relate it to
Any usefulness; in this, having
Less of a function, even, than some

Oildom's backscratcher, following his
Chevrolet to the gaming tables
In a Super Snipe. I wish to feel
My complaint is better than a mere

Chafing memory of a child's hours
Waiting and waiting; it sees the point
With a cool rationality; it has
The courage to reject some things. . . .

But – 'If they want to', drones out some
Fool-libertarian voice, 'let them. Why
Shouldn't they do as they like?' (You
Have heard – or maybe used – that very tone!)

Passing in High Street rain, I repeat
My glance at that window and its line
Of faces locked in hives. No. I can't
Wish I were as liberal as that.

49   *Common Sense*

An agricultural labourer, who has
A wife and four children, receives 20*s* a week.
3/4 buys food, and the members of the family
Have three meals a day.
How much is that per person per meal?
                    – *From Pitman's Common Sense Arithmetic, 1917*

A gardener, paid 24s a week, is
Fined 1/3 if he comes to work late.
At the end of 26 weeks, he receives
£30.5.3. How
Often was he late?

– From Pitman's Common Sense Arithmetic, 1917

A milk dealer buys milk at 3*d* a quart. He
Dilutes it with 3% water and sells
124 gallons of the mixture at
4*d* per quart. How much of his profit is made by
Adulterating the milk?

– From Pitman's Common Sense Arithmetic, 1917

The table printed below gives the number
Of paupers in the United Kingdom, and
The total cost of poor relief.
Find the average number
Of paupers per ten thousand people.

– From Pitman's Common Sense Arithmetic, 1917

An army had to march to the relief of
A besieged town, 500 miles away, which
Had telegraphed that it could hold out for 18 days.
The army made forced marches at the rate of 18
Miles a day. Would it be there in time?

– From Pitman's Common Sense Arithmetic, 1917

Out of an army of 28,000 men,
15% were
Killed, 25% were
Wounded. Calculate
How many men there were left to fight.

– From Pitman's Common Sense Arithmetic, 1917

These sums are offered to
That host of young people in our Elementary Schools, who
Are so ardently desirous of setting
Foot upon the first rung of the
Educational ladder . . .

– From Pitman's Common Sense Arithmetic, 1917

50   *Class Incident from Graves*

Wednesdays were guest night in the mess, when the colonel
expected the married officers, who usually dined at home, to attend.
The band played Gilbert and Sullivan music behind a curtain. . . .
Afterwards the bandmaster was invited to the senior officers' table
for his complimentary glass of Light or Vintage.

(Good-bye to All That)

At the officers' table, for half an hour afterwards, port,
The bandmaster. He accepts, one drink long,
All the courtesy of the gentlemen. They are suave, and equal.
'I expect with your job . . . Do you find . . . Oh well . . .'
The bandmaster edges the shining inch of port along the grain
    of the table,
Precisely covering one knot with the transparent
Base of the glass. He crouches forward over the polished wood
Towards the officers, not comfortably convivial,
Eyes always going to the face speaking next,
Deferential, very pleased.
The band put away their instruments out at the back, having
Drunk their beers, standing.
The detachable pieces of brass lie down
In the felt grooves of the cases, just as they should.
Nine-thirty strikes.
There is laughter of men together, coming from inside.
'Mitchell's still in there, hob-nobbing with the officers.'

51 *A Sunday Breakdown*

Crossing the coarse pebbles with scrupulous tread, in
His Gracechurch Street clothes, poor Ludbrook
Goes out on that long jutting wall to the end point
– Where, evilly foamless and smooth, the sea
Lurches over it – and sits down with his *Times*
Where it's three inches deep, and puts his umbrella up

And waits (reading the Court Circular and Birthdays Today)
For the police, or the lifeboatmen, or the Civil Defence
To be the first to come and argue that what
He does is irrational or dangerous,
And would he stop because he ceases to amuse,
And he is driving away the custom from the place.

52 *Trio*

He has now gone with the toy gun into the greengrocer's shop
And is using some mock ploy with the greengrocer's girl.
She is cramped up, uncomfortably half-sat on the long ledge
Of the frozen food Cool Cabinet. She looks
A suitable imitation of absolute fright, she raises
Her hands and gives a visible but inaudible shout
– The traffic is so loud – as he gestures with the Xmas gun
Towards the celery or the till. She is a tall excitable
Girl of the kind wearing tinted, attenuated glasses
And patchy coloured nails. He is a thick, blunt, overcoated
Wedge of a middle-class man with several parcels,
Including the toy gun. Now suddenly the proprietor, in a green
    coat,
Comes out of the store at the back and throws a horrified stare,
And shrinks himself, trembling, against the potatoes
In their brown, stolid banks. The man with the wooden red gun
Speaks, you can see, but you can't hear anything he says,
And all of them are standing in these postures still,

As they might be if the gorgon glance of a photographer
Had taken them all in flagrant tableau to present to the future:
On Xmas Eve, behind the green leaves and pink paper
Of the lighted trade window of 'Mackin's Best Fruit', between
Frozen plaice fillets and South African oranges.

53 *The Lost Surprise*

Your dog I hate strains from you and would run.
A dead-leaf dust confirms the arid grass.
My eyes, faint from newsprint, watch some odd man
Prowl round and round in a feigned casualness
– Voyeur, today, of different lovers. How
Could we two serve such curious interests now?

And yet I think you brought the dog in case:
He was your good excuse lest I should move.
Not that he would protect, but just increase,
By simply sitting there, your chance to have
Some breaking sentence said: he could run loose
At any tiresome moment you might choose.

I have to relish, though, this flattery
You build for both of us; that dares to claim
That lost surprise you need for you to be
My main quest still, the reason that I came;
And brings this dog out on our autumn day
Squatting its aged cunning in the way.

54 *The Suggestion*

Consideration says you lose a moth by sliding a card
Under a quick glass shut on the wall patch where it sits
And carrying it out, perhaps to a light, to the midnight street.

I am saying to you, then, have understanding ready to devise
Your equivalent trick: get friends, have activities ready to
    divert me
Coming, unignorable and restless, to fret your neat room.

55   *The Victory*

I think it's yours. Furrowing the
Sweat-nights groping for metaphors
– Like the bed's cool patches –
It was hope even then. And other fluences

Carried me somewhere: as, telepathy:
Winging blind wires to carry somehow
News to you. Mad, but it all allowed
The thing to continue. Now, though,

The wires are down. My brain can't ever seem
To stop still enough to think you. My
Bland words talk alone about themselves.
It's yours, this victory, then,

By simple waiting. And, if only you
Might find just what you truly wish through
That same patience – building where
You use it now to reap such disrepair.

56   *The Situation*

For it was that the cousins never came,
And so we could not know what they were like.
They never did walk out in their overwhelming way
To stand by the streaming water-butt, or
To hold the fence with their girls' adult hands.
This garden can't be remembered having them laughing,

So they remain a possibility:
That after our disappointment with man
And with dogs and with travel and with remaining still,
From our last armchairs we shall come to know
That there are the cousins left; who, that day,
Were to come, and did not, and are there to be tried yet.

57   *In Crystal Palace Park*

One January day, among full frail light:
The new stadium shut in blessed silence; sun,
Of the mild midwinter, glossing the gorilla's haunches;
The lake-sheet above the refreshment-room staying
Quiet, through the trees, as the Consort's white elk facing it.

But slumped and crooked at coffee, I think: Only
Beings like these trees can renew. Teachers or foresters
Could point out endless ring on new ring of survival;
Rafters are told of, whining in sympathy with storms;
Gateposts have launched unearthly leaves; and our Commission's

Dense, patterned groves elsewhere grow for when we are all dead.
Trees outlast us. Seasons – how many have *we?* – make no
        difference
To them, through centuries of vegetable time. – Yet use
Your human reason. Should we feel outfaced by even
These mere park glades, in all their bareness now?

At these moments of disquiet, take any single
Individual tree: your face (you can feel the grooved bark on)
Can almost defy it: for after ten years you can
Think its wear equalling yours. Even the inexpert eye
Can spot decay (like your own: each sad spring bravery of leaves

Seems like the brashness of rejuvenation drugs.)
And then you, councillors, murderers, can ride over
A Preservation Order; or citizen, set your crudest pedigree dogs
To do their natural work at some one tree. It surely was
As abstract 'trees' they had that lasting look.

– It's late. I leave the coffee cup, and step out warily
To the mild air again. Away from gulls, many separately
Walking the grass as one to some unattained place,
I hunch, and stride downhill. And pass each tree,
Not blessed with human reason, living its sober term.

58   *The Space*

Then why see it? This 'flat and ample
Space over which you walk at no one angle,
Led as by something very like your will?'

*You could go on with proper concerns. You
Are boiling tea, typing some letter, listening
To politics when it comes. Why let it, why let*

It come? – That pale, clean stretch
Stays small, and won't usurp the whole. So
I let it come. There is no harmful freedom.

*But where do you go across that space? Do you
See things, see anyone?* I don't go anywhere
But across it; taut and clear, though the wind leans at me.

Further, it might be a world, and not safe:
It might be stayed in. I keep it unfulfilled.
Its colour? Certain shadows, shades of green.

– And whoever she who walks there, and stands,
She won't tremble into definition, isn't
Like Fournier's girl, say, on the steps and real.

Then why let it come at all? Only, that to this
All common facts yearn to approximate,
While time strains to reach it. And it

Won't be otherwise, it refuses, and must
Return as plainly as before; nothing but
A kind of sober walking-space. – I see

You are not answered why, nor sense why I let it come.

59   *Skipping Rhyme*

   / /   / / / /
Pain of the leaf, one two –
   / /   /   / / /
Word of the stone, three, four –
   / /   / / /   /
Foot of the dark, pit of the hand,
   / /   / / /   /
Heart of the cloud, five, six, and
   /
Out!
     /
   Skip.
   / /   / /
Nora she had white eyes,
   / /   / /
Mary she had black –
   /   /   /   /
Helen looked in Grey Man's Wood and
   / /
Never came
   /
Back!
    /
   Jump.
   /   /   /   /
Nora draws a green thread,
   /   /   / /
Mary spins it blue –
   /   /   /   /
But Helen will not bind it till her
   /   /
True Love makes it

/
True!
   /
  Quick!
 /   /   /   /
One, two, leaf of the pain,
 /   / /   /
Three, four, stone of the word,
 / / /   / /   /
Five, six, dark of the foot, hand of the pit,
 /   / /
Cloud of the heart, and
 /
OUT!

60 *Nasty Habit*

The sky is so white, the paper is so white.
The unattended leaves of January lie in the damp.
The girl who ran upstairs wrote
Her face, pausing, on the blank of the white wall
(Or on my eyes) with black and pointed hair.
That clock is very fast, the time exists.

And, well, the emotional components exist
For something; for one of the three or four
Attempts at answering 'loneliness'.
Here is a chair comfortable for meditation,
Arms long enough to stretch on, back facing
Towards the window and concealing any

Thought or action I might have or take.
It's up to me. I can sense the moral framework
Even now expanding to allow
A lot of things. Virtually every gesture
Takes on its altruistic look, and
'I had to do it . . .' feels an honourably

Far-off last resort. . . . So I start to write.

61 *Office Party*

We were throwing out small-talk
On the smoke-weary air,
When the girl with the squeaker
Came passing each chair.

She was wearing a white dress,
Her paper-hat was a blue
Crown with a red tassel,
And to every man who

Glanced up at her, she leant over
And blew down the hole,
So the squeaker inflated
And began to unroll.

She stopped them all talking
With this trickery,
And she didn't leave out anyone
Until she came to me.

I looked up and she met me
With a half-teasing eye
And she took a mild breath and
Went carefully by,

And with cold concentration
To the next man she went,
And squawked out the instrument
To its fullest extent.

And whether she passed me
Thinking that it would show
Too much favour to mock me
I never did know –

Or whether her withholding
Was her cruelty,
And it was that she despised me,
I couldn't quite see –

So it could have been discretion,
And it could have been disgust,
But it was quite unequivocal,
And suffer it I must:

All I know was: she passed me,
Which I did not expect
– And I'd never so craved for
Some crude disrespect.

62   *A Few Syllabics*

You said you couldn't
Do other. You were
That conventional
You just walked 'into
The night.' It hurled rain.

They had left on the
Light in the builders'
Yard to stop burglars,
And you had eight wet
Miles' ride. But what was

Not usual was (and
I didn't know) you
Carried a man's child
Two months uninter-
rupted away in

You. It wasn't mine,
I loved you, and by
This bit of chance, your
Not telling me, you
Left, to take her on

Till birth, and to push
Her onwards down time
To stand here (a child
Two months in her too,
Which I do know, and

The new child not mine
Either) where the light
Left on in that yard
Again shows me that
Shape I love, as we

Look at your photo
She holds (bit of chance!)
And I wonder if,
After all these dark
Things, I'll let *her* leave.

63 *Affinity*

He. This thing we have, one means by it what starts
Between two people not near to one another
Who have hardly met and never spoken,
Yet know some faint intangible linking
– Neither to be made firm, nor yet to be broken.

She. I don't see it like this at all, but
In opposites: a sudden image of this woman,
Myself, set off on this dark road unaccompanied,
Pacing between blank hedges, her feet
Leaving and reaching echoes, behind and ahead,

And all at once this new thing arriving,
The darkness thinning and varying, the car
Rushing the channels of her ear, its light
Climbing the sides of trees. And her one doubt is to
Ask what *kind* of man he is at the wheel that night

(Is he lover, enemy, casual messenger,
To give all her landscape that white leaping look?)
Since although she cowers back in the mist, bent
In self-protecting fear of what he means,
She has called and craved for . . . this new element.

64   *Ode to Felix*

At that tired eye-level point where
Impulse buying starts, he
Was there in flush, banked rows in
The supermarket: Felix the Cat.

Two dozen cat-food packets, patterned
For sales appeal, repeated two
Dozen static gestures of his face who
Almost first made cartoons animate.

I remembered that black-and-white
Stroll, brought back on the t.v. screen
About twenty years after: undoubtedly
Smart for its time, the commentator said.

Yes, he had all the possibilities
Already, little early Felix. His
Famous walk was even then the quaint, quick
Cartoon swagger, his features were

The easy prototype of all
Those smirking descendants, capering
In slick, flourished lines, richer
For the primary colours, and running on

Down and down a million celluloid frames
Hand-painted in endless studio rows by
Patient, paid artists reducing everything to
That clear-cut, lucid world, while

Elsewhere other grown men sound-tracked
The basic squawk. – This way was
The world infested by your
Charming animal kingdom, Felix, having

Driven out real beasts. Numberless
American children responded to
The uncle-funny voices, actually came
To look like Mickey Mouse. In the

Demure eyes of innumerable
Homely girls and wives lived
Bambi's primal innocence. Felix,
You were first of all those lovably

Blundering and resourceless dogs and
Elephants who helped to make our
Gross and failing natures bearable.
You set off Li'l Abner, firm and strait,

Shouldering over fields with no effort, as in
Our own fulfilment dreams, you
Tamed with Snow White all our dwarfs
And witches, you helped to paint

Donald Duck on the fuselage of
The bomber for Hiroshima. If today
A man in the *Sunday Times* Colour
Supplement makes t.v. commercials

To pay to make his very own cartoon
Satirizing agencies, the credit's
Partly yours, and you can be proud to think your
Walt Disney voted for Goldwater . . .

I would not buy your food, I have no cat.
I can pass on down the stacked and shining
Aisles to other violences (the frozen red
Chops glossed in cellophane on puce, plastic trays)

But I'm not to pass without that sense, again,
Of one of my more elementary sorts of
Going mad: Your thousands of representatives,
Felix, walking into my world, writing my

Morning letters, modulating from the shapes
Of strangers outside the house, answering
My alarm calls for Fire, Police, *Ambulance*. In
That last nightmare trap and maze, they

Strut and chirp their obscene, unstoppable
Platitudes, Felix, while I run round and
Round and round to destroy their pert, joking smiles
And scream my own voice hoarse into their cute squeak.

Last and most hurting stroke of the wide,
Inescapable sunlight, a flash from some turning car's windscreen
Streaks across to my eyes and blots the whole day black.

I walk on looking out through a pulsing cloud
At the disfigured street, planting a
Seething blur on every face and dress:

They move, half-black and writhing, towards me,
Not knowing, in their late afternoon. They
Are talking and smiling and conducting their

Own concerns beneath my surface of wounds. And
Who am I to tell them they are
Scorched blotches in an insane ignorance?

They would think me the mad one.

66   *Girl Counting*

She lifts up her fawn head, nodding
Rapidly into air; she rests tensing, then
Untensing fingers on the table-top;
She closes her eyes;
And she counts, counts, with a flicker of lips breathing,
In a sort-of ecstasy of computation
– Which she gets wrong.

Such processes of icy reckoning
Seem somehow endangered by this
Devotion of her complete creatureness; by which
She renders her whole, quick, committed
Pulse to contradict all
Numeration's neat sterility:
The figures tremble as they add and rise.

And it seems all the more wrong that
We worry to put in the programming that
Conscious suffusion of some
Warmth like this, alleged to make
All the clean lights and unagitated
Dials tolerable.
While it looked only wise to bring

This human mildness in somewhere,
We should have known the struggle
Long lost before anyone ever
Began on those cool, implacable
Constructs of order and tabulation
– Clicking us into place like straight
White sticks crossed on mass graves –

And should have sensed that to
Start so late, even, was as to
Wake up that fallible, routine sentinel
To see the gulls' possible
Missile flight over his waiting screen, and
In his cavern room, to lift
His one telephone, once.

67   *Winter Appointment*

Now, after too long,
A fool's courage flows back again, and assists me
To the dentist's chair and his unheavenly lights.

The vanished space between me and this house has been
Like the gap scaring
Some anxious lover and all that he dared not risk.

Horse, hawk and debutante in the smooth magazines
Soothe, in the waiting-room, me, with tired coat and grey
Mouth. Rising, I think:

Scales of sharp justice
Appear to be carefully balancing this out:
For those gropings at pleasure, this payment of pain.

Two weeks gone since my first daring venture, when I
Knew he would not start,
And I only need fearfully submit to that

Quick, sinister, flicking parade of the wan street
Of my mouth, that tilting of searching mirrors, prods
At each drab structure,

Surveyor's verdict:
No site to be cleared, or buildings to be shored up,
Though some cleaning, for appearances, would improve.

But! – *I'll take a small X-ray of that one, in case . . .*
And two weeks of fright
Till today's visit, even if swift certainty

Soon now. (Yes . . . take a large X-ray of Diana,
I'd still not know what meant reassurance and
What shaking terror.)

*

So. Today's the day . . .
Well, I *could* have shirked it . . . What more helpful than to
Put off yet another painful self-attrition?

Do sit. Bleak time of revealing: no comfort here.
A train grates, roars down
The cutting outside, the smooth cat flops off the sill.

Something will have to be done . . . You see there was this
Shadow like a sin I didn't think I might have
On the X-ray plate.

Nothing but to *sit*
As the cotton wool dabs at the affronted gums
And his white arm slopes to the swivel tray. But – please –

Talk, please – Rhodesia, anything – till the
Injection takes . . . I'll
Lie open-mouthed at the honour of van der Byl.

A sort-of napkin fitted below my neck. 'Not
Where he eats, but where . . .' (Diana-pray-grace-this-meal-
Before-and-during!)

. . . Christ! anything *must*
Be painful to be salutary. His foot pumps
The chair close (think of her, think of her, think of her,

Seize her presence with some poet's metaphysical
Calling of her to
This moment: for example, though he be a man

I'll allow Diana to visit the dentist:
His drill is the one of all the violations
Which purges and mends.)

Jarring suddenness;
Intermission; recommencement. *Take a good rinse.*
We are come now, I would say, to the nub of this . . .

Pain accurately descends his cold, angled crane
Of quivering wires:
Bleak hysteria of the burr changing its note.

*

And how long do these renewals last? What hope place
In his painful skill, or in any curative
Promise I might have?

There are no answers;
Except to make a quick leap in equivocal
Relief and faith from his chair, and, to myself, say

That to have no trust in tooth mended or promise
Kept, helps no raw nerve . . .
A cavity clear, metal could firm in the space.

A sure, pure flame melted his amalgam. At last
He has carved a surface, he has stripped that napkin
Away; so I rise,

Convinced. With ball-point
I fray his dotted line, sense comfort in the gift
Of this restored street in hopeful mid-afternoon,

Down which Diana could be ready softly to
Walk, as down some now-
Cleansed and part-shuttered Piccadilly, quite alone.

68   *Hedonist*

It was not the religious pleasure-principle,
The supposed, long quest of the libertine; nor
Was it any kind of arrant desire for
Immolation in some seizing mode of brief
Forgetfulness. It was no sort of strained belief,
Or meditated act; but much more simple:

It was the sense of the sufficient good-ness
Of the next thing beyond the present thing:
The food after a day not eating,
The landing after the stairs, the prospect of some
Prospect filling the ten next minutes, should they come.
It was sleep, sometimes. But simpler even than these,

It could be just the sunlight, as an amiable event
To walk out into after the thick
Complexities of his room, leaving cigarettes, stick
And tablets and trusting, for once,
To his own feet and the friendliness of distance,
And to mere walking alone on the bright pavement.

69   *Old Company*

What is there underneath this tight and
Scarlet creasing at their eye-corners,
As the mouth-stretching laughter-spasm holds
And stacks each man's entire, shuddering
Body on top of his stomach folds?

Their faces seize in this concerted anguish.
The spread-out, cumbersome limbs around the circle
Look like helpless pain to possess.
But they will laugh, and stay. Their risen steam
Muffles each window, hides the street's greyness.

Gregarious mankind . . . Old company
Can ride down any fear as the stale
Seconds of their present unendurably tear
Them piecemeal away from those fresher
Seconds of their mutual past, where

The first laugh started. Each one's ageing face
Makes now a shield for his flesh, here where
All shields grip together grimacing
On phalanx-night against the terror
In one expressionless, unchanging thing.

70 Song

The pheasants rightangle away into the thicket;
The mill sails appear on the right, as the map ventures;
The sedge bends to the light wind politely, not constrained;
             I love you as detail.

The church has a tower the miniature of its tower;
Finished sacks, thrown down, glitter and litter on the field;
Three day-owls scatter towards the approaching wood;
             I love you for detail.

The lane turns into two ruts with a thick grass centre;
Rides of pines come thinly down to entreat at the hedge;
Hay-blocks provide for the month under polythene sheets;
             I love you in detail.

Turned soil rests and waits in the damp, clean and unharried;
The concealing flat cloud glows, in foreground to the sun;
One gust flicks beads of wet from the grass at crazed angles;
             I love you through detail.

71 Disposed to Sleep

To cry, in the near space
Between the unfolded pale screen and the bed,
Would be late, late; and would be water only.
My fluids have been less, always,
Than that impartial, other blood which now
Drips from poised foresight into
The channels under his skin.
I have not given, this or other ways.
I have, like this, gone in and out
Of bad sleep, not grasping;
Working

Dry-lip-words to half-recognize
Those faces, what they came for.
                                    And here the dark sister
Stands too soon by my own breathing side.

72   *Fourth Lover*

That fourth lover you mentioned, the dangerous one
Only to be talked about carefully, the one
Closest of all, still: him I will not demote too far.

I may even be generous, and allow him
One small particular duchy in
The Holy Empire of your consciousness.

Its name? – Insomniac nostalgia.

73   *Mad Animals*

In comic, unthreatening circles, the spaniel
Ran mad and fretted round the college cat;
Which sat still and just, only, looked

With at most a mild, unequivocal
Compassion. What this spaniel did was a
Sort of obsessed, yelping, bewildered

Orbit of this inexplicable creature
For a long time. It was not dignified. It was
An insanity, reproached and warned by

The gargoyles on the chapel gutter, who
Presented like frenzies, punished with
Being congealed in stone and permanent.

This was a cat of super-elegance; and
O spaniel, you to have no dignity,
Dog as you are, and self-possessed really!

What use was it to yelp? – And yet, and yet,
On an inside page in Rees-Mogg's *Times* there was,
Against all reason, news and a picture of

A cat some man had bred with spaniel's ears.

74 *Pathetic Fallacy*

Now autumn's rank enforcement of
Fawn-pointed thistle and tip-faded iris
Leaves us with this garden as an
Indifferent waste, we tend to let it alone;
We tend to light the rooms early.

We dispose to think mostly indoors, for
Outdoors only stay the limited
Tactics of inanimate things: the stray
Of blown leaves from the heap, dabs of rain
Blurring the fences, grass become irrelevant.

Nothing to think about there, we think.
Let's hug to itself the self of winter,
Glad of the close fire's flattery, happy
For winds to slam doors on us as if
It was worlds happening against our very will.

75   Balls of Sweetness

Before James Carra knew Anne Furlington
She made love, often, the first in both their lives,
Under a slipping mauve quilt in a seaport,
With nightlong traffic noise disturbing;
There being wallpaper the same as in her
College room; and it was Peter Daines.
It was the world. No one seemed later hurt, or
Finally betrayed.
                              It was not of consequence.

When Hester Lang told Cavan Benther that
Hidden in some long spell away from him was
A week when Philip Quernier was prepared
And it happened three times (but each time one of them
Pretended) an hour was enough for Cavan's
Fury. Nor were these people heartless. It was
Not of consequence. Such oddness at such distance
Could be healed.
                              It was the world.

Elizabeth Pender felt that past could be
Contentedly left as past concerning
William Stennett's beds where Margaret Bourn
Fought conscience and hindering fear. She
Only nodded; and thought. Such guileless frankness
Gave a lot of help. This would leave
No injury-traces . . . It was the world. In minutes
Their hands came coolly together.
                              It was not of consequence.

76 *For my Son*

Not ever to talk when merely requested,
Not ever to be the performing child,
This is what you would establish;
                        always keeping
Private and awkward counsel against
All coaxing; and going – one hopes –
The way of a good will,

To your own true designs. Which is
The way of some human institutions,
Growing not as any collective urge
                        would have them
(In its own placable image) but into
Their own more wayward value – strong,
Untidy, original, self-possessed.

77 *Twenty-Third Day*

The moon, a rejected
Gift to your disconsolate nature,
Is wasting on you its good literary

Pause in the elm branches across the river;
So that your hand leaves mine on principle, and
Complains that I make you too much the moon,
An uncomfortable ideal . . .

There is, in that, a kind of unguessed truth.
One knows, by now, the moon to be
Pock-marked, with routine mountains; thick
With feet-deep uninteresting dust
Which chokes its incursors; and worse,
She is attainable for the worst of motives.

In all, she is only a little, pale thing,
Ordinary, and human in her way (going through
Phases? You have your bloody ones; sometimes.)

– And only just staying, through inflictions
Of time and knowledge, the same, white,
Round-faced, acceptable creature.

78   *In the Room Above*

In their bed of loss they are
Like sea-things.

Her cries, like drifting gulls',
Lie ancient and somehow
Small about the air, as if wanting
Unction or pity.

A metropolis sways outside,
But in their surge of two griefs they are
Not disturbed.

– I think I know why pity comes to mind.

There was her choosing to cry,
Which she had heard was so; and there was you.

It was your silence, silence,
Made her lost and bird voice pitiful.

79   *Pictures*

Terror at night, that turns precise:
Sweat of the firebell chills my skin
With fear you lie in swathes of smoke
Too dense for rescuers to break in.

I could fling back the sheets at two,
Shake myself into waking and
Run all the roads half-clothed to where
That gaping ignorance would stand

Watching your slimness, blanket-wrapped,
Handled down ladders into the snow
As I recall those bodies were,
Was it four Boxing Nights ago?

– But then, mortality extends
To any step in any street:
There's dog-bite, or there's poison in
What small amounts of food you eat.

'Friendship is lovely' – yes, but who
Knows of all opening doors which one
Closes in velvet kindliness
And stands you facing someone's gun?

This way, the horrors flock around,
The fears come pestering. – And yet
Their idiot multiplicity
Provides a kind of safety-net:

If I decide sometimes to dread
Your falling down on every stair,
Just as irrationally I could
Think you strode safely anywhere.

If death could wait on any step,
Conversely you might stay intact
From any earthly wound or stain
Your sort-of innocence might attract.

And leaving every profitless
Anxiety which coats the breath:
There is one fantasy I feel
A *little* likelier than death:

A day in sultry weather, soon,
To sit and think, idly, to where
Some momentary fatigue has bent
Your shoulders . . . With a casual air

You stretch; and all that row of beads
Rides upwards on your stretching dress
– My fingers stretch out miles to touch
Their spacing red-and-yellowness.

Would this aspiring gesture set
Some small telepathy in train?
Encouraged by the thought, I go
And try the telephone, again.

– Anna's voice. You are called. Downstairs
You answer with far-off surprise,
Slow, as you yawn and curse, to see
Anything with your naked eyes.

You take your glasses from the shelf,
Hold, and unfold, them, to the light,
Flick them across your sleeve, and put
Them on, so that your world seems right,

– And speak. Although you often hate
Suggestions made when you are tired,
This time some sixth and lucky sense
Tells you what answer is required.

Distance can cancel out itself,
But slowly! Thought is faster than
Speeds at which engines or mere feet
Can move to carry any man.

But finally your street, too warm
Under that gathering summer cloud,
Arrives. And when the intercom
Takes up your syllable aloud,

The lock releases. As my steps
Run to the inner door upstairs,
You stack some records on, and make
To rearrange the couch and chairs . . .

Some time earlier in the week,
We cleaned this room. These cushions take
A gentler attitude, one feels,
For every kind and prescient shake.

The window's wide. You jump to see
Your curtains snatched into the storm,
But something lucky I think to say
Makes laughter of your half-alarm.

The Indian shade veiling the lamp
Clicks, in the draught which shuts the door.
Anna is out. The phone is dead.
You nudge four shoes towards the floor.

Braceleted and bare, your arm
Stretches to drop on a low shelf
Your folded glasses. How the rain slants.
Gently the record plays itself.

That table-lamp again. It has
Horsemen mounting a fawn hill.
The edge of its hushed arc of light
Quivers; and yet the draught is still.

There are some fish that drift about
And at each breathing close their eyes,
As if replenishments of air
Came each on each a sweet surprise . . .

No matter . . . Half-an-hour in one track
– A kind of blues, but sweet enough –
The automatic pick-up arm
Achieves its end and switches off.

Much social detail you don't need.
Fuller descriptions of the flat?
Or names, or times, or what we drank?
Invent your own. And leave it that

As well as pictures in each eye
We get slipped discs and are let lie
In some large, liberal, hospital
Bed together, so that all

The learned doctors might come near
(Oh, not to diagnose, but) to hear
Wild, whimsical, allusive range
Of talk, on questions rich and strange

For, laid on boards to straighten us
For all things curved and tortuous,
Day upon day we languish there
And talk, from Twardzik to Voltaire.

80   *Breaking Eggs*

It is as if she chose to exist
To scathe forgivable sins
– In which she could be right;

But to watch her way, for example,
With pardonable pride, or any faintly
False dignity or ceremoniousness

Is somehow terrible.
                              And to prepare a meal
(Though no one should dare to asperse her skill),
She will unclasp each poised, mature

Vegetable's grip upon itself, leaf
By pathetic leaf, intently; or crack
The fragile and decorous eggs

With rapid and curt fingers, not smiling.
It would look like no more than cold spite
If it were not her own kind of care; and

If she could not also, with a mere knife only,
Take up (precise and chilling miracle!)
Each omelette into surging fabric-folds.

81   *Seven Activities for a Young Child*

Turn on the tap for straight and silver water in the sink,
Cross your finger through
The sleek thread falling
                              – *One.*

Spread white sandgrains on a tray,
And make clean furrows with a bent stick
To stare for a meaning
                    — *Two.*

Draw some clumsy birds on yellow paper,
Confronting each other and as if to fly
Over your scribbled hill
                    — *Three.*

Cut rapid holes into folded paper, look
At the unfolded pattern, look
Through the unfolded pattern
                    — *Four.*

Walk on any square stone of the pavement,
Or on any crack between, as long
As it's with no one or with someone
                    — *Five.*

Throw up a ball to touch the truest brick
Of the red-brick wall,
Catch it with neat, cupped hand
                    — *Six.*

Make up in your head a path, and name it,
Name where it will lead you,
Walk towards where it will lead you
                    — *Seven.*

One, two, three, four, five, six, seven:
Take-up-the-rag-doll-quietly-and-sing-her-to-sleep.

This coarse road, my road, struggles out
South-east across London, an exhausted
Grey zigzag of stubborn, unassimilable
    Macadam, passing hoardings pasted

With blow-ups of cricket journalists, blackened
And not-quite-Georgian terraces,
Shagged-out Greens of geraniums and
    Floral coats-of-arms, lost pieces

Of genteel façade behind and above
Lyons' shopfronts and 'Pullum Promotions',
– Journeying between wired-off bombed lots glossy
    With parked Consuls, making diversions

Round bus depots and draggled estates
In circumlocutory One-Ways,
Netting aquaria in crammed pet store windows,
    Skirting multi-racial bingo queues,

And acquiring, for its self-hating hoard, old black-railed
Underground bogs advising the Seamen's Hospital,
'Do-it-yourself' shops, 'Funerals and Monuments', and
    Victorian Charrington pubs. All

Along its length it despoils, in turn, a sequence
Of echoless names: Camberwell, Peckham,
New Cross Gate; places having no recorded past
    Except in histories of the tram.

It takes out, in cars, arterial affluence
At week-ends, returning it as bad blood
To Monday mornings in town. It is altogether
    Like a vein travelled by hardy diseases, an aged

Canal dredgeable for bodies left behind
On its soulless travels: Sixty-Nine,
Thirty-Six, One-Eight-Five. It takes no clear
    Attitude anyone could easily define

So as to resist or admire it. It seems to hate you
Possessively, want to envelop you in nothing
Distinguishable or distinguished, like its own
    Smothered slopes and rotting

Valleys. This road, generally, is one for
The long-defeated; and turns any ironic
Observer's tracer-isotope of ecology,
    Sociology, or hopeful manic

Verse into a kind of mere
Nosing virus itself. It leaves its despondent, foul
And intractable deposit on its own
    Banks all the way like virtually all

Large rivers, particularly the holy ones, which it
Is not. It sees little that deserves to be undespised.
It only means well in the worst of ways.
    How much of love is much less compromised?

83   *The Clouds*

The craftsmen in my line bred out.
I drive, but could I mend a fuse.
My fathers handled founts of words
My brain would catch and fingers lose.

I find a fair excuse, to serve:
There has, in our society,
Been 'social change', which makes these skills
Much less of a necessity.

Beyond your shoulder I can see
A saucer – stamped out by machine –
On the formica shelf near where
We lie on quilts of terylene.

No sort of ancient expertise
Goes to create these modern things:
To them, no craftsman's hand its pride
Or love for their completeness brings.

Their very make and feel rejects
Any thought that such loving powers
Nurtured their shapes to what they are
Through someone's calm and patient hours.

That care seems obsolete. – Yes, I know
You were your parents' artefact,
Your perfect head, shoulders and back
Made in a sort-of skilful act,

But when I move a care-ful hand
(No craftsman's art its legacy)
And dot a pattering line to count
Your poised and tensing vertebrae,

It's not *great* numeracy I want,
Or flair for cold technologies
– Such details are not wanted in
All kinds of loving enterprise.

Nor do we need such skills to lose
All sense of this room, house and street . . .
And don't doubt, though we use no craft,
That love it is makes this complete.

– And, well, on looking up I see,
As a sweet end to summer's drought,
Some wholly unskilled clouds which pour
Blessings of rain on Baron's Court.

84   *Comforts*

The precisions of idleness:
A ball hit through a hoop on a lawn,
The table-top grained and bare, to which
You take a thin, scrawling pen and paper.
Also, rain is at the green window, scratching.

– Or, posing a record, leaving it
To settle itself, to play;
Or, an immovability about certain white cards
In a shelf-row . . .
Such things, therefore. And, I dare
You, I dare you, disorder.

85   *Fortune*

Whirling through January, a conclave
Of echoes under a parapet, sleet furring the sheep, and
A cord of salt unthreading onto the table:
            A yellow bell, an orange, a yellow bell.

Circling round April, a syllable scratched in ash,
And flicking past arches on a motorway, though
A white cat waited and washed at the downstairs door:
            A yellow bell, a yellow bell, a peach.

Turning through August, the complexions of two
Terrains various as Iceland and Romania,
Then that important ladder she walked beneath:
        A grapefruit, a yellow bell, a yellow bell.

Spinning in December, and snow spinning, and her
Feet drawn in close on a tall chair, when
Somehow the mirror fled her superstitious hand
        – Three lots of grapes in mauve, ironical clusters!

86   *To Sleep; on St Lucy's Day*

Shadow containing all shades, glad
Enemy or eluding lover, rabidly
Changeable and sly one, here then
Is the shortest day's tribute, made
In merging, unaccountable images:
Chestnuts fallen on the random
Grass at Hales where the blood once
Lipped the barbaric phial; crude
Skull-bone under a woman's eyes unable
To hide or feign; men wounding
Sweet animals and weeping; music
Becoming phrases becoming music.
                            Who
Could hold and follow these back to
Say the loose paving stone in the adult
Street this morning, where it
Tripped the crying child? Shadow,
They are yours to understand, and
To repeat; wilted
Wreaths in nightly giving.
                        Where
Gods are most firm and ancient, you
Are new always, and never certain;

Youthful; a slow, calm hand, or a face
Followed and escaping. Those whom
You love hardly need to dispose limbs,
Or resolve on blankness to invoke you,
But wait merely, only a short time.
Those you despise,
Their bodies char and live in sullen
Fires of wakefulness, quartering and
Rejoining at each chime. Between, lie
All your various supplicants, meditative
Or sad-uneasy, sensing
– So many hundred ways – their
Thoughts meet, link, dissolve into
Illogic, leave consciousness.
                              Why
Are you, in whole Valhallas of
Straight gaze and iron purposings,
Most sickly and inconstant, working your power
Through unexpectedness (we never
See you, but only, ever, wake
To know that you have passed)?
You stay invisible; and yet, last night,
Ruining and re-begetting, you
Came without terror or long delay,
Your footfall unhurried, your words
Kindly and sure, telling no lie, and
Your arms folding round without
An ambiguous glance, and you were clear and
Quick, as petals quivering in daylight.

The North Lancashire Ballet Group is coming
Next month, and Miriam Granger-White is giving
A Francis Thompson reading in the Public
Library. So we are all well catered for, culture-wise,
And don't really miss London. It's interesting
How many talented people do in fact
Choose the provinces: you seem to get
Room to breathe here somehow, and so many

Advantages (for instance, the post for London
Goes as late as *eleven* on weekdays!). We have these
Musician friends – the husband's often having things
Done by the choir of Radio Chesterfield, the wife
Lectures in a College of Education – they're like us,
They gave up London because it just didn't seem
To offer the scope somehow. Robert's work is
Going awfully well; as I think I told you, it's

An open-minded, progressive sort of firm, and he has
The chance to do a small, quite modern, country
Cottage for a retired solicitor. He's pretty sure
The standard is as high as a lot of firms
In London. I do several hours each week
Helping at the Family Planning Clinic, there's plenty
To occupy us. Yes, we keep in touch, we can
Get most of our old friends on S.T.D.,

And people really do exaggerate about the northern
Weather. I wouldn't at all like to have
To drive the Anglia in London traffic. I don't think
I could. There's a design shop in the Market Square
Where you can get almost anything, a delicatessen
With every kind of bread we like, and
A fabric shop as good as Oxford Street. Robert
Is on the Third Programme Listeners' Panel.

We are growing lobelias for the local Help the Depressives
Flower Show, which keeps us busy. It's
A good life. Would you like to come down?
We have an enormous spare room and it would
Be lovely to see you. You could stay as long as
You like – we wouldn't bother you. It's
Quite possible, don't you think, to be 'provincial'
While actually living in the metropolis? Anyway,

Write soon, tell us your news, love to Amanda.

88   *Taking Amanda back*
      to St Winefride's

As I drove,
to see what
came I was
looking in
the driving
mirror and
saw Aman-
da's face glazed
at air, at
some turn of
the talk. This
was danger . . .
Switch the talk
to something
else, quickly,
please.
        It switched.
We ran up
between two
hedges of
spurting flowers,
the soft clouds

flocked above
to the sun,
quite a fine
afternoon.
I smoked.
          Three
people in
this car in
a country
trip to a
– a house: so
obvious,
easy and
Amanda's
eyes clear now.
Yet I still
saw it there,
another
closing face
seen elsewhere,
with its own
purposed kind
of rigid
calm, and blank
light; and guessed
the intent
look it had
was someone's

very mad.

89   *Peter Daines at a Party*

Oliver Cromwell and Beethoven both
Died in the middle of thunderstorms. Ruth
Didn't know this, but knew Kierkegaard's Dad
Cursed God from a hilltop, or so it was said.
Yet none of these things was at all familiar
To Mary, or Nora, or Helen, or Pamela.

But Pamela knew of some laws of Justinian's,
Helen listened to Schutz and had read *The Virginians*,
And Nora and Mary liked Wallace Stevens,
So in general terms it worked out evens
– Except that none of them, only Amanda,
Knew that Oliver Cromwell had died during thunder.

Still, here were these women with items of knowledge
Picked up in one and another college
– And here am I with not quite all their gaps
In my knowledge of all these high-powered chaps,
Doing well with the female population
And their limited but charming conversation.

90   *Sestina in Memoriam Vernon Watkins*

When, that October, he was at Attingham, I first
Saw him in the early evening: treading with a good
Relaxed stride down the kitchen garden, only to then
Pause under a little brick archway and wonder
If there were really time for a walk before supper, and at last
Turn back, avoiding the rain, to the great

House, to unpack instead.
                                  Out of a great
Metal trunk lashed up with ropes, he took first
His poems and notes, then some very orderly clothes, and, at the
        last
Moment, nearly missing the meal, needing to be a 'good
Listener', on the stairs, to a lady full of wonder
At the naturalness of a famous poet, he ate his roast beef, then

Signed a few copies of *Affinities* over coffee, then
Told precise, nostalgic anecdotes of the last
Time he encountered Dylan Thomas; stopping to wonder
How it was he never somehow got beyond the first
Shots at teaching him to drive, on Pendine Sands.
                                          Though good
For several more hours' talk, we did at last

Wander off in search of our respective rooms, the last
People to go to bed; but not knowing where we were, then
Had to grope our way, lost, through innumerable great
State-rooms of irreplaceable relics, probably a good
Half-mile from the room where we first
Sat – and were finally caught up by the Warden, starting to
        wonder

Who it was prowling about . . . I do wonder
Why, when most men drop *two* shoes on the floor above, the last
I heard of Vernon Watkins that night was his dropping first
One, then a second, then a *third* . . . It must have then
Been well past two . . . But he was up early working on a great
Pile of other people's verses, which he covered with neat good

Advice; and at eleven gave his Yeats memorial poem, a good
One to finish with, a fine bardic rendering, from a lectern. I
    wonder,
Still, how his taxi got him to the station in time: it could be, great
And mysterious assistance saved him, in this last
Frantic departure . . .
                    Still . . .
                                Mere irrelevant scraps? But then
He had this sort-of quality – no one's first

Virtue, and not *his* first, but one power his good-ness had,
Then as always: to give all quirks and details a sort of odd wonder,
Each last, least, great thing asking wry gratitudes.

91 *In the Visitors' Book*

Straight north across Norfolk, the lanes
Lead on past shrines and staithes to assuage
All thirst for greenness and lucidity,
And present at last the Meals and Bights of
An exhausted, exalted coast.
                                And there start
The contradictions. The spring tide in April is
No resurrection of crested energies, but
A cagey, persistent ripple towards us
Under ghost sunlight, quietly
Marooning the yellowed freshes. Boards
Painted with warnings compromise the apparent
Calm of a sea you could walk into
For placid furlongs. It doesn't feel right, but
Here there seems nothing in the world except
Paradox, any more; and to
Wake after afternoon sleep is a
Reincarnation to the inconsistency of
One's existing at all with this archaic flesh,
Combining, like this place, such aged

And such fervent weathers.
                              Inland,
The mills casually circle, the cattle
Diffuse in an amiable way over
Ample and undulant clovers, and
The land is quite logically patterned
And fruitful. The silences there
Add layer on layer to themselves, in
Immense stage pauses; disquieting, but
A less ambiguous peace than the sky's
White wideness here over these ancient,
Incredible sandgrains.
                              There is nothing on
This coast at all comfortable: even inconse-
Quential things are ominous with a hint
Of the not-to-be-explained: little metal
Grids in the water, abandoned
Clothes in the dunes, a quick wheeling-
Off of birds for no detectable
Reason.
              And unless you love them, this
Many antitheses would amount in an hour
To a request to go elsewhere; which
We, at least, did not obey until,
Rising from the reed-cries of love we saw
Five black undrowned sisters of chastity
Receding in the very naked light along
The foam-line, with footsteps arrogantly
Murdering the assoiled sand.
                              It was
Tribute of a further contradiction, almost
Deserving what we had just quite freely
Taken: the freedom of the place.

114

Born fourth out of five. Mother
Had maxims about sunrise and godly
Demeanours. Father went
Away and it wasn't allowed to . . . She
Made him a 'very famous
Scientist'. Fostered, on various
Homes of indigent Florida,
Calling from the table, 'I'm
Starving!' Swam early. Told
Sister at ten, 'If you let the bath-water
Run on you *there*, it gets
Like you kind-of can't *bear* it . . .'
And lay with her, nights, pretending
It was Elvis. Went to High
School, was once voted
Student 'most likely to succeed'
In the year. Collected a
Pack of girls for constructive
Depravity, sat on a long bonnet
For a boy's camera, proposed
Club colours black and grey, was
Fired and let other leaders
Mess it up latterly. Cheered, danced,
Wrote the club song and found
How all the boys tried making it on
Peppermint tongues and false, sun-
Hot leather in coupés. Ran
From the house when sister could
Nearly have been dying; and blamed
Herself. Looked a long time with
Brother, for a Coleridge, to
Complete themselves. Lost It
In five jerks of a quarterback's
Ass . . . homo ludens . . . he hasn't ever
Married. Saved up for U.C.L.A., nearly

115

A Republican; Civil Rights
At Berkeley. Stayed Karl's
Flat in the poor quarter – and
Went to Mexico for the first one
(Corner of the avenue: 'Americano?'
'Si!' Christ lifted her away
Through the pentathol). Good grades,
Naturally, and surfed on the beaches;
Broke down about obsessions with
Filling, every, single, moment . . . met
With Joe Missile, that being
The second time: a phone call to the flat. 'Say,
Did you get your . . .?' 'No.' Done in
San Diego. Crying in a
Waiting room, yet bored by
Comforting in only six weeks,
Went six
Thousand miles, married, carried
Her mother's admonitions. Adopted
Cats, put down a mortgage, was
Pursued across rooms with knives.
Ate and ate and spoke about it,
Invented William and Rosemary, covers
For lovers. Recalled how
Last summer started working the
Harmless fantasies: Greeks, Finns,
Admirers, haters, blackmailers, mechanics,
Lecturers; had thought to let in
Some of all the professions that . . .
Left, for her own flat; found
The tap in the *centre* of the bathroom wall,
Had 'waited all my life for such a tap – but
The water was ice-cold!'
Taught some people, wrote an exercise,
Lived in a station, lay with this
Frenchman, Saturday, above
Knightsbridge. Today

Cut her forearms in unimportant
Places over the sink, writes, 'Leave
Me, forgive me, this
Is the tomorrow I have chosen, the
Suicide it will mean.' And now the white
Sun rises as we drive south, with
The power-station ambiguously
Applauding, and
Tomorrow is happy
Birthday, Lauren, happy
Birthday, Lauren, happy
Birthday.

93   Ballad for a Birthday

I cleaned up the house, and moved the telephone;
I had a look to see if the plant had grown;
I put Tiddles outside, and sat on my own:
    I feel the same, but I wouldn't want to call it love.

I arranged my dresses on laundry hooks;
I pulled out the table and set out my books;
I went to the window for just one or two looks:
    I feel the same, but I wouldn't want to call it love.

I wanted coffee, so I marked the page;
It should have been over when it got to this stage;
Can I *be* the same girl at a different age?
    I feel the same, but I wouldn't want to call it love.

What if he phoned, and I heard the bell
With my feet on the bath-tap, and I couldn't tell . . .
Well, I heard it . . . should I answer it as well?
    I feel the same, but I wouldn't want to call it love.

If he wrote a letter, saying Could we meet,
Or if we met by accident, in the street
– When something's finished, is it *always* complete?
    I feel the same, but I wouldn't want to call it love.

If he drove round here and knocked on the door,
Would I answer his questions, let him ask me more,
Or could I tell him I was absolutely sure . . .?
    – Oh, I feel the same, but I wouldn't want to *call* it love.

94   *The Packet*

In the room,
In the woman's hand as she turns
Is the packet of salt.

On the packet is a picture of a
Woman turning,
With a packet in her hand.

When the woman in the room com-
Pletes her turning, she
Puts the packet down and leaves.

On the packet in the picture
Is: a picture of a woman
Turning, with a packet in her hand.

On this packet is a picture: of a woman,
Turning, with a packet in her hand.
On this packet is no picture

– It is a tiny blank.
              And now the man waits,
And waits: two-thirty, seven-thirty,
Twelve.

At twelve he lays the packet on its side
And draws, in the last packet in the last
Picture, a tiny woman turning.

And then he locks the door,
And switches off the bedside lamp,
And among the grains of salt he goes to sleep.

95   *Ode to Melancholy*

(for Martin Bell)

I have made England
almost
unusable with associations. Every

beach, square, terrace or
shattered chancel has its
touchy girl, saying

'Don't go back *there.*'
                    So
on Bank Holiday I walk
home, home in the sun. Little

cats jump their heads into
my hand, but I can't talk
to *people*. Closing

my door, it's eight hours
playing and refining the
games of melancholia:

cushions, records,
crumbling sugar-heaps,
self-love. O gentle, helpful

119

melancholy, give me
one good doodle on a
white page for

all my afternoon's journey;
rescind time's
importance for me so I don't

care how the days of the week are
seven, the days of the month are
seven plus twenty-one; and

feed me black coffee, black
cigarettes, black socks
(toujours

la délicatesse!) – that I can
wait so happily for
darkness to require

all those curtains to be pulled.

96   *White Night*

I did not dream it, no I *was*
A t.v. screen left on shining, and
Insensately vibrating, and
Blank, in a shop at night: like a
Flat yet restless pool.

I could picture nothing; but
I was alive and was shivering and
Wanting to hold more and think more
Than grey, sudden flecks and bleak dots
Momently repeating.

O nice insomnia, fastidiously
Beckoning the abrasive dawn, and tuning
The mind to that first, drab
Water-table where, out of such cold depths,
    came
Monsters on which the hurtful body rode.

97   *Weathers*

The man rummages the intonations of her voice.
He wonders if she will proffer the cigarette.
The filament of the fire clicks once.

She rises with the cigarettes pointing.
She goes to the second woman first, who refuses.
The lights flicker as if his eye had blinked.

She goes to the second man second:
He accepts. She goes back poising her own cigarette.
The draught teems at the stopped-up door.

From her chair she offers now the first man
A cigarette. He takes it quickly, and nods.
A spray of rain patters the reflecting glass.

It is not that they speak. The first man leans
Rapidly to the matches on the table, strikes one.
The clouds of the night outside shift among themselves.

He lights the woman's cigarette, the second man's,
And then his own; relapses eagerly to his chair.
A pitiable vain wind hawks the marshes in darkness.

And that midnight raced across
Down the sand, James Carra first. And
Though the air drenched his eyes,
Suddenly he saw the thing, the figure, his
Own shadow running terribly forwards onto

Him, out of the water; because all these four
People were running straight down the
Headlight path in the dark to the shallow
Sea, and had met their ghosts rearing
Up from the tide-edge. Where

The water stood them, the four stood
In quiet and disquiet, trying to trace
The invisible lip of the retrenching
Tide. The sea was unseizably dark.
This distance, the car lights couldn't

Choose out one wave-crest; but then the water
Was blankly calm where the four
Stopped, and couldn't speak, before
Their huge grey shapes hovering
And diffusing upon the Atlantic. Such

Ghosts they were content to own,
Knowing their nature, the un-
Measurable powerlessness of shadows. And when
They turned back up their glaring track
Those vast greynesses comfortingly

Dwindled again (slowly, because they walked)
Dwindled into the sea again, that did
Nothing. Only James Carra, walking,
Thought more than this, as he measured out the
Dark sand and caught at his disrupted breath

122

– As he knew she would catch, who
Lay across the water in the
Drowning sheets, checking her
Breath for a lover on whom no
Writs or shadows he could cast could run.

99   *Connection*

The first take was an offer in eagerness,
With every white finger so quickly threading,
Those hands went on as if they didn't think.

But they thought for the second take; which was
A slow agreed advancing, and a
Watching with eyes to see what eyes would tell.

The third take was from longer forethought, becoming
A turmoil and grating of little, decorated
Bones; neither hand wanted it.
                              In fact,

The fourth take might never have been at all,
Except. . . . some kind of separateness travelled
The arm to the shoulder, the shoulder to the brain

And there it spoke: to separate, such hands
Needed to have been joined
                              and been confused

– Once more those fingers did as they were used.

Sea-crabs live in
And near the sea,
Land-crabs go back
Occasionally.

After these many months the old crab was out of the water,
And into the full, blank air and wanting the sun.

A crab has a very strange
Sideways walk
And eyes placed on
A retracting stalk.

Wide sheets of wet light covered the level beach
As he came fumbling and peering over the gnarled sand.

Two kinds of bodies
For crabs there are:
The oval and
The triangular.

His ten legs carried his squat bulk gravely
and slowly like a burden altogether too sad to keep long.

A little crab only
Really begins
To be adult when he's
Cast five skins.

This was his last stroll of years out of the bitter flow and
Hard swirl of the winter water, dragging from pool to clear pool.

A crab's feet are not
All the same, because
Some are for walking
And some have jaws.

His old mouths muttered on the windy silence as he walked.
In his funny clumsiness and misery he was man-like.

101   *Elizabeth Pender's Dream of Friendship*

When all these men and
women came, in
the sunlight, to that
                    tower they
found it
was embedded
in the earth. And
to get inside, you
crossed over this
iron bridge, to meet
spiralling
                    downward
steps;
which they did,
and proceeded down
-stairs to a room
with only a
white
telephone in it and one
window looking out at hills
barely holding back the sea.
And when the
telephone immediately
                    rang,
a voice told them
don't

go, whatever
else you do, out
by the middle stair
-case door if the
                    horse
is standing in the field with
tresses of blood-wet
silk at its mouth.
How then to
                get away,
all these lovers and friends,
because when
they
        opened that door,
they saw, in blank fright,
the enormous horse
waiting
            and looking
and waiting,
and they must not, could
not go out. Still,
at the top of the spiral of
steps, it was a
hundred fears worse:
a darkening
field of
broken
inscribed
            graves, which moved
and edged to
-wards them,
and utterly white
funerary
            statues,
embracing.
At that top door, they
held one

another tightly, but
                        who,
when they looked,
exactly
            who
were their friends?
Because one by
one, everyone
                not
thoroughly true to her,
or to himself,
or to herself,
was irrevocably
                        dissolving,
and it was starting to
be, very suddenly,
                        night.
It was so
            black now, they
couldn't even make out
which of each other's
faces
were still
truly
        there,
in which fear,
she, and they, tried
hard (it was so
hard now) to breathe, and tried
to speak, and tried to
think how possible in any
-thing like this, any
-thing like
        dawn
actually

was.

In the convent vegetable garden the nuns
Have erected a scarecrow in front of the runner beans,
And it has an old wimple on its head.

In the spring the beans will climb, will climb
But the crows are coming:
The wimple will chase them away.

In the convent vegetable garden the nuns
Have erected a scarecrow alongside the cauliflowers,
And it has an old wimple on its head.

In the spring the cauliflowers will rise, will rise
But the daws are deadly:
The wimple will drive them away.

In the convent vegetable garden the nuns
Have erected a scarecrow behind the marrow plants,
And it has an old wimple on its head.

In the spring the marrows will expand will expand
But the tits are terrible:
The wimple will turn them away.

In the summer the marrows will fructify completely,
And will be scrubbed under rubber-nozzled taps and peeled
And sliced and cored and mutton shoved inside

And the scarecrow will be taken apart
And at the long tables in the cool refectory
The Mother Superior and the nuns and the novice nuns
          and the symbolists will sit and stuff
               themselves for a considerable
                    length of time.

We used to be some self-absorbed people living
In a compromised age about twenty years ago. We hated it, it
Was a terrible age, and underneath we liked it in a way, it
    Was because it gave us the chance to feel like that.

Now it has all changed, and we are older,
And we hate the age completely, not nearly so
Entranced with our hatred. But now there are lots of younger
    People entranced with hatred of this terrible age,

While underneath they like it in a way, because
It gives them the chance to feel like that. We ourselves feel lost
Because we can't tell them they are compromised like us,
    That being hard for the self-absorbed to see.

And all the time the ages are getting worse and worse.

104   *Formosavej*

The tramway ran out along into the night,
Its rails were wet from the rain and the tramway continued.
It met houses, it met shops, it met parks, it met cafés,
It met dogs.

        And in the shining of
The light of the lamps in the rain on its tracks
It went steadily on with its own quiet, metal
Wilfulness all the time.

        On it, the brittle
Narrow, bright, single-decker trams rang and
Rattled: busy and green-grey frameworks
Of glitter and rightness.

At the many turns
In the wide streets and the by-streets their
Brakes drew in breath and groaned, at
Jolts and bumps on the track all the dainty
Lights went off and came on again.

Overhead, through all this,
The wires droned and thudded and crackled
And at sudden halts all the empty red-leather
Seats reversed themselves.

When the terminus came,
It was a splendid aggregation of trams on
The circle of tracks at the end of the route,
A stupefying, fascinating, memorable
Clatter of numbers

And lights and signs and conductors and drivers
And cheerful spitting sparks at the knots
In the overhead wires. Readers, you would have
Enjoyed this as much as I did.

1970s

105 *Epithalamium*

Two by two this Saturday you little animals
Step with your decoration of hymns and flowers in-
To your waiting compounds; taking your place among all
The ancient objects of living, those graceless
Gifts that will stick for years, like burrs out of reach;
There being, always:
                    Blankets to cover you,
Curtains to curtain you, clocks that will thread your
Disquieted sleeps with duty, and sets of knives.
In all South London a misted orange heaven
Haloes the nurtured hair and suits of smiles.

But in some other uncertain sunlight, of a bad dream,
Such things may rise like some
Sortilegious army, shuddering the compounds,
Greedy to seize their own power and
Wailing in rancour: Can you depart us,
Dismiss us, divide us? – And will need to be
Put down somehow in baskets and sacks
And cases and bags and pockets and
Arranged elsewhere, in a place where they can always be seen,

With snarls that stay on their faces until you die.

106 *Told by a Monk*

'When the Saracens overran the shrine at Jerusalem the monks of Little
Walsingham announced that the spirit of the Blessed Virgin Mary had
taken up residence there . . . the resulting flow of pilgrims brought great
wealth to the monastery. . . . Early in his reign Henry VIII walked barefoot
to Walsingham to pay homage. . . . Later, at the dissolution of the monas-
teries, the image of Our Lady was taken to Smithfield and burnt there. . . .
The Walsingham shrine is again today a flourishing resort of pilgrims.'

Norfolk guide-book.

Our Blessed Lady who
Dwelt in the Holy Land
Rose from her shrine that was
Soiled by the heathen hand,

Soared from that martyred place,
Ransacked Jerusalem,
And for her dwelling chose
Our Little Walsingham
Ave Maria

Then every godly soul
Who would make offering
Unto the holy name
To our new shrine did bring

Alms and ten thousand prayers
For her sweet charity,
So that her presence here
Made us prosperity
Deo gratias

One of that long array,
In cruel barefootedness,
Great Henry came this way
To give, pray and confess.

Walking, a pilgrim, with
Hosed and shoon courtiers he
Tore his royal feet on hard
Stones to our monastery
In nomine Dei

Suppliant and penitent,
Asking her mercy for
All the sin covered by
The majesty he wore,

Henry bowed down his height
Under her image here,
Many an hour bowed down
In holy pain and fear
Miserere nobis

All who attended him,
On reverential knee
Fell at his ordering,
Prayed there as long as he,

Then when he rose and stood,
Promised with him to bear
To us and Her always
Tributes of gold and prayer
To help our holy work

Great Henry went; and was
Cursed of our Heavenly King
For the vile mind he showed
In lustful wandering,

And, for the gold he gave,
This way again he came
Bringing for penitence
Edict and sword and flame
Instead of naked souls

He who was holy once,
Festering with vanity
Thrust his royal power into
Filth and carnality,

Pillaged our golden shrine,
Taking the Image there
To burn in heretic
Fire at a Smithfield fair
No better than a Saracen

135

Great God is just upon
Avarice and lechery:
King Henry died in grief,
Stricken his treasury,

Useless his proud decrees
Who in sin plunged his . . . head,
Heresy earnt him the
Pox on his dying bed
No more than he deserved

Now again in that spot
Glows our new modern shrine,
And pilgrims render their
Gifts to the Form Divine;

In painted village shops
Priests sell on holy days
Pictures and statues and
Rosaries in her praise
Who gave us all we have

Thus has God's wisdom done
Justice on princes' sin,
And his strong love made gold
Where dross had entered in:

Where shop and shrine lay de-
Cayed under godless feet,
Sweet truth and goodness fills
All the teeth of the street.
Amen

'For the first time did I engage in armour,
which I found but a dull satisfaction.'
                          Boswell's London Journal

I think they hardly happen any more.
But once, the mettle used to go on with
Such subtle forethought as was a pleasure
In itself: happy cumbrances, sweet slow
Anointments to give safety in the joust.

The tourney was more honourable then!
Little was quite so quickly gained as now,
And yes, there were some kinds of gallantries
Peculiar to the garb. . . .
                          But now, to wear
(Half-way, or more, through your warrior's career)

Nothing but naked ease, this disconcerts.
You feel you need a ritual to mask
The lack of mystery in the mystery,
Some few pretences round it all to hide
The mawkish fundamentals of the war.

Or else it gets to be a woman's thing.

A soured mellowness creeps into the light
After the start of July; because
The best of summer is just about now
Worked through, and the evenings seem resigned
To the season having already lost out.
These short fierce stalks are all
That's left in the shorn fields, with someone's hay harvest
Reeking off towards the barns. And my
Birthday comes around the middle of all this,

Arriving just past the place when
The marvels assumed of midsummer are dreamt of
As having lain, somewhere untraceable, back,
A little way back, under wet June days; being
There if one only could really have known.
My birthday is therefore a case of thinking
What was it that could have been worth it, if it
Had not unnoticeably gone? The day itself
Inserts a chill under the August sweat,

Especially towards nightfall, especially towards
This time of life; and stands to summer
As the next circle out stands to the bull on
A target: each approximate hit is challenging
Me back to try for summer again. So that
I feel death's final supervening might come
Like a hand holding back the arm which draws,
Still hopefully, the bow; while my voice, thin, and just not
Natural any more, is screaming – 'Look, I've only just *begun!*'

109   *Clerk*

Is a lady of twenty-nine in a
Green, neat tailor-made two-piece, a
White collar, tortoiseshell spectacles and
A smooth skin nourished with the pallor of the Court.

There is a cool one, you say, and are right:
It's in the swift, sleek balance of the wrists
Over the documents, and the voice
(Of the deputy senior prefect of
Her public school) that whispers all day so
Accurate a continual
Transcript of proceedings into
A small white mike.

One dull Tuesday, the sort of day that
Can hardly lift its head to speak its name,
I saw her; from the public seats, thank god.
As usual, the sick with power were busy
Afflicting the sad with none, and she
Was in on this, as she would have to be.

I thought she had a stare might disinfect
Whole seas of toxins.

Part of the time she read the charges out.
Part of the time she jotted little notes.
Her fountain pen was a Parker Duofold.

At the end of
a line of
good, elderly squires
came
this last one,
       geared
to the forces of change,
Master of Foxhounds
but also
graduate of Surrey
(honours
in Business Studies)
and a collector of wines
– who one day
called in his
sharpest tenant-farmer
and his best
shepherd from the
slopes of the dale
       and *his*
smartest
sheepdogs, Rover and
Gyp,
       supreme at
heading
the woolly drop-outs off
– and showed them all
a letter and a
newspaper report;
their valley having
suddenly
become measurable
in terms of a
       capacity

of a different sort from
rearing
sheep.

Because where
conurban
corporations thirsted,
the streams of the mountains
might
            give,
and a full
valley might quench,
and besides the need
was
            paramount
and the squire
quite liked
the idea.
Three years gone,
only ten letters from
affronted Hampstead and
one defused
time-bomb in a
biscuit-tin,
            Gyp
and Rover laze on
the café shores
where the boats
are tethered for
sailing
            on
the reservoir,
the shepherd
stands in charge of the
            tea-urn
or dowses the plastic
cups, the farmer

papers the walls of
the clean new flint
cottage from which
he walks out to
             oversee
the embankments,
and the squire is
addressing a
conference of civil engineers
on 'Landscaping for To-morrow'
at a week-end
             school at
the University of York.
Warm Sundays in summer,
nose-to-tail
in long, loveless
processioning after
what neither
water nor anything
else can provide,
the well-cooled
cars from the conurbation
sidle the new road
to the concreted
edges of the lake,
while back at home
the sprinklers
rotate in solitude
on the lawns of Croft and Mead.

111   *Weeping Doll*

A trapdoor in the pink tin knickers
Of the weeping tin doll set down outside
This chemist's in Notting Hill is
Padlocked, tight, in a little bronze clench.

Open it wide when the key is fetched, and all
Your donations will tumble out, every coin
That activated her high slight wail for
The mortal disease she tells of in

This pitying locality, when you dropped them
Through the slot in her downturned lips.
One need not name the incurable demon (a
Crutch carries one unwithered shoulder

Of this articulate creature) but better celebrate
The goodness of the people spending coins
To make her weep and help her, so she
Lives a little longer on their small change.

Twice a month, a man drives round W.11
To all the dolls, stops his painted van
('The National Society for . . .') and
Unlocks all the knicker-trapdoors and takes away

Pennies and even sixpences to prop
Her twisting bones. This man has children, too,
Works for them as an accountant for a big company,
And does this voluntarily at night

– It keeps the whole thing personal, and he
Is rather proud of fifteen pounds twelve shillings
Taken from seven dolls in just one trip.
                                        A sunlight
No pestering State could hope to intercept

Shines sometimes on this area, where,
Who knows, the very same company may even
Own some of the houses where people try to live
– Enjoying the freedom of their choice to help

Others, and save taxation, and show a lovely
Unforced charity passing by and feeding
The weeping doll with enough stray pennies
To set her wailing many many times a day.

112 *Pastoral*

Some pining cows – with unenchanted sniffing –
Browsed the wan grass. Straggles of green wheat lay
Thrown down by ill-conditioned winds near where
A river dragged past, in a surly way.

Between two stony, grubby settlements,
There was a bend in a connecting lane
Providing, helpfully, some pallid verges,
And here the foxhunt met, in spraying rain.

Sound flesh and arteries swelled boldly outwards
Over the confident bones; the usual
Red coats and leather trouserings were sported;
Their little caps were the identical

Hunt gear for anywhere; and each man had
A placid piebald which, as he proudly sat,
Fumed feathery steam from nostrils set in faces
Looking well-pleased to do what they were at.

An indoor lighting, very blue and feeble
– A sort-of paintwork of the high sky-shell –
Fell on the hounds, brought up in snarling batches
And loving it, so far as one could tell.

Then, at a billowing horn-call from the master,
Each creature fled off, with a huge sultry bound
After a prey let fly for their pursuing
And chased across a grey and powdery ground.

In all these men and women pride was burning
To have this ceremony in such a place:
The air-locked air smelt grand, the beasts were sprightly,
The clothes were filled with arrogance and grace.

The faces, just as furious and paltry
As were their ancestors' before their births,
Joyed at the springy touch of lunar pastures
As had those solid forebears' on the earth's.

If some forebears had dared to be the first ones,
And radioed back, and from a special bag
Took cameras to photograph each other
And set them up a little national flag,

And gave rehearsed extempore impressions
Of how it felt on their historic day,
And walked around collecting bits and pieces
On screens two hundred thousand miles away,

All this was so that natural human measures
Could dance themselves wherever men might be,
With nothing fine or beautiful neglected,
And nowhere closed to oafish liberty.

113   *Calypso for Sir Bedivere*

But it was not only a sword to me,
It was a symbol, like, of virility.

King Arthur said, 'Take the sword away,
Throw it back into that lake today.'

> *Now King Arthur was a*
> *Wise old king,*
> *But why should he under*
> *-Stand everything?*

145

So I went down as a loyal knight should
And looked at the lake in an uneasy mood,

And was shaping to throw the sword in the water
When suddenly a very subliminal thought oc-

Curred to me: 'Whoever *wants* to lose
A trusty weapon that is still some use,

'A rational man would want to retain
His faithful tool and use it again,

> King Arthur may be a
> Wise old king,
> But is he tuned in to
> Everything?'

So with this sensible reasoning,
I stashed the sword and went back to the king,

And to change the subject I stood and lied
About the marvellous, marvellous countryside.

But the king said, 'I can quite well see
There are one or two things you are not telling me,

'Go back and throw that sword in the lake,
Tell me what you see, make no mistake.'

> King Arthur was a
> Wise old king,
> But why should he have to guess
> Everything?

Well, a second time I went down to the edge
And took out the sword to fulfil my pledge,

And cast it, for the king, out into that mere,
When suddenly I thought, 'No, I *can't* stand here

And fling this thing into that dirty pool,
It's a work of art, and valuable:

> *King Arthur may be a*
> *Wise old king,*
> *But does he know the cost of*
> *Everything?'*

So another time I went back up along
And told the king how I'd stood there, long

Time gazing at the lovely scenery
– But still he was not believing me.

He said, 'Go back down and take that blade
And throw it in the water just like I said'.

Then I thought:

With the king being terribly stern to me,
Can I prick against the kicks of authority?

So a third time, then, I went down to the brink
And looked at the water, as black as ink,

And picked up the sword (what else could I do?)
And with one strong, well-meaning lunge I threw

It right out *there*.
. . . . There was a clatter and I saw it drop
On the flat of its blade with an almighty plop,

Making little muddy bubbles in the foggy light
As it awkwardly, gradually sank from sight.

Well, King Arthur was a
Wise old king,
But he didn't hear the facts
About everything.

The lake was murky and the light was dim
And I saw no mystical samite limb

Or anything else that I pretended,
And thus when I turned around and wended

My way back up to King Arthur's shrine,
I had to invent things – tell him some fine

Story of how I plucked up courage and then took
A mighty throw, and with a beautiful, incisive look

About it, the sword fell and entered the water clean,
And the smoothest arm I had ever seen

Came up and eagerly clutched it through
Into the silky depths of the evening dew

– It had to be a story, you will surely see,
Fit for a symbol of virility.

But let's come to the
very revealing point of the
whole discreditable episode –

King Arthur was a
Wise old king
But he didn't tell the truth
About everything.

King Arthur listened while I had my say,
With a gimlet look that gave nothing away,

Then he rose on one elbow and put out one hand
And pretended he could suddenly understand.

And he said: 'Reversing that history,
Yes, exactly the same thing happened to me,

And the way you describe you finally shot it,
That was the way I originally got it:

The arm that came up to grab and take,
Handed it to me out of that lake.'

> *King Arthur was a*
> *Wise old king,*
> *But no, he didn't tell the truth*
> *About everything.*

And you can blame me and you can blame the king
If you've never done any equivalent thing.

If you've never told some fancy history
To make art cover up for reality.

114   *Ode to Centre Point*

One of the most
Paradoxical of infertil
    -ity symbols
Lately contrived, a vast
    Barren phallus of
Egg-boxes without eggs, it
    Simultaneously wav
-ers and maintains its own

Projection into the
Soft depths of the sky, a
        Thing of monumental
Insignificance, making no
    Impression and
Quite ignorable, unless for
        Its huge vac
-uity. But in so rapidly
        Appearing, it rased out
Everything lively on its site:
        Small blocks of
Usefully inhabited mansion
        Flats, various
Helpful shops, a passable
        Ristorante, an
Experimental theatre, and
        All of the navigable
Pavement on one side of the
        Charing Cross Road,
Substituting, at ground level, a
        Blue pond inside
Crass concrete walls with square
        -Fingered fountains jetting
The water; and above, shooting upward
        A weird, implacable
Cliff of patterned stone, glass and
        Air, a hive of empty
Cells, tilting, apparently, as the
        Clouds above pass over,
And at one dizzying, approximate
        Count, thirty-three stories high.
Therefore, it impinges on us all,
        Notwithstanding, and needs
To be taken into account; which
        Is why strong men with de
-termination and research have
        Gone grey trying to

Discover why it is there
    (But then who, exactly,
Wanted and actually willed Shell
    Mex or the Euston Road?)
– And what it is to do? Such
    A thing is like the
Clothes without the Emperor,
    Flaunting what looks like
Purpose in order to cover weakness
    And chaos, proving again
That somehow, in our time, all
    Towers are peculiarly
Bad, contraptions of anti-sense,
    Contraceptions of truth,
And things which one day might,
    With the clarity of simply
Looking at what is there, be just taken
    Down and scrapped. Indeed,
What couldn't we do when even
    The few square yards on
Which we base giant follies were
    Fruitful and even
Innocent again, with perfectly
    Natural weeds? To
Have *this* one as a play-space for
    Technocrats to
Run around and play utterly
    Virginal games of Bank Robbers on,
Instead of the real thing,
    Might be a splendid
Idea for its owner to instal
    If he ever repented
Of the tremendous non-use to which
    He put one quarter
-acre of our possible grass. And
    Perhaps one damn good
Roundabout with small, wry,

Cynical horses' faces to
Ride on, going perpetually grinning
        Round and round would be,
Though futile, a bit more sense.
                                Mean

        -while, until the world
Turns thus inconceivably pure
        And benevolent, the whole thing
Will rear up in front of the eye,
    Narrowing into the heavens and
Widening at its base like some
        -thing unnatural and
Unmotivated found one morning
    In any man's life, and
Probably the result of some
        Nasty and unremembered
Dream.
        Well, in a way, I'd hate
– With its uniformed toughs, trained
Alsatians and all, to knock it down
        And spoil anyone's happy
Fantasies, an act for which I may
        Have no moral right after
So much indulgence of my own,
        But . . . one's most citizenly
Sort of impatience sometimes rises,
        Just as suddenly, wishing
It lugged with it some uncitizenly
        Substance which might go
Off, and reasoning: Reality ought to be
        -gin somewhere, so why not
With somebody else, who has thirty-two
        Storeys less of it than me?

115   *Ballad of Scarlet and Black*

Waking at her lover's knocking, or
So she thought, she crossed, running,
A carpet twenty yards wide
To the curtains at the window, scarlet-
And-black,
And drew them.

Or so she thought.
                  Because
Behind the first curtains were
More curtains, and behind
The second were third,
And behind the third were fourth, none
Of them opening into daylight and onto
Her lover's face waiting at her door,
But onto only
Scarlet-and-black and then
Scarlet-and-black and then
Scarlet-and-black.
But several seconds later truly waking,
She drew
The curtains which were not in her dream,
And were one foot from her bed,
And were scarlet-and-black
And let straight daylight immediately in.

So now she combed, at her mirror, with
Fingers over open eyes, a parting in her hair, counting
Which day of daylight this was, and counting
The years of her life again.

And when her lover called, she
Went across town with him talking of her dream
    and what it meant,
Talking of their parting, and joining, and their
    endless counting of time,
And she was trying, trying to uncover
His daylight face.

Up the stairs to his room,
Their blood was the blood of veins returning to the heart,
Returning as if with ritual nostalgia to the heart,
Between scarlet and black.

There, pulling the black,
Lying under the scarlet, curtains, unhooked from the wall,
They made again the love of years,
With his face in darkness;
And then, with fingers across closed eyes
She sorted apart her hair
And slept until the next daylight arrived to be counted.

116   *Sadly on Barstools*

Sadly on barstools, in a city which doesn't speak
English with their accents, two have come together
Of whom one is asking the other advice, very frankly,
About a third – to whom neither is connected
By blood, or sexual ravin: just anxious friends,
And wanting to save Amanda's and William's marriage because
They prefer it that way.

The drinks, the bar, the barman, the fast bar clock
Are spun away to nothing among a cat's cradle
Of lovely information and speculation: who
Should, for whose future good, intervene
With whom, and if possible when,
And as between Friday in Greenwich or Sunday in Islington,
It isn't decided yet.

Common citizens unlike them, and more usual in this place,
Are flocking round,
With ordinary drinks that have not seriously, ever,
Strained the cellars of the Bull. The television,
Shoved on the shelf above the forgotten picture
Of part of the local docks in 1910, is showing
A retrospective tribute to Michael Miles.

117 *Sporting Event*

Wimbledon. Centre Court. Blank and pitiless sun. Many
Eyes misted with, as it were, emotion.

The Old Fox is playing young Kenny Trabner of Australia.
The Old Fox sticks to a baseline game, Trabner is
Up at the net for the volleys, leaning back
At unthinkable angles for the smashes. Cunning,
Age, and experience facing
All the burnished arrogance of youth, Trabner
Playing the ruthless tennis they play now,
And things not going too well at all for the Old Fox.

Trabner, too, in immaculate shorts and Sassoon
Coiffure, the Old Fox, bald, in full-length, pre-war
Flannels, and wearing a green eye-shade on his forehead
Above his bifocals;
But the crowd is on his side.

Can the Old Fox do it this time, *can* the Old Fox do it again?
Things don't look too well. First set
To Trabner, 6–0. Second set
To Trabner, 6–0. It is a crafty tactic the Old Fox is trying.
Third set, Trabner leading 5–0 and 40–0 in the sixth game,
On his own service.
This will need all the Old Fox can pull out, but
Throughout his career the Old Fox has somehow been
Strangely able to pull something out,
So to speak, in moments of crisis.

Now the crowd is utterly still, now the princess
Fingers the Cup, in the Royal Box, with excitement that
                              mounts weirdly. Trabner
Is serving for the match, three balls bunched
In one broad hand, and
The first ball lifts. And as
The thunderous, upward, apparently final trajectory
Of Trabner's racquet begins, the Old Fox
Pulls out from the pocket of his flannel trousers
An ancient flintlock pistol such as might be hired
For commercial t.v. serials about the Jacobite Rebellion,
And fires.

And Trabner falls. The crowd is on ten thousand delirious,
Cheering, swooning feet. With a last
Expenditure of feeling the princess accidentally shudders the
                              Cup from its plinth.

The Old Fox leaps the net and shakes Trabner's dying hand.
The newsmen, as they are said to do, crowd round.
The umpire calls out, 'Game, Set, Match and Championship to
                              the OLD FOX.'

Max Robertson says, 'Yes, the Old Fox has done it again!'

118   *The End*

(*for P.C.K*)

Not simply human, but all,
But all matter dying there,
Dwindling and tottering away to
A much-more-than-cosmic pit,
An ultimate dark,
An inconceivable collapse:

If so, a tough
Test for the relationship (of matter with
Logic and physical laws)
And as tough for you and me.
But I
Should like to think we could be there, and see:

On the brink of the last collapsar, surviving;
Linking us, ten finger-tips dwindled already
Into two precariously-poising fives.
A touch commemorating all our
Mutual matter's scars from a thousand
Previous little deaths, and falls. Would

We balance, balance,
Humorously on that very final edge
(Such as we often stepped to) smiling
As ever before in that dark, waiting the worst,
Elated in our own, as its, contractions,
Feeling no vortex greater than ourselves?

119 *April Fool's Carol*

Celebrate today belladonna and shot silk.
Women will do what they are for.

Belladonna: poisons in
Certain quantities are a cure.
Women will do what they are for.

Shot silk: it changes at a look, you move
It varies, contrary; but
Is completely one, its feel
Will rub the best and nothing, ever, more.
Women will do what they are for.

The Marys are at every birth, and grave
Delivery, at every marriage too they wear
Their ancient finery: *Women*
('Sing all a green . . .')
                              Will do what they are for.

120 *Knightsbridge Display-window*

Thrown out and buried from the colander,
The peelings struck. Potatoes flowered
Blue, white and green,

English republican colours, on
Our wartime flower-beds.
                              I see
My great-aunt now, thrifty

And foresighted patriot, calendar
Of Winston on the wall, bending
To dig. She grew tomato-plants

And forsook zinnias, she planted out
Saplings of wilted lettuce which would
Hold the invader back; well,

Indirectly. Thus the war years were:
In things like this, a concen-
Tration of particular sensibleness,

A living-on by what would keep
Us living on; not blitzes,
Factory pep-talks, flags on maps,

Not shining uniforms and Alameins,
Or V-signs, tanks and refugees, oh not
That annual stutter of King George VI,

That Churchill-rant – simply making ends meet,
Cutting bread thinly, having
Just enough things to wear, etc., that.

We'll grumble now at imposts on Montrachet . . .
Sometime we'll get perhaps
A commonwealth of sense, and not with guns.

121   *Unnumbered Road*

(for S.L.W.)

She walks in bleeding and smiling from a midnight road/
   she can't remember it/she remembers all of it/
   her hair is black and grey at once/her
hand trembles to be familiar/it is
   calm with its familiarity/her face
      smiles and bleeds/the car turned over twice
   on a road at midday/she can't keep
      her hand from shaking/she can't keep it

shaking/her friends were all there/none of them at all/
           they said her hair was grey and black at once/
her face bled while it smiled/her voice
           talked while it was silent/
       he could understand/she
   turns the car over in her head/her
       hand is calm when it trembles in his/
which holds it for the first and hundredth time/
       it is now/it is months ago/the friends have all gone/it
   is night/it is morning/they are all coming back/
           the night is black and grey at the same time/
   the dawn is black and grey at the same time/
           her lips close to open/
       it is all calm/it is shaking with strangeness/
           he puts out his arms to hold her for the first time/
           she holds him before he can touch her/
           he turns the car over in his head/
       he turns her body over in his arms/she
— is night and dawn at once/she is
               black and grey at once/she is
           smiling in his arms/she
       is bleeding in his arms for the first time/
           for the hundredth time/he is smiling in her arms/
   they are calm/they are shaking with strangeness/
       the friends are constantly there having gone away/he
   is constantly there having gone away/he has
               come back from a midnight road
           turning over a car in his head/and
   she is smiling she is smiling/she is bleeding she is bleeding/
       he hears his voice saying her name her name/
   they are crying/they are smiling/
       it is night/it is dawn/
   he has at long last without a second's waiting
               temporarily meshed his contradictions
                               with hers for ever

In the Cornwall wind
I stood with the mine-shaft behind me.
Something said, a toneless kind-of-voice said, 'Don't
Walk on that ground.'

The ground was plain mud and stones, a grey stretch, safe.
But, 'Don't walk on that ground.'
I had flung and heard the pebbles in the dark shaft
Fenced off under the brick stack, black.
Was the grey ground not safe?

The wind worked at the firs' tops,
It had that whisper, 'Don't walk on
That ground.' The pebbles in the shaft
Clanged, and hit echoes. The echoes touched out
Echoes. The echoes said, 'Don't walk on that
Ground.'

The death-shaft gulped and trapped the echoes of the pebbles.
The ground was mud and stones, is mud and stones,
A grey stretch, not fenced off now, thirty years
Safe, still. People have walked on it,
Thirty years.
I did not walk on it when I was ten.

I stand here, thirty years after, in the Cornwall wind,
A man, looking at the grey ground. The firs' tops
Work and whisper.
The day is a clearer day, the sea visible,

The sun is out. A woman touches my arm.
We are standing with the mine-shaft behind us swallowing
Echoes of thirty years ago, of a minute ago,
Pebbles we have both thrown, smiling.

Something says, a toneless kind-of voice says
'Don't walk on that ground.'

123 *In Hertfordshire*

Not very meek are the polytechnics, they
Shall inherit the earth; what there is left
After Construction Units' rummagements. – Come
Hell and the low waters of this stricken place,
I might elude it by transmogrifying to
A cat safe with ninety-nine lives on
A Hemel Hempstead walkway, or a muddied

Reservoir swan, or a magpie fumbling
The scrawny grasses of roadhouse roundabouts,
But this would be enduring, not enjoying:
Single-manned nearby, the Green Lines would
Rattle on, more slowly than the stagecoach, past churned
-up verges stuck with signs, and it would make,
Like other people's, a sort-of country life.

But living, a human in all this, system-built
For profit-sharing, for Helping to Build the Firm,
One would feel all the prep schools, in big Victorian houses
Among arranged glades eking out the hopes
Of the techno-bourgeoisie; dance, young, in the formica
Discothèques of Letchworth; rent house where Ebenezer's paltry
Cities are nailed down in the duckboards of Hatfield; carry

One's young in wire Macfisheries baskets across
Littered precincts of pools and statuary; grow old
In the Community Centre in front of screens pocked with
Supersonic interference; get interred
In somewhere undulant and discreet behind
A subtopian hill. Against all this, in Barnet perhaps,
Some poor bloody Blake might frenzy a while, then

Take out a mortgage himself, or move to Leeds. – Though
Consumer Groups rampage, and the Hadley Green Fabians
Plan, plan soft turquoise bathrooms in central heating,
And the spirit's life goes on (flocks out
On Sundays of Vivas and Dolomites to wafers and
Lollies of sweet consolation, New English
Sermons and Welwyn's holy ice-cream chimes),

All around, in securest sunlight, the
Brownies parade for Thinking Day, the Rugby Clubs
Run their Development Sweepstakes, the commuters play
Aryan golf and buy private treatment, and
Telescoped Avengers lie on the reservations among
Sprays of demented glass as company
Jaguars bray, and scream, past.
                                        So don't get there if you

Need not, you'd find your escapable future ready,
                                              grazing
With jaws like Corporations on miles of forgotten
Scrub forty miles from the centre of the boil:
It has fangs of reinforced concrete and triple glazing,
Its eyes are huge stacks of strip-light in Industrial Areas
Refining precisions to blur life, imprinting so tidily on
Clicking cards the specific patterns of your death.

124   *Texas Book Depository*

I am writing my text-book of modern American history
It will sell in all the schools
Every school will buy fifty dozen copies
One for every child in every class
In a given year
It should appear about 1963
My book will sell in millions
To the school authorities

163

It will be stored ready
In millions
On the shelves of great depositories full
Of textbooks for schools
My book will make me a fortune
It will have fine clear diagrams
Fine clear expositions
And be a fine text-book yes
The depositories will be full of it
The depositories will be air-conditioned
Men will walk around the depositories in grey coats
Counting and packaging the books
Including my book
They are wonderful places depositories why
You could get lost in depositories or hide
And not be seen for hours
You will be able to get lost even among the copies
Of my book
I will have done a humble service
Publishing my book
I shall be able to say to myself
I could have done innumerable worse things
Than publishing my book
Than helping to fill with books like mine
Depositories so big you could hide and not be found
Now tell me what harm ever came of depositories of books?

125   *The Ship of Death*

First, prolonged and weird estuarial waters,
    And so wide before you realise: full of rusted,
Sunken, purposeless objects; or creaking guide-lights
    Offering unclear channels, curving paths
Of a grey water greyer than the rest. And now the eager
    Sea-birds that followed have dropped back for the shore.
The strip-lighting blinks on in the Dining Room, the cutlery

Scintillates. But you don't enjoy their small-talk at the table, as
The white-coated band on the platform lilts into selections,
  Selections: it's a musical about your life they
Are playing them from, and it could not have run long in town.
  Now the ship tilts, and the crockery slides downhill; and
There is a tannoy announcement from the captain:
  Welcoming you to the ship, hoping you will be
Comfortable, and reminding you there is no destination.
  You leave the table for the bar. Already it's dark, which
Might be more interesting; though you expected, looking out,
  That a scattering of stars might show; and the sky's dull.
Far off, is it west, you can pick out an esplanade
  With lights like a frippery of beads; you
Never attained that one, wherever. Your drink hasn't lasted,
  The print in your newspaper blurs and you can't see faces
Very clearly. The map, of the route of the ship in
  The frame on the wall, is practically blank. Is there a rest

                                                    room?
The stewards don't attend to you, they are attending
  To the bed-makers in the cabins. The duty-free shop
Is a shut grille. The handrail in the corridor misses
  Your hand, upstairs both sides of the deck cant you into
The bullets of the spray. The wake is dark, the prow is

                                             chained off.
  You go to the Engine Room for the monotone of the
                                             drone,
But that is no anaesthetic. There should be
  Amusements aboard, surely? What about the staterooms
Looking so sumptuous in the brochures? And the gilt lounges?
  Something worth having this ticket for? God, this ship feels
No different from being alive; because
  Your seaboard walk shakes like your walk on land, and
All your thinking ends at the same advice: it's time, no
  Other choice, to go down the metal steps to
Where it says Men, and lock the door; be alone, alone,
  You may find, there, what's wrong that you couldn't
Name, that nobody found out.

                                        – So this you do, except
    That when you have closed the door, the door locks
On you. Rust runs in lifelong trickles from the welded
    Bolts of this cubicle; everything shudders, even more,
In you and the whole ship. No hammering for help,
    Or calling, it's H.M.S. Death, death: the eternal
Accumulated store of everything life became: just
    Yourself, as you are, and your face in that bowl. Smile,
                                                    you're free

To vomit your self-regard for the rest of the voyage.

126   *An Elegy on Mademoiselle Claudette*

Mourning the final death from disbelief of one
Who lies now farther out than her rival's sword;
The sea, having had her at last, being
A fit receptacle and outcome. She
Was thirty-two when she died, I having
Given her first credulity when I was eight,

And the ideal reader. Somewhere they met,
Her fatalism, my childhood, and made strange friends:
She held her world with fingertips of ice
On chalices of poison. She was in the eyes
Pulling mine at fifteen over café floors, she stared
Out from trains, she dared in time to come near and be

No different, even when she undressed. The spell didn't
Break, because she was always gone next morning,
A skyline figure on horseback, not leaving a note.
And this continued some while, her cloak
Flowed at numberless parties, and she nurtured
Linguistic codes beyond mine, and had flats

(Which I never went to) all mauve lights and white divans,
Acting indestructible enough to be
A life-force in her way, a fuel for one kind
Of imagination. But what could she keep when
Life coarsened, and truth walked in? Well,
She thrived for a while by updating her devices,

Like – playing the metropolis, all the sleights of
Communications, the trick of the very new:
She was good at sudden taxis, away, in the small hours,
Had a dreadful skill with things like the letter
Never sent because of the promise to phone,
Never kept. And she had this vague gallery of

'Friends' to refer to, in a sensual, significant abstract,
No names vouchsafed. She was trying hard, was desperately
Applying the cosmetics of decline. – But she's
Abstract herself now; finally dead; not
Struck down by some other in contest, not replaced
By odder enchantments, not vanquished by any

Conversion from Snow Queens to Earth Mothers, none
Of that: she just couldn't keep up the pose.
It was not so long back that her last departure
Took place. She put out one entreating hand in velvet,
But it looked like something ghost-written for her.
I tried to feed those plaintive metaphors, I searched

The depths of my compassionate soul for faith
To keep her alive; but all the same she died.
And sad the way daylight lastly saw her sink,
Poor Mademoiselle Claudette: leaving shadows of stances only,
Vague rags of garments, tawdry stage properties,
And terribly dry pink tissues on bedroom floors.

My dancing is, in my opinion, good,
In the right, cramped circumstances, and provided
Other people are too preoccupied with
Their own to notice mine. I am happy
To have lived into an informal age when
Standing and shaking in approximate rhythm, not
Bowing and guiding, is the idea. Because to
Have to know regulated steps and be skilful was what
I could never manage at all when it was the thing.

So I do dance. But I'm never entirely sure.
It's a kind of movement you would never make
In the normal course, and how much it always seems
To obtrude on the natural in an embarrassing
Way wherever people get it started!
Set it apart, on a stage, with a large
Orchestra, it's all right, it's undoubtedly clever,
And the costumes are glorious to gawp at, but
It still looks a little bit foolish, moving like *that?*

To speak of how all its origins are so
Utterly primal – the planets, the seasons,
The rhythms of mating, and so on, and so on,
Is to list a lot of fundamental things,
Explain them, and exorcise dancing:
Because simply why dance if you've come to understand
What dancing mimes so roughly, or makes such
A repetitive pantomime of? Sleights of courtship,
Postures of delight, grief, vanity, idolatry I see

All around me more sharp and subtle for not being
Done in a style. Dancing has social uses,
I know, but so did elemental spears and punches before
They invented tables for eating and conducting
Verbal negotiation (and does hands
Gripping slyly under a table ever happen
In the middle of a fandango?)
Moreover, if the elemental stuff
Of dancing is banal, the ancient, ritual and customary

Panoply of 'the dance' is incredibly peculiar:
Fellows in feathers, or kilts, or puma-skins,
Guys trinkling little bells down there in Hampshire,
Or folding arms over black boots flicking in the
Urals . . . one surely turns away to find somewhere quieter,
Where one needn't be part of a silly circle
Of grins, clapping hands in moronic unison (I once
Took a pocket torch in, to go on reading – *The Listener*,
I believe – all the way through a Gene Kelly musical).

For ostensible moralist reasons, the
Puritans disliked dancing: but they also
Opposed all giving and wearing of jewellery,
In which they may well have been right; so with dancing,
They may also have come at the truth
From a wrong, religious direction. But, down Oxford Street
These days, whatever the mortgage rate, there jogs
In shine or rain an irrelevant group of chanters
Shuffling to the rhythm of tiny cymbals, opposing

Shaven sublimity to the big, crude, selling
Metropolis around; and *dancing*, in sandals, for converts.
They'd like to see everyone join them . . . how unlikely,
I think; and how such unlikelihood shows
That most of us only don or discard our
Finery, to dance, in a fit of social desperation.
I recall that outside the Hammersmith Palais,
There once was an illuminated sign announcing
A group of performers known as THE SANDS OF TIME.

For months, the words, I surmised, were a motto
Of that establishment: a thousand grains shaken
Nightly in that vast box, a thousand softies
Sifting for life-partners as the hours and days
Ticked on in tawdry, implacable rhythms. Yet the
Dancing prospers – telling how many the world leaves
Despoiled of words, of gestures diverse and specific,
Of shades of forehead, or hintings of finger-tips,
Or any more delicate tremor that speaks the whole thing;

And this is the crux. Tides vary, exact shelvings
Of pebbles on shores don't repeat, while patterns of clouds
Are never the same, are never *patterns*. Raindrops,
At unforeseen moments run, and weigh, down, minutely,
A million particular grass-blades: movement, movement,
Everlastingly novel shifts of a universe not
Gracelessly ordered, not presided by a setter of
Regulations. Vanity is so sad pretending to represent
Nature with humans dancing. Those who can move need not
dance.

In the same post, the Old Fox receives
Word that he is in overdraft at the bank,
And a gas bill for £3.69.

Ten days later, the Gas Board write again, in red, 'They would
Be grateful if . . .' The Old Fox waits.

Two weeks later, the Gas Board write, in red again, some
Phrases underlined, 'Regret, you do not tender payment within

Seven days, supply disconnected, charge for re-connection.'
The Accounts Officer's signature is stamped below.

Six days later, the Old Fox carefully writes a letter:
'Thank you for, apologies for any inconvenience,
Do not wish cause difficulty, wonder if payment
Of sum outstanding *by instalments*, very grateful, Yours etc.'

A week having passed,
Drinking coffee made on his undisconnected cooker,
The Old Fox reads, 'Must regretfully state, not customary,
Payment by instalments when sum entailed so small,
No alternative but to ask, within five days,
Supply disconnected unless, Dictated by the Accounts Officer
And signed in his absence . . .'

Four days passing, the Old Fox writes, 'Thank you courteous
                                                    reply,
Recollect (which is untrue) kindly permitting me
Payment by instalments, previous occasion, some years ago,
Comparable sum, possibly consult your records, appreciate
Your looking into this, regret any delay caused,
Only anxious to settle account as soon as possible.'

The Gas Board writes after a week, ignoring this.
'Supply disconnected unless . . .' The Old Fox rejoins,
'May I direct your kind attention, my letter of,
Possibly held up in the post, possibly crossed with yours of,
Sorry to put you to this, Yours etc.'

'We have looked into our records,' the Gas Board two weeks later,
'Can find no precedent in your case, not our custom with small
                                                    amounts,
Must insist on immediate settlement, otherwise steps
Will be taken, supply disconnected, recovery of sum
By legal action, Yours very truly, Accounts Officer'
– Personally signed.

Sadly, then, the Old Fox writes a cheque for £3.69,
Omits (on purpose) to sign it,
And posts it to the Board.

In eight days, the cheque is returned, 'For your signature,
Yours truly.' The Old Fox waits.

A month later, 'We do not appear to have received cheque
On which your signature was requested, bring this
To your kind attention.'

It is winter by now, and the gas fire gleams.
The North Sea roars on the cooker to heat
The Old Fox his supper of Irish stew from a tin.
Lighting his gas water-heater, he runs a bath.
It mellows him. He writes his name at the bottom of the
                                                    cheque
(Which will come back 'referred to drawer' in nine days'
                                                    time.)
Returning from the pillar box, he picks up the next quarter's
                                        invoice from the mat.

I take a long lick of this envelope,
Getting an unsweet, unAmerican taste:
The glue of England, which does not pretend.

The middle-classes drink precisely
From the far side of the other person's cup,
But kiss more deeply than the workers do

– Say sociologists. One day, we parked outside
A backstreet house in Wandsworth, kissing
In just that way, not thinking of social class,

And this in broad daylight, very visibly,
When an aproned lady came out quite displeased,
And motioned to us, literally shaking

Her hand with her wrist as if her hand
Were shaking a duster, wanting us to move on.
The moral disapproval was very clear.

And the point is, do you remember this at all,
Which came to me as I began to lick
Your envelope? Since, if you don't recall,

Invisible dust, from a hand shaking it, may
Have settled on us and on the whole Atlantic
– Covering also what this letter means.

And need I have unsealed it to say all this?

Shallow: And is Jane Nightwork alive? . . . certain
she's old, and had Robin Nightwork by old Nightwork
before I came to Clement's Inn. *(Henry IV Part 2)*

1

Loathing the day-, if not the candle-, light,
Old Nightwork burrows by unsocial hours,
Preferring heavy curtains: velvet pelts,
And under them, so warm to sooth and seethe.

2

By definition working by darkness,
Nightwork can freely imagine it is anyone
Provided she is of average shape and size
Assuming she is not much different in behaviour
Given that she stays silent
As long as his head is not plagued with associations
Granted the place is anonymous and dark

And until his eyes grow used to the dark.

3

This epitaph for British Standard Time,
So hatefully abrupted in its prime:
Let it lie, if it must, in peaceful rest,
This kindly scheme, which succoured the depressed
By giving them at dusk a longer day,
And in the morning holding dawn away
For one sweet hour.
                         Soon may it come again
To help Old Nightwork and his screwed-up Jane.

4

Love as light being a figment of chastity,
Nightwork keeps, as a brief lamp, only
The after-image of the crass filament
On his eyeballs: all senses then are bent
On the tactile patterns of the blackness,
Where legs and hands tangle and wrangle and press
Into their feeling places, making shivers
Out of the dark fiercer and fierier than slivers
Of clean sun by morning on shrill waters –

Nightwork, perforce alone to-night,
At sleepless 4 a.m., hating small hours radio,
And a scorner of unassisted self-abuse,
Has a very bright idea: rings Dial-a-Tit,
And listens to the wobbling.

What frankly feeble lover, even some hellfire
Sticker-up for Nature, does not go
Spare as Nightwork when the dawn chorus starts? That seeping,
Officious rant from the whole *Book of the World's Birds*
(With five hundred bloody colour plates.)

Night and its stations pass with clamped-up eyes.
What sleeping with adds up to is: an hour
Before you sleep, and later on, an hour
After you wake up, but before you rise
– Between the two, some eight hours spent so dead
You, like Old Nightwork, might as well be dead.

if I went, thought arrogantly the Duke, someone else
would have to be saved from it all by my coming back.
This time he was not humble and did not go.

Christ! things were bad. Ignoring Government appeals,
the plastic bottles blocked up the underpass. Build
us a flyover, their spokesman demanded.

the people were urged to economise by Ministers.
One said: Using the cores of toilet rolls
as toilet rolls, would help us at this time.

the militants had halted the mushroom farms.
Fungi were growing on the mushrooms.
'Their wives say "Go back",' showed a poll.

the Duke, not having left, could not go back.
He could not even come down like a god
from a Supersonic-Channel-Tunnel-Machine.

the thermometers offer to the mercury: Accept a cut
to Centigrade rates for now, and we will consider
talks about Fahrenheit scales next year.

yes, television slashed to seven channels, only six coloured,
closing down at twelve, the intelligentsia
forgetting the words of the commercials.

students, disguised as guides, got into the grottoes, wiped
the drips off the stalactites, caused tourist
income to plummet, never caught the swine either.

exclaimed the Duke: The breathers are behind all this,
breathing in, out, day, night, agitating to share
the very air with us who – respire.

you must conserve rubber corkscrews, said an announcement,
    steel corkscrews are just as good, in twenty years
        all bottles will be made with corks again.

the four faces of a public clock showed each a different
    time. Thought the Duke: Some liberal, giving
        the workers four chances of being punctual.

photos of an agribusinessman fondling a battery hen
    were printed by conservationist subversives,
        and sparked off a community crisis.

to reap the full benefits of restriction, a newspaper wrote,
    we must face higher prices for things which will be
                                               cheaper
        when less is more available than it is now.

after a hundred years or so of this, people were saying:
    Are we sure we need a Duke, whether he knows
        he is coming or going or not?

132   *Recollections from a Death Bed*

Waiting circa 1949, in the little waiting-room
Beside the single track, with the small stove crackling,
Reposed on a bench, reassured by a verified connection,
The journey onwards going twenty miles
To a destination feeling remote (no seagulls
Floating in this far from the unreachable marshes)

He listens to the quiet and contemplates distance:
The long miles slowly to go in the two carriages,
Then the light in the wrinkled panes of the door,
And the known face opening and greeting.

Three hours before he had been: a philosopher,
Recounting in a lecture *things we can be certain exist,*
The other side of the moon, for example, which cannot be

               seen

But may reasonably be inferred. An hour and a quarter
To wait.
    A low fence exists, he sees it, on the far
Side of the track, and a dimmed field beyond, leaves lying
Dulled by the rain, circa 1949 and autumn.

The stove, for now, inextinguishably secure;
And hard corner-arms to repose on, in the straight seat
In the somewhere surely-coming small train;
Then all the villages ahead, reached singly,
The place with a market, the one with a harbour . . .
Trees brushing the windows, darkened grass along cuttings,
A known face of the moon veiled above the coppice.

And the little room was secure at the time,
And stayed so, carried in the mind when the station
Closed and the track was wrenched up, and the
Stove broken out of the wall.
Life, Elizabeth, he said, *is certain to get*
Imperceptibly faster and more brazen. And later, *You*

Were always some distance to reach, but
Today, how everything feels too close . . . is much too seen.
We die, these days, of the obvious and the near.
We die of the marshes towed to the caravans in
Half-an-hour.
    He is dying today, in a twelfth floor room
With a high steel crane veering outside the window, higher.

But delay, blessed delay, yet. Thinking time. An hour
And a quarter to the end.

Dear Elizabeth. Just to say
I shall come by train in the usual way.
I shall have the wait at Charnham for contemplation.
I ought to be with you by just after five o'clock.
Don't trouble to meet me, I have little to carry. And

It is a mere ten minutes' walk from the station.

A Song of Good Life (133–153)

133 *Natural Order*

Over the dainty
Crenels of a dynasty,
The sweep of old, walled,
Outspread estates:
Pheasants fumbling through hedges,
Trotting peasantry.

In one high, green drawing room
A photographer is spreading a tableau out,
Standing, seated, sitting on the floor;
A dynastic tableau.

Try to look royal and natural
At the same time. Try to look
Ordinary. Is it so hard?

Sweeping in hushed cars,
Naturally,
To platforms of bunting,
Shaking dignitaries and their hands,
Stooping a solemn wreath to green again
The limbs and bones written into historical mud.

At births and weddings and deaths,
In dynastic succession,
Outspread sweet fanfares,
Gold Stick Extra-

ordinary,
In black, trotting carriages,
Dynasties of quadrupeds.
Can it be natural, please?

Today it has to be natural through the streets,
Learning to fix quite ordinary
Poses into the viewfinder,

Learning to green a nothing
With a mask of naturalness,
Ordinary smiles, no crenels,
An outspread dynasty of masks.

134   *The Telephone in his Office*

The answers are freshly delivered, complete,
Infallible, natural, good-humoured,
In the light of, thank you
To the press of cameras and questions at ten,
After rising, shaking, at six,
After a session of member countries till three.

Now flying to Washington Moscow Saigon
Cairo Jerusalem Brussels,
In power above the cloudbank in the light of
The sun, hands shaking with heads-of-state,
Or talking to them on the telephone
In his black office, in an ordinary morning.

Ceremonial luncheon for the Ambassador of,
And Madame. Avoiding the migraine lights
In the prisms of jewels. The working together
For the common good, in the light of
The historical bonds.

The index shaking through the afternoon,
The mind, if not the face or hands,
Shaking while conferring to curb the,
On measures to prevent the,
Review surcharges in the light of.

In the light of an ordinary afternoon like this,
He could go into his office,
Pick up the one, coloured, one-coloured telephone,
And in twenty minutes
Fifty million people would be dead.

135   *The Majesty*

Wishing to be thought of brisk but leisured at toilette, the decisive, scrupulous shaving, the braces bracing the Queen's Own shoulders for the day. Not this no-man's land between pulsing half-sleep and the muddy light of the forecourt.

And breakfasting at six off immaculable silver; lifting, on a sideboard, burnished salver-lids like domes from an imperial age, coffee attentively poured, and one bending who trots out again with an oiled flip and whisper of the door. But: fumbling from cupboard to table with slices from a polythene wrapper, time only to open at the obituaries . . .

Still, the scattered particulars of the outspread city, the bus queues in the rain, the underground, the people about their occasions, can all be swept together into the purview and protection of the Law, comprised in its ancient cohesion, chastened by its sanctions.

This evening, addressing a society: 'A High Court Judge Remembers': *We enshrine all our age-old, historical, meditated wisdom in the majesty of the Law, which holds, through all its manifold detail, our Christian society together. If the Law is brought into disrepute, if the Law is flouted . . .* And, colloquially: *Many other comic, and indeed tragic, sides of life come one's way in a day in Court.*

Home to the nightmare of the giggling crucifix.

Caption: *Simon Kemberton – things moving fast
Among the Op-Art*

Unruffled, King's Road-suited Simon Kem-
berton of Paramore
Is the type of the new, young executive with a bright
Eye to the European future. *Forescan* found him
In his Op-Art panelled office on
The nineteenth floor of the newest Seifert block
In the City Centre, eight multi-coloured
Telephones blossoming around him. The story
Of Kemberton's rise is amazingly simple,
Based on accurate, split-second
International contact with his fifty million
Market, getting producers to package the product
Brightly the way supermarkets can sell it
To the lady with the little wire tray. Business
Has grown just ridiculously fast since Paramore
Adroitly skirted round that take-over bid
From Dave Walker's Hubris empire.
The future, a bright one,
With branches in Brussels, Jerusalem,
Cairo, Saigon, Washington, you name it,
Looks to be a rather pleasant trip
To the multi-million level.
Forescan asked Kemberton how he, why he,
What he, etc., etc.

137   *Rustic Wedding*

The son of the plantation farm that takes
A company name
Is driving from the edge of the fen to his wedding
In one of the collapsing churches.

His bride in the mistery
Steps out of her Vanden Plas in a turquoise cloud
Of unnatural fibres for which a thousand hens
– In no particular order – have pecked in the dark.

Worming into the pews for New English maxims
Under high Norman vaults, their guests are there by treading
Down hedges and trees for miles, and renting
Wet cottages out to 'peasants' and the wind.

At the reception hotel,
A sweet lulling music blows, all the time,
Through every sort of room.
                              They'll sit and talk
The latest, lucrative, pollutants; over Veuve Clicquot.

138   *Interview with a Creator*

No, not the idea of slamming at people with the stone
From the start.

We begin with the product itself,
And make it into something which people can be persuaded
To want of their own free will.
What we do is, we adapt
The image of the stone.

Take this picture of the stone in the Supplement,
The grain of its firm arm around the brunette
On the undulating fields of County Down.

– Or, if you like,
We soften the stone.

Between the News and the Quiz the
Giggling little rubber stone frisks
And carols around the screen
With a backing of sweet music from a combo
Of pliant pebbles.
A voice confesses:
I never bought any other stone since I first tried this.

Walking the outspread supermarket glades, Mrs Bourn
Sees the price reduced on the turquoise packaging
Round the offer of succulent stones. And some stones
Nestle in her tray at the check-out instead of bread.

Two minutes only in lightly-salted water,
And they slip down the smiling throats at the table
With no trouble at all.

*Mrs Bourn's young family of seven can't wait
For their dainty stones.*

139   *Arranged Blossoms*

Peeling itself away like a morsel of skin,
There's another petal to be seen to,
Deranging the antique order of the room.

She must get Mr Fernlock to cast her again.
Knowing the right things to do, the investments,
The Settlement, the family, is so hard.

Angela can be so very hard.
One can't give straight advice as one can face-to-face
When the two of them are in Johannesburg.

Well, I can't stand the weather here either.
But this is my home; and Angela,
You might try writing more often than you do.

Dust the Wedgwood now, not later, it's waited two days.
She must get herself cast again, horoscopes
Can alter for the better, she has heard this.

Tuesday already, and so much to do before Friday.
Friday is the car to Mr Goodman's
To get the codicil witnessed.

And things going wrong she can't manage herself,
Yes, that tap thumping ever since last Thursday week.
A dirty man, who smoked, and it still won't stop.

140   *Warmth*

What made her decide she'd
enjoy being a wee-hours disc-jockey,
well it was something about *giving*
to ordinary people, and well . . . And
did she like the life now (and how!)
she was part of it, yes she thought
it was a great life, what did she
especially like about it, providing the
sweet music between the News
bulletins, what made it a good life
for *her?* Well, maybe, like she said,
she felt she was doing something
for people. But switching this
round, what was it people did for
her? Well, people were quite
wonderful to her, she couldn't
describe it, it was a kind-of warmth,
you know, coming over to you from

people. As to being the most
popular girl in England to phone in
to, she could only say, giggling
shyly, she loved talking to people,
and though you did get those who,
well, just couldn't get *over* to you,
well, most of the time, you know, the
kind-of warmth, she thought it was just
great. Would she sum it all up, then,
in the same kind-of thing, the kind-of
warmth she felt? Yes, she couldn't
describe it exactly, but it was maybe
just that thing, a kind of . . . warmth
she got from nothing else.

141   *In the Trade*

Pre-empted places in the breakfast car,
Death commuted to the Midlands by
The mercy of trade.

Having to really know the ways
Of the production line, the likely
Delivery dates and everything,
That's the point.
And smile and be at ease, make the customer think
He has thought of it for himself.

Eight-ten.
The older man instructing the younger
With age-old wisdoms nodded quickly and taken in,
As curios, as bygones. Off-the-hook talking
To King's Road hung-on-you, wily eyes
Watching the trade for years,
Wily eyes for slugs on the lawn at home.

We shall have to work even harder, and watch
The Japs, we really will. It's not the old
Shoddy stuff now, you know, oh no.

The Midlands are coming, Birmingham coming nearer
Past grey sheep chewing
At scrubland fields. *That's England for you,*
This table-cloth should be absolutely white.

And *I left him the literature, you never know.*
Now you and I, being in the trade, we know . . .

The firm is, for the moment, in the trade.

142   *Going Up*

After a year or two among the drop-outs,
One motivated drop-out
Dropped out, & took his paperback Tolkiens & his
Guitar to another part of town.

It was high summer, the workers were striking, & he was young;
& he bought himself a girl by computer, because
He had dropped out after getting a 2/1 in Maths
(& that after smoking a lot the night before).

& to borrow the money he went to a father
Who clutched at straws, & he set up in business
With a shop full of bygones and modest antiques
In a district where a famous estate agent used

Meat-porters, working spare-time, to get Vacant Possession.
But to be fair, he did not cut his hair
(Which Jani trimmed) and he did not chuck his jeans,
And he even smoked a little now and then.
                                                              Well,

Soon the fully-converted, waste-disposing, Georgian
Terraces filled with young sales executives,
Barristers, painters, young dons with a line on linguistics,
And their shop was full; and this pair sold Vic-

torian jam jars, Valentines, oil-stoves, tea-urns,
Shelves of pith helmets, sugar-tins, chamber-pots,
Phonograph cylinders, pincushions, ballads
With flaked yellow covers; and old solitaire boards

On which dainty marbles, quick and bright,
Ran round the bevelled edges, round and round
Going 'Clink! Clink!' They bought a villa in Minorca,
And they called their children Siddhartha, Demian and Tim.

143   *The Card*

A young dark suit
A tie with crests
A death's head sheared bright
From a two-pin plug
Over coffee at eight
Yes by all means phone
I'll be in my office
Would you like my card
That's the number here
I've written my number at home
Any time except Sundays
(The roadhouse Sundays
Lunch at the Motor Hotel
A bar with leather sofas)
Take as long as you like
You'll forgive me a moment – ?
Well you might like to think of
You'd be well advised to consider
No we don't give a discount

Don't hurry about a decision
The other possibility of course
In the light of the surcharge
Not the same depreciation
I have one of them myself
Yes perhaps think it over
Yes call in to-morrow by all means
We stay open till six
Lightly walking in every
Morning over the forecourt
Supple death's head
In the plate-glass
Biro and Handy Guide
On an alcove desk yes
By all means by all means by all means by all means

144   *She Made of It*

Cords hitched up, sweater pulled down
Over a plain human body absorbing itself with semantics
Among the dried leaves.

Walking along this path, this October,
Having committees to talk with Bill Stennett, and
Uncategorised air to now and again
Replace hair from in the wind.

At the wheel of the Renault, later,
Towards her flat with the two upstairs levels,
Two steps down from one to coffee on the other,
Thinking, if pressed to say,
Of bubbles in a steel tube neatly rising.

Faint photostats from *Mind,* uncurled and
Flattened from the copier, clammy, smooth
And grey, at angles to the bevelled
Table-edge. – Straighten them, in passing.

Eight years ago those two nights
In a borrowed room when some people who, at the time,
Were in Colorado, left them the key to use.

Not since. And she never made
Notes for the bother of nostalgia (for example:
The cactus paling stiffly on the ledge,
And the klaxons blaring meanwhile for sins downtown.

And she wouldn't recall the place-mats of *Berkshire Scenes.*)

145   *An Evening with Anne*

Don't stop what you were saying, I'll see to another record;

Where was I? Oh yes, at *that* I sat up and opened my ears and put two and two . . . He'll evidently be moving to that Division in the New Year;

Where he'll have to try to learn to live with Benther, agreed, which I wouldn't care to have to do myself. But for him it'll be a decided step up all the same;

Someone, perhaps I shouldn't say who, told me Pat (Ferguson) would be going to the Regional Department in the Spring, working on the nineteenth floor. You can guess how she arranged *that;*

Which means Peter Daines will be bound to get the Senior IV post at Colswell (unless they appoint from outside, which they hardly would). And he's only been in his present job one year;

Anyway, not to bore you, but they've asked me to move into Jean Levitt's office, temporarily anyway. Yes, quite a surprise, and I'm not so sure I can cope; but I said I would. I mean, it seemed a chance, and it leaves me the option of getting out later, or moving up higher when the time comes, if it does. It leaves me completely free.

Try again. No? Vivaldi actually.

146 *Vital*

I think my work is important, I am a link
In a long chain.
I had to have the training for it,
And I had to dirty my hands.
They ask my advice when they want to know what would be
best.
I might move up even higher, in time.

One Sunday I woke up shouting. She said,
What on earth's the matter, we're supposed to be
Going out to dinner later; or rather lunch.
I dressed, and played with Lynda, and
Felt a bit better.

I was called into the office from the shop
Floor. 'Mr Fletton, up from London, wants to see you.'
But I was hearing the mutter-mutter,
The kind-of giggling noises inside the machines
Through four thick concrete walls.
I could not read the words in front of my eyes.

She said last Thursday, you haven't said a thing
The whole evening.
I said no, I've been watching.
. . . I couldn't name a thing I'd seen on the screen.

Today is vital, people are relying on me
To get ten thousand packages out on time.
I am part of a chain, a link, they ask my advice.
I open the front door. After the wind,
It's a lovely cool morning, and sun;
Very bright.
The keys of the Toledo are clenched wet
In my right hand. And I don't move.
I am standing shaking. I am standing, shaking.

147   *The Image*

Vampires are said to be living in Essex this Sunday morning. And the paper he buys for serious reading says, in the Supplement, 'Most of us would resort to cannibalism if there was nothing else we could do.' As if it were a sign, the shaft of cool sunlight strikes down through the R.A.F. window onto the Communion rail and young Mrs Mountacute, with leukaemia, kneeling. The Christian and Property, The Christian and War: people like to have it all made clear. Or, shall we say, the context for their personal decisions made clear. He tidies the bookstand in the alcove, and shakes the box inquisitively; but wouldn't wish to be seen opening it just now. Down the gravel path past the graves, past the Dormobile (it won't depreciate as much) and into the rectory, and the cooker is pinging for lunch. Must ring and check with the group performing after Evensong.

148   *Metres*

Reads, alone, last thing at night:
Make life a rhythm,
A strenuous, glorious rhythm,
Live it, feel it, in every muscle and limb,
A beautiful, disciplined, natural
Rhythm.

And every part is ready for waking:
The shoulder that hinges
The arm that flexes
The wrist that sends
The finger that stops
The alarm at 5.45.

Pill from the phial in the cabinet,
And click the cabinet shut to fix
The mirror of a really healthy face.
– Washing to a rhythm, cleaning teeth, etc.

Slapping the streets of Wythenshawe with fit plimsolls,
The stadium-terraces, the crimson number
Jogging on the vest
On the drizzling Saturday screens.

Back, and eating sensibly, lightly,
The Corporation offices, 8.30 exactly
– And make life a rhythm
On through your working day;
Whatever your work, it can be done.

I hear the new appointment in the Data Section
Is a bit of an athlete by all accounts.

149   *An Actress*

The part for now: kimono and Bianco,
A finish to the long day at the agency.

I couldn't live in small rooms these days:
'Spacious, second floor, deep freeze provided,
Just off Gloucester Road.' Rather garish
And 'a slum really', I read somewhere . . .
But I like it.

And visited once in three months by a father satisfied with a
Capable girl, he shrugs and supposes.
Can look after herself.

A Range Rover using the Residents' Parking,
A French registration. *René!*
Hi, I'll let you in! An Entryphone
Can keep out anything that threatens to be
Embarrassing.

Réne, have a seat, dump the books on the floor.
Oh, you're harder at twenty-six, I feel that.
Christ, a hell of a night, you can say, and then
– All over!

Yes, if life is responding I do respond.
Yes, I'm sure I respond,
There are lots of things I respond to.
I think he called himself René. (An actress
Will make any noise she considers suitable.)

– But Amanda, Christ, what a giggle, did he
Talk in French when he came?

150   *Imposing*

In the middle of late September a commissionaire,
Outside, from the pavement in front of, the curtilage of,
The Majestic Hotel, kicks a scrawny
Leaf away, underpaid;
A leaf that must not be allowed to stay.

He can summon taxis in a chocolate brown, braided
Majestic hat, even when it is
Chucking it down for bus queues.
He can impose it, on even such a street.

What it is is to have grown into his hat,
His long long coat, his bright thick shoes,
To have grown into this from being a sergeant once
(Now, for the management, ordering a leaf about)
And the matching suit, and the accurate watch:
The time, for the residents.

You do not grow out of it if you are in this,
Ever. But leaves
Will somehow enter the front, revolving door.
And there will be, the week after next, a leaf
Scratching inwards somewhere on the second floor.

151   *Circle*

Chris's place . . . They'll have something . . . Last time a whole week coming out of a bad one & not eating. Nothing but beautiful books at first with blossoms on the outside, & he read them for years & saw unending spread-out brown stone valleys of these thin millions of bodies dipping their limbs in supple mud & flowing slime . . .

then the words were suddenly changing into these smiling faces or masks, altering as he looked from yellow & black to sparkling green, above a cloudbank. & he tried to fix his mind on them as words, but they wouldn't mean themselves, they were the faces. & he tried to fix on the letters in the words but the letters were faces as well, & through the circles of the O's like pulsing vaginas he was trying to get out, but they clenched . . .

& out was a succession of streets & streets of food-shops, the food in them, the meat, was bright packages of muddy bandages, or shit, or little glittering clusters of hazy lights & blossoms & beautiful books, everything changing colours & then going dead flat & going dead flat . . .

he said, *Don't come to me with white coats & sympathy.*

152   *The Gloves*

Bent with close eyes in the late afternoon,
Concentrated alone at a nearby bare
Velveted window which spreads out
Exquisitely a random few pedestalled pairs
Of grey gloves carefully drooped.

An infinity of care gazing at
An easy deployment of care
– The gloves not visibly priced.

She would need to go in to enquire the price,
In a voice that would not fit
From a voice that has learnt to fit.

The long sour ache of being this much poor
Was earned through generations, and comes
To such aspirings of the menopause:
Treating herself with the gloves,
With the look of the gloves.

The dustless tableau of the window
Stays where it is, where it always has so far.
Better to go back, as she will,
With bare hands on the underground, on
The disappointed journey, her fingers keeping
Apples and a small loaf covered in the polythene.

153 *Twilight*

Outside the window,
Over the black brick wall,
The hearses were there again today,
Black hushed carriages
Passing and pausing, the stench in here increasing,
The shapes through the curtains I pulled across.

He was late again last night, so where had he been?
The hearses were bigger today,
Standing or sitting I could see them,
And the thump of the box I could hear
In the heart of the cold tap. And it's dusk now,
Like lids of boxes on us all.

I told you, stop that, stop screaming,
The seven of you.
He'd been round to her again, I could
Tell it by his eyes, they faced me out
As I stood at the table, and washed the things, and asked.

So I told him.
Yes, I was positive, the doctor said, and the doctor's nurse
said,
I imagine that's the answer you wanted?

No, he can't himself, and he won't recommend,
It's the Law. No one will
Recommend anything, no.
We shall die, I suppose, and be bones in their mud.

Because they won't stop the hearses every day,
They won't stop, the streets of them,
The streets and streets of them,
The streets and streets and streets of me.

*   *   *   *

Seven Old Men on an Inter-City Train:
A Yeatsian Poem

The First.   Is that a flood or a lake?

The Second.   I saw a lake.
And were there flooding there would not be
                                   swans.

The Third.   The swans could have come from a lake, with
                             all this rain
A lake could overflow and spawn a flood,
And cast out swans on it.

The Second.   Yet I look again,
And see they are not swans but clumps of suds
Engendered by detergent. Had you but looked
You would have seen all their necks were under
                                 water.

The Fourth.   But it is unimaginable that suds
Should drift in wandering pairs as if designed
To have the look of swans. Now the train has
                               passed,
I speak it with an old man's memory,
Yet say that nearly all of them were in pairs.

The Second.   Why should not some base tycoon-man, who
                                desired
The pride of an environmentalist,
Discharge the effluent of his factory
So that, upon a sudden dreaming glance,
It looked like swans?

The Fifth.   That would enhance
A desolate vulgar place, could it but have
Appearances of companionable swans.

The Sixth.	The poet Yeats loved real swans on real lakes,
	And had a penchant for using them as symbols.

The Third.   And Yeats, I have heard tell, wrote of swans
on floods.

The Second.   But what would Yeats have thought of clumps
of suds

                                  Reclining ceremoniously on a foul scene?
To forge his symbols would be difficult.
Yeats was not of an age when factory waste
Was put on show as swans as a P.R. stunt.

The Fourth.   But Yeats himself was a bit of an old . . . tycoon,
And symbol swans are just as shadowy
As foam that moves upon a twilight flood.

The Sixth.
Yet
Yeats

                                  Would not have cried the praise of effluent-swans
To sanctify some tycoon's greedy till.
Yeats was –

The Seventh.   I think that Crewe is the
next stop.

155   *Spring Elegiacs at the Sea*

High on a ladder just began
The checking of the fairy lights for spring;
And a hundred yards on, a man
Digs about in some concrete tubs, planting

A glossier little-flower-decor
Than the girls – out of uniform, all white-
Faced in the wind sweeping the door
They shelter in – provide, on this first bright

Day of the new season. Menus
(Re-photocopied, but with changed prices)
Inserted into glass frames, views
Of the beach all now in colour, ices

In virgin, unexcavated
Blocks in the freezers, early posters for,
One would say, uncelebrated
Entertainers all start to beg favour

Of visitors. It's not yet May,
However, so the lights, blue, white, red, green,
Blue, red, green, white, a neat array
Of regulated colours, have not been

Time-switched for the evenings; but come
Easter and the first arrivals they might be,
And all the girls, and even some
Of the boys here, will start vaguely

Wondering what the season could bring,
And trek the long promenade, up and down,
Hoping out new faces dropping
Into their transitory gleaming town,

Which vanishes inside itself
In winter, hiding such summer young.
And so I walk here round about 12th
April, when the last spring tide which flung

Grit all over the forecourt of
The Pier Hotel is a week behind;
And they stand here, boys in half-love
With the girls, and the girls in a thrilled kind

Of love for themselves and for what
A girl is, unknowingly confined to
Their ancient, sweet limits.
                                    One, not
Twenty-five yards away just now withdrew

From her quivering assortment
Of growing-up friends, and ran to an old
Lady treading the strait pavement,
Calling 'Gran!' At which, forgetting the cold

Day she shuffles through, the old one
Turns now and smiles, and the two stand to chat
– Linking the young, in the white sun,
With the very old, in the old skin that

Clothes her, a shrivelled Olympian
Admiring the girl with an elder's wise smile,
A sudden warm in her face when
She sums up the pursuits of the child while

The holidays last, all the parts
Of her granddaughter's body trembling for
Their inheritance, all the arts
Her nature will learn for itself: the lore

Of being a sexed creature,
Though the girl would not think of it like this.
The girl seems happy, in feature
And gesture, as she talks; then, with a kiss

For her ancestor she goes back,
And the elder goes on, with that old pride
In children's children and their lack
Of foreknowledge.
                                But mostly she will hide

Her close, quiet thoughts about today,
Which are these (though not so worked-out, of course):
'My own body has gone its way
Through the ways of hers, but come to no worse

'Or sadder place, in the event.
From where I am, out of the surge of things,
All her mild being looks intent
On questing after toys. Her small age brings

'Her nothing, no, that I would have
Back again, having seen the whole game through.
It was all a dance of warm, slave
Shadows that I remember. And, when new,

'It was too strange to be enjoyed,
And as it went on, it was just craved for
Out of a habit. Time destroyed,
But cleansed me, also, I am sure

'– All this you'll learn, my eager sweet,
By living thousands of bewildering hours,
Starting this moment, in this street,
Arranged in sunshine, playing at being flowers.'

Curious about her seven daughters, in turn came
The seven fortitudinous knights. And the first
To sit by the swarming fire, sipping mead with
Mother and eldest daughter, saw with much delight
The white cat pace to him, as he loved them,
Cats.
        The creature was unbleached to a queer
Shifting shade of green by the colours of the room
– Green hangings, green velvet on the couches,
Green branches at the window, green eyes in matron and girl,
Green even in the flames of the fire because
They cast salt in the crevices of the coals to
Make matching colours.
        So the white cat
Mewed at him, nudged his ankle, mounted his lap,
And the mother murmured, 'You are honoured, she
Has never before walked in such a way up to a man.'
This flattery went deep, proposals were made, and the pair
Duly wed.
        And since daughters must dutifully marry,
And mothers must needs be mothers, and marry off,
A second knight came seeking the second daughter
And chose a green chair by the great fire while
The mother poured wine.
        And willingly again the white
Cat rose on her green cushion, stood stretching,
And pattered the flagstones to the handsome second knight
To form fond figures-of-eight round the man's thin legs.
'There's a something about you that attracts her, she
Has never lingered with a man,' the lady said;
And in this style was her second daughter secured
To a cat-adoring knight.
        This way it went too

With the third, the fourth, the fifth and the sixth, on
A succession of green days with the cat casually
Trusting its truly-said-to-be-untypical
Affection to the different knights, whether of
Transylvania, Tartary, Aragon or Tibet, being
Similar only in their peculiar pride at pre-empting,
Uniquely, an unsociable animal unsure of men:
Cat-lovers, but gullible with it, which is rare.

On the last and greenest day, green curtains gathering
Across the storm which sent green branches seething
Over the sky in a frenzied trellis-work of green,
The seventh knight finally knocked; one who knew
And loved cats more than any of these lovers, and
He yearned for the youngest daughter's hand.
                                        Her mother
Decanted liquor as usual, and the lovely daughter sat,
And green flames flashed in the hearth as the cat
Began again, greenly, its meaningful trek of the floor.
'She will not go to you, she has never yet greeted a man,'
The matron predicted; but the cat pounced all at once,
From no definable angle, onto the very codpiece of the doting
Knight, and neatly nestled.
                                So the mother and girl
Cried equally with eagerness and ecstasy as before

– At which this knight bounded up from his bench of green,
Shouting, 'I am getting out of here at once!'
And 'I know what sort of a situation this is,'
Dropping the cat, flat-eared and snarling with dire dismay,
And decapitating the thing with a dirk;
With screams from all, except himself and the evil cat's
Head, which jeered, and rejoined itself to the body
And said, 'What was that intended to imply?'
'The true friend of cats,' said the knight, 'knows
That cat in ninety-nine which walks for women

And not for itself alone, the animal which is
The familiar of witches.
                              But it seems as if
I did not exorcise this one quite enough.'
'You are remarkably right,' said the reconstituted cat
Sapiently, 'and for this wisdom you will wend,
By a promise you will here and now provide,
One year through numerous travails of the world, and come
To the terrible temple of the cat-goddess,
Mere pictures of whom inflict fevers and death on
Temerarious beholders who brave them, and
Leading lady of many a savage psychotropic
Trance. There we shall truly meet again,
And I shall take my turn.'
                              So the seventh knight
Ground on grimly over the bogs and crags of the world,
Lodging roughly, going rudely his slow way
On a bewildered horse through innumerable bleak,
Colourless, sleazy, subtopiate regions,
Demoralizing tracts of megalosuburbia,
And came, just after eleven heavy months, to a splendid
Castle, where his welcome was very grand.
                              And there,
In the course of prattle at dinner about property prices,
He thought he might try to elicit where the temple
Of the great cat-goddess stood, half-hoping it had not
Survived redevelopment.
                              'My fine fellow, I can
Tell you the lie of the land,' said the lord his host,
'But linger a little while here, enjoy some relaxation'
– And his lady smiled in sly sympathy and accord –
'While I do some terribly tiresome hunting. And, by the way,
Be good!'
        With a feeling of distant *déjà vu*,
The seventh knight agreed; and for three successive days,
Was allowed to lie lazily in his bed while his host
Went hunting and left his lady (just as he had read);

Because, in short, truncating a tangled tale,
Coming in sleek, scarlet, delightful garments,
She insisted on sleeping with him thoroughly each of the three
Days her husband was happily hunting the evening meal,
Which the knight agreed to with an anxious sense of
Compromise; and suspicion.

                  Each night, the master,
Hot and bothered and scenting himself, brought back
The special spoils of a strenuous day in the field;
For this supper asking nothing in return and reward
But the knight's good company in anecdote and carousing;
And on the last day, as promised, he provided
Instructions for reaching the great cat-goddess's place.

It proved a daunting plod over muddy areas,
An extremely unclean excursion, so that when the knight
Arrived there, both he and his horse exhausted,
Spattered in the saddle from travel, he thought it was his

                                  tiredness
That stopped him from seeing where it was. But suddenly,
He saw it: a low, brick thing nearly hidden in the grasses
Of a thistly field, with peculiar peep-holes from which
Any occupant, sitting safely in a nook, could
Scan out.

                Dismounting, the knight called, clearly, and as
Loudly as he was able, on whoever lurked inside to
Emerge; and there expeditiously appeared a
Truly tremendous cat, the size of a full-grown woman.
'As I promised and pledged I would do, in all duty,'
Stated the knight, 'I have travelled to the temple
Of the great cat-goddess, to pay the penalty for
Following up certain suspicions too rashly,
And acting in anger.'

                  Then the cat mysteriously smiled,
Saying, 'Listen. As an artful knight, you showed
Some shrewdness in discerning a witch's cat;
As a truly brave one you moved boldly

Against a defenceless, domestic beast; as
A plodder you showed profound persistence
In going your way through the world for a year
To find out this frightful place; as a seizer of chances,
You lay three times with the lady of the castle,
Obviously not having offered any oath you would thereby
Break; thus an immaculate code of knightly
Tactics you have most tightly kept, and
Will be rightly rewarded.'
                     At which the vast animal
Cast off its outer cat-costume and calmly stepped forth
As the seventh daughter, dressed in the delightful,
Scarlet, sleek garments of the mistress of the castle.

'I was,' she said, 'all the time secretly concealed
In the little anatomy of the cat, in the body
Of the lady of the castle you came to know a bit,
And the knight of the castle, my loving master and lord,
Was all the time my own dear mother in drag.
So on the basis of all that, you may bow and beg now
The hand of the youngest daughter you came to collect.
There is no way out.'
                So, haltingly heeding
These dreadful words, the dumbstruck fellow put
His proposals, too perplexed to do other, and the pair
Were rapidly wed.
                  And they went on to work through
Many years of irrefrangible, retributive wedlock
(For the daughter turned out termagant as well as witch);
But concerning these travails I cannot truthfully say
I am sad or sorry, and cannot make this knight seem
An object of proper pity: as a grown-up, I regard
Knights and knighthood and the mores and weapons
Of a warrior society as both juvenile and degrading.

The Old Fox glimpses the little bag passing
Furtively round. They are secretly
Collecting for him in the office, he is going to retire.

The little bag, something tells him, will be light;
Not with an excess of paper money either.
The Old Fox is not popular where he works.
The typists have given 2p, the Under Manager
Ten, the Manager puts in a fifty
And takes out thirty-eight.
. . . It might not reach two pounds.

For forty-three years' service, two pounds or less!
The Old Fox cogitates quietly at his desk
(So quietly not even his secretary divines
He is cogitating at all).
Well, he could act the martyr, he could break down and weep
In front of the whole staff at his presentation.
He could make an acerbic speech and scathe the lot.

He could, out of humility, refuse
To have them make such a fuss of him: 'Forty-three
Years in so happy a firm seems not so long.'
But he has another idea.

The Old Fox knows where they keep
The key of the cupboard where the little bag
Is hidden in a teapot at night.
                                        The evening before,
On a pretence of tidying up loose ends,
He stays altruistically late, the last to leave,
He fetches the key, he opens the cupboard,
He takes out the bag,

And he puts in the sixteen five pound notes he has drawn in

the lunch hour

Through the youngest clerk in the bank.

At his presentation next day, the Old Fox
Breaks down and gratefully weeps in front of the whole staff.

158   *Point of Honour*

On a wet South Coast night when even
Believers in rain and luxuriance are resenting
How drenched the leaves are on the trees outside
Their pelted windows, a dark-haired girl lies lamenting
How far love seems from any dreamed-of heaven
– As this egotist who has just straddled her, and cried,

And slumped into a heavy shagged-out quiet,
Says, reaching for a well-placed cigarette,
'If I'm hurting your right leg, dear, please let me know.'
And oh, it is her *left* leg which he needs to get
Clear of to reach the matches; having come to lie at
A clumsy angle during his last, slow,

Gratifying turmoil, which has nonetheless
Been too fast for the girl by half.

Now she has heard
Sam. Johnson's words, 'To scratch where there is an itch
Is life's greatest pleasure.' And she forgives her absurd
Seducer's selfish haste. And she feels worse distress
That he thinks it her *right* leg on his right side of the bed

– Since a gentleman could tell which limb was which.

I

Look down into hotels where girls work
    In their vacations,
And in the early evening, managers, averaging
Forty-six years old, induce them to upper bedrooms,
Empty because business is dropping off:
Think of the protestations round the coasts of England,
The moaning on the candlewick coverlets,
And the girls so young, this the first time for most of
                             them,
And the managers cautious and honourable,
Saying they won't go too far, and going
Too far, the girls done with A levels,
And the managers pressing and leering and the minds blown
                             for days.

II

Look down at one manager at seven-thirty, all his girls
    Heltering through his mind,
And fewer girls each year in the last three years,
But this year more girls than for three years past,
Five girls to be exact, so it is spring once more
And the blood sparkles, at an average age
Of forty-six. There he is now, leering in the glass
Behind the lounge bar, tilting, adroitly, Chartreuse,
Thinking of his five girls this season: Tina, Prue,
And Elaine, and Kirsten, who pulled the scarlet
    Curtains herself, and Rosemary, queen of impermeable
Silence, who will come back of her own accord.

III

Look down there at the window of a room at dusk
  Where a pensive manager,
Letting the twilight change to dark, sits alone
Without a light at nine-thirty, run out of cigarettes,
Sits alone, eyes open, in a crumbling swivel chair.
Now he hears the feeble whine of a slow lift,
And a girl comes in who understands his sadness,
Business declining and years declining
– And a good love quickens in this very young girl,
Or a love upgraded from pity (she has brought some
           cigarettes)
  For a manager pining heavily in a hotel
Not doing particularly well . . .

IV

Look down at a boy friend emptying fruit machines
  On the pier at ten-fifteen,
After a fair day's business. The ogling machines
Are adjusted finely to concede just a little
And grasp the rest to themselves,
And this girl is adjusted finely in the same way
– Because of a manager of a hotel (where they
Spend the early evenings in an upper bedroom).
She is meeting the boy in the Bull, and
For him life feels like a nasty row
Of mocking variables, apples, plums and flags,
As he filches the coins with which he will buy the drinks.

V

And look at this boy friend at midnight
    At the girl's gate:
Now cradling the sobbing girl, who has told him
Everything all at once in a sudden gush.
She says she could be sick, which she could not,
And the boy is sick instead because it has taken
Eleven pale ales to her four bacardis-and-coke
To bring her to this point of revelation.
Thus: the manager, his girl friend, and her boy friend –
It's a bad time for all of them (though at this moment a
                                          letter
Is on its way to the girl to say she has
Two D's and an E and a place at the North-East Polytechnic).

VI

But look again at this boy friend, who is feeling better
    Up the hill past the Cats' Home
On his long walk back about an hour later.
He is compassionating the manager in question,
Whose letters he has been shown: 'Dear Tina,
I long for you all the time . . .' and similar things.
He can guess the timeless agony of the man,
Longing so much for the girl he more or less
Longs for himself, and he is not so jealous.
He could be in the same position one day.
He could be in the same . . . He is overcome
With a selfless presagement of the nastiness of time.

VII

Look between the chink in the curtains
    In one hotel window,
Where a manager, at one-thirty, is turning a coverlet
Down, the only coverlet he ever turns
Down, to slink into bed beside his wife.
Groping the pillow in the darkness, this manager
Thinks of that day's baffling girl: 'You've never
Read any Gary Snyder or Frantz Fanon, you've hardly
Heard of Claes Oldenburg or Roland Barthes,
Or of Simon or Garfunkel,' she had said in reproach.
'Do you call that living?' – 'Yes,' he thinks,
As he thinks of her left breast flipping the back of his knee.

VIII

In the terrible small hours look over
    Everyone fitfully asleep,
And do not imagine they do not have complex dreams.
E.g., a girl is at the bottom of a slimy pit
With smooth sides, and hairy managers are toppling
Hairy managers in rockers' goggles down on her,
So that she screams; only the scream
Comes out a bit ecstatically and she can't
Explain to herself why this should be really so,
Or how she should have come to be here at all.
It stays with her while she dresses for another
Long day at the hotel. She can't wait for the early evening to
                                  come round.

IX

Look into a corridor where a girl at nine-twenty a.m.
        Walks carrying sheets,
And a second follows, to shake them out with her,
One girl moderately appealing and the other
Less appealing than her, not least in her perceptions
(Which she keeps to herself). The conversation
Is equivocal, since they are discussing the manager
And the first girl has more to disclose than she says,
Though she is hinting, continually hinting,
In the faint breeze from the sheets. Small tabs with
Laundry numbers fall off the outflung linen,
And the bedroom radio sings of '*leurs déguisements*
                                fantasques'.

X

Lastly, gaze out there at the crematorium.
        Having consumed fourteen
Tequilas in half-an-hour, a manager
Is being consumed to rest. His wife comes first,
And behind her follow forty-six girls in all,
The youngest sixteen, the oldest thirty-four,
And all in states of nostalgia or raw distress
According to how lately they knew the man.
So wife and girls compassionate each other
As the clergyman, noting an ancient English
Ritual of mourning, shakes each girl by the hand.
If this can happen, the world must be good. It is ten forty-five.

160 *Ruse*

Lastly my turn to hide, so
The other children instantly
Scattered among the scrubland grass,
Blanked their eyes, began
To count aloud.
                    Away downhill,
The traffic thundered less
In the hazed streets, the orange
Street-lamps suddenly lit in
A necklace of twilight mauves. I was
Expected home from this game, to eat,
And read myself to sleep. Besides,
There were so many ruses more
I wanted to devise.
                    Before
They counted out my time, came
Running to look for me, I ran
And left them there, I ran back home
And left them.
                    Turning today
A tower-block corner, I saw them
In the gathering dark, bemused
And middle-aged, in tattered
Relics of children's clothes, still
Searching even now in the glittering
Scrubland of my Precinct, for
What had deserted them, what had
Cast them there; blank-eyed, and
Never to tell what I had built,
What I had left them with in forty years.

161   Scare

I laughed about it afterwards,
But it frightened me at the time.

Yes;
And in entertainment, one axiom is
That scare can be terribly funny:
Those floors that tilt you
Ludicrously here, there, here
In the House of Ghosts;
The wicked fangs on the posters
Dripping hilarious red.

The real worst of horror is
Its shabbiness . . . How nice
If all private scare were awfully
Amusing to retell,
And much better still
If it really, rather wickedly,
Entertained.

– I could hoist my habitual
Skull at its fixed
Mirror in the morning, go at it
Over its shallow covering with
The razor, and receive
Such a comical thrill.

I could open its mouth, gape
Wide with it, make a sound,
And laugh about it afterwards.
It could be a real scream.

162 *The Information*

When the Library of Congress is finally
Reducible to a cube one inch by one
Inch by one inch, you are going to need to lose
Absolutely nothing: stored and retrievable

A pear-core once left gangling on an ashtray,
The moment of Amanda's purple scarves touched
Sadly into order, the whole of *Le Figaro*,
And the accurate timbre of all your departed
Cryings-in-the-night. None of this
Will be vanishing any more.

Up there, instead of shining empty sky
(The still clear sunlight you are walking in
With terrors in your head) will be
A building specially built to set this right:

In any of a thousand rooms it will
Be possible for somebody to remain
For all of life after infancy till death,
Fed and evacuated and re-clothed
In a see-through cubicle, flicking up fact after
Fact and image upon image, actually
Playing his infancy back; working with his keepers
At the reasons, there, for needing to do such a thing.

163 *Afternoon in the Fens*

Then the farms ended, and the last dyke
Gave onto reeds, to mudlands; beyond which
A lightship blinked in the haze where the mud became the sea,
And that afternoon, two black and circling specks
Droned like gnats in that distance beyond our reach.

A dubious peace, the water shrunk down in the channels
Under clumps of bleached, unstirring grass;
A drugged end to August, the dyke-track
Dusty under four people's shoes where we stopped,
Gazing at a high square of wood braced

On a frame of iron in one field-corner. – And suddenly,
Out of the faint waters, the two droning dots
Enlarged towards us, two furies homing at this
Target we were standing near on the dyke, coming
Each ninety seconds and screaming and screaming

At the square of orange-painted slats clamped
On black poles of iron rusting into the rich earth,
Laying down fume trails onto smoke from the
Straw-fires left by farmers affluent on
Their steady reclamations of mud.

After two screamings our hands held our ears
As we moved aside along the narrow path,
But the two planes turning again over the flats
Avoided the target, were diving at, screaming at
Us, furrowing the air with billowing smoke-lines,

Homing at the four of us walking this bank
Between farms and land-finish. Out on the far sea
The lightship blinked to no one in the shallows,
And no one elsewhere moved in the fields
Under a sky impenetrably clear, curiously

Dulled by the heat-mists. Again and again,
Turning and screaming ancient, reasonless
Hatreds, they followed; then finally wheeled away, back,
Out over the sea, where the lightship continued to warn
Among sandbanks stuck with wrecks from recalled wars.

Sixteen miles from anywhere larger
On the map of a renamed county,
With an ancient market-square to which
Sore-faced farmers drive flocks in brown, tiered
Lorries every Thursday, is this
Country-town: a pestle-and-mortar
Restaurant, a glinting pharmacy
With rows of touched-up tincture jars, a
Salon of 'Gowns', one minimarket
Grocery, and a furniture shop.

Past the last black-and-white traffic sign,
The last lights in small manor-houses
Go out, and one more squirearchical
Day is done with; county magazines
Lie smoothly on their own in the dark,
The warm engines of the GL-12s
Click and settle in their garages
In villages where old bachelor
Campanologists tire, and hunger
At last, leave their ropes and sprint off home.

Through the glass of the furniture shop
A sleek room gleams, indescribably
Tidy and perfect: purple wall lights
Allure and chill, and a magenta
Carpet sets a table and two chairs
Fast in the specific attention
Of two poised lamps. This is a ghosts' room:
Two especially, two spectrally
Immaculate-feeling people could
Stop and repose here at two a.m.

As exactly pure exemplars of
How things ought to be. It would give them
That virgin bed with a canopy
In the background, spaced silken pillows
Asking those who have walked at a fixed
Distance for so long to lie, chastely
Apart, until the first unpolluted bird
Announces dawn. Shall we step inside?
I can't think we or it will ever
Suit each other quite so well again.

165   *The World Outside*

When poetry was a landscape art, arranging
Syllables in a noble sweep to gaze up, the vista
Was the big house of order and seclusion, stately
Between stiffly regular lines of most proper trees.
The world kept out was the goatherds and their pipes.

When *civitas* seemed quite possible, the view
Was the city square, across a purified *parole*
– Incredibly kempt, and engraved with some token bourgeois
Respectably strolling out. Small in the foreground, the rest of
                                                    the world
Was the mongrel dog that whined at the flawless space.

Seeing the lift 'Out of Order' he mounts the stairs
Helped up by a loosening banister, and sees
Poetry striving to root in a tub of dying plants
Put down on a vinyl landing. The poor pale thing
Is hungry for sense and sanity, wincing at

The sight from this fifth floor window, and craving
Simply to understand: four lanes of a freeway
Mesh with six lanes of another below him, and the sun
Amazedly glitters off the flank of twenty-two
Office-floors across the street. At the ninth landing,

He knows that this world won't be excluded. It goes with him
Into a room where fifty are gathered together,
All drinking to efface the scenery. Traffic management,
Retrieval systems, God, can't contain this world;
So words will somehow have to.

                                    'Hullo,' he says,

'I've read your book, I think it's really great.'

166   *Breach*

Within a mile of a sea, which could be heard,
On a Chesterfield much too narrow,
On a night that was much too short,
These two achieved a rare sort of victory:

They carried through a completely unselfish,
Unkind-to-no-other-people act of love,
Between twelve twenty-seven and twelve
Forty-four, while the latest oil slick

Slurped at the sands in the dark.
Nightlong coastguards fought it with radioed
Data about its location, helicopters clattered
To neutralise the thing with chemical sprays,

And half the resort was out next morning, waiting
As for some dismal, predicted second coming.
But these two made their protest about
The general soilure of the world at the hands

Of the effortful and the crude by just one
Once-only, uncontrived breach
Of its chaos with love. And there should be
A plaque on the esplanade to this effect.

167   *Lost and Found*

The knights on his first chess set were mounted
On horses with close-together eyes and narrow noses:
An amused look whichever way they faced.
One day, the set was not complete. A knight
Was lost, he played half-heartedly for thirty years
With a plastic pepperpot instead. She walked into his room
Eventually at forty-one, with a set smile
And amused eyes close together under her forehead.
She took a step, and turned aside, smiling.
Consequently life could be played properly again.

168   *Procedural*

The Old Fox sits at the front in the Chairman's eye, he
Questions the Apologies for Absence, he
Questions the Minutes, including
The accuracy of the amendments in these Minutes
To the Minutes of the meeting before last, he
Raises Matters Arising for half an hour.

Then he
Carps at the order of items on the Agenda,
Queries the omission of items *from* the Agenda,
Interrupts, interjects, raises Points of Information,
Asks innocent (loaded) questions, has serious Points of Order,
Puts down motions, puts down amendments to motions,
Puts down amendments to amendments, questions the voting,
Wants the Chairman to state again exactly what it is
They have decided by the voting,
Wants his disagreement with the Chairman's decision minuted,
Quotes the Constitution,
Waves the Companies Act.

The Old Fox proposes the creation of
Sub-committees, steering committees, working parties and
Working groups, and declines election
To any of them himself. Any Other Business
Is devoted to matters raised by the Old Fox alone.

When the time to decide the Date of Next Meeting arrives, he
Objects on sound grounds to every possible date.
The desk diaries wearily rise from dispatch cases once again,
The overcoats stay unbuttoned, the great white pages
Turn and flutter and the flutter becomes a wind
And the wind becomes a gale tearing
At the darkness outside the window,
At the darkness in everybody's soul in the steamed-up room.

When the storm subsides, the Old Fox
Has disappeared until the next time.

169   *Representational*

His mother's wrinkled gloves have been warm enough
For the glass of the table where they lie to steam a bit:
These three are sat on gold-painted cane armchairs
In the middle of a spa, the man quite readily benign,
And smiling at the seven-year-old boy, though he hasn't
Much to say, and he sucks a thin cigar.
                                                              A lady
In a purple topcoat leaves the counter and brings,
On a green tray, coffees and orangeade, she glides
Into their circle deftly with a quiet, adaptable
Smiling. This December is cold, but the sweet
Orangeade shrills heavenly up the waxy straw, a cool
Perfect runnel over his tongue, it's 1974.
                                                      His mother
Is flushed and laughing with the man, there they are
In the great wall-mirror on the far side of the room,

Laughing and flushed the two of them, the freer selves
They could always be if this were only art
– Oh, if this were only art, or even fiction! But still,
Small rewards and mercies hold good . . .
                                        And the little boy
Now draining the last sacramental droplets from the glass
Quite likes the man, and the sun is coming out.
The lady with her emptied tray makes an adult smile
For the adults, and a children's smile for the child;
Her petition forms on the counter, to which she returns,
Are nearly filled, so the Ring Road is nearly prevented.
                                        The man
Will have paid off the Datsun in just under five months' time.

170   *Dea ex machina*

The woman with legs long for her family,
And the man with short legs, a short-legged man,
Match perfectly in the kitchen before Anna comes:
Anna, after a decade, at the wrong moment, back.

The crockery is streaked, and rattled dry,
And will have to be re-washed better by hand.
'Start over!' Anna will say, being American,
And they will have to unmatch their thighs, which
Will be aching, and may be slightly shaking,
And wipe at least forks to make a snack for Anna, back
Oh God, on the scene after ten years gone and not regretted.

It took no little time for these two to match,
For each to find the words, and their legs to lodge
One against the other and the other one
Against the other one, respectively,
In a sort-of logical comfort.
                                        So may not
The telephone, vicious in voice or in silence,

225

Or the neighbour, preening her jubilee rosette,
Or finally Anna returning, any second now
– An emanation from her own dishwasher, all
Streaked with happy tears – break
This decent duo up.

171 *Night and Sunrise*

The cog-wheel abrasions are at it again
On this first glinting day of March,
Swerving over any pale surface, fastening
Blips of a crazed illumination on
The walls, the carpet, the half-typed page.

So again the old half-humorous yearning starts,
For the life of the darkest months:
The sunless heavens, the velvet hours
When action soothes, and shadow into shadow
Glides for a shadow-satisfaction.

– And truly, the heart of the educationist
Rises in autumn, as dead leaves drift
Round blocks of switched-on light in heated rooms;
The colours of that season moderate
The strident freshness on those shoots of green . . .

Reproached one late June day, when she maintained,
'Dark nights, cold weather, cold women,
Those are what you seem to want!' I tried to say,
'Exegesis is so difficult in summer,
My eyes can't tell the words from the spaces

In a book read out of doors. Besides,
Your sunshine only lights the surfaces,
And deep down things the dearest darkness lives,
Where profundity waits to be dug for'
– When she put the book aside, and we went indoors

Discussing my eyesight and my character,
Regretful or happy that the nights were already
Drawing in, and she closed the curtains.
                                        Who had won
I could not tell. We let things rest between
The dark and light . . . But I was glad she stayed

To try the night, and see the dawn up for me.

172   *On the Day*

He thanks whoever-she-is for her thoughtful
Beneficence to him, in that visitation
In the early hours of the morning on the day
He travels up to hear what the X-ray meant:
Appearing out of a carmine snowdrift and
Lustrously uncovering; then extending
Such long quick legs around him, and pushing
Him widely awake to smile at the dawn for once.

If he remembers ruefully that no one now
Visits of their own free will, that you visit
All your dreams on yourself, still, either way,
His world comes right for a while. In the lift,
As it drops to the snowing street, he knows
That either some she, or some part of himself,
Wants to will him even yet into life again
– Something is pushing schemes for winning time.

It may rain on the crags, but down in the resort
Only a sunset breeze billows and fans the grey
Nap of the boating lake into pink ripples, like
– Like scarlet ripples. Now, swiftly, she closes up
Her curtains on their small and disappearing day,
And turns with a wan smile. He sits with one hand warm
From her electric fire, and keeps the other cool
On the smooth rexine flank of her armchair. They dress
Formally, for tonight. And on the sideboard next
The window, on her right, stands a neat cut-glass pair
Of sweet aperitifs. He will not look her way,
But focuses the ashtray on its leather strap,
Where she may lately have set down her cigarette:
Nothing has yet deranged its drawn-up thread of smoke.
Whatever they may do when dusk has turned to dark
Is hidden from us yet (was hidden from us then)
So all we might conjecture from their perfect poise
Is that the most she feels concerning his profound
Conviction of her cold, impermeable grace
Is a sympathetic spiritual regard;
And envying their world of carefully-defined
Limits and chances (they need never travel on
To places where correct patterns of gesture make
No real impression on the bloody flux of things),
I can see reasons why, some forty years ago,
The self I am today should 'Spend a Day in Hove'.

174   *Find*

The waxwork chef once gripped in two wax hands,
Grinning over it at his readers, a menu
In a square wooden frame. The frame is empty,
And the chef lies grinning on his side in an overlooked yard
Behind a washeteria; presenting his lack of choice

To the gush of a drainpipe.
                              When they learn
The value of this site, and finally all
The bulldozed earth clumps down on him, he will make
A find for a commercial archaeologist: he will mean
Someone's failure to make it in this world.
He did not work. He does not work tonight,
In the little darkening yard.
                              So call it flesh
To ashes, and wax to wax: in the crumbling
Sewers of the city the waters are rising, the eating
Is going on in another, lighted place.
On this raining night, successful faces elsewhere
Shine out like artifacts of burnished wax.
                              They read,
Through their private spectacle-frames, what wine
Might gush from the list held out by the living hands.

175   *Syllabics*

At a deep pool left by a high tide high on a beach,
Rather sinisterly dark green even near its edge,
And rapidly shelving away to an unknown depth,
A various, bustling, organised family
Plays happily on through an overdue summer day
At the forming of little well-fashioned knolls of sand
With the help of improvised spades hacked out of driftwood,
And the scooping of narrow, regulated channels
So that quantities of water transferred in cartons
Might be pushed and manoeuvred from one point to the next.
You can never say ants are organised while one ant
Pisses off in quiet serendipity from the ranks,
Or that humans are individual while these nine
All dispose themselves in such unison, and delight
In the antics of brackish sea water and grains of sand
Gone black with the dull consensus of the polities

To crowd out our oceans with mercantile detritus;
And you could even say that a literary eye
Was giving itself unnecessary dilemmas
In pondering whether to organise such data
Into structures of formal sense, when the thing might prove
A sociological question, a case of how
An extended middle-class family runs itself
In nineteen-seventy-eight, as it cheerfully finds
A scheme of elaborate play on a tarnished beach,
The elders pushing their young to be entrepreneurs
And learn a tremendous work-ethic learning to coax
The spillings of obstinate water to the right spot
. . . I suppose one might let it fade, a small cameo
Of a decorative kind, quiet plastic enjoyments
Going dimmer as the figures merge with the twilight,
And the calls die distantly in the nostalgic dusk
(The parents retiring, the children turning into
Young Eurocrats, or producing some kind of let-down,
And the future arriving with its ancient, heartless,
Recurring prospect of *déjà vu* and *plus ça change*)
– Except that it glows in the mind with a feverish,
Even wilful colour, on the memory's small screen:
The cavorting torsos crazy about their rituals,
The sun blazing uncontradictably, just this once,
On a long terrain of water and sand resplendent
With an unexpected heat-wave; an erratic case
Of forgivable weather in a summer that gave
Not many days to build castles in the open air.

176 *Especially*

To Frank and Rita in Bracknell, greetings,
And greetings especially to those listeners who,
On this weatherless February day at half-past four,
Have risen from first long lovebeds in small warm rooms
To lie again in magenta baths together,
And dabble each other's steaming thighs with suds.

I especially feel
For those who have long-delayed essays on Tennyson to write,
And have switched on their English transistors to discover
Some Third Republic operetta tripping out
On Radio 3, all coquettish plaints
And cavalier manoeuvres, happening out there
In the distance and the past, and so near and true.

May you, especially, recline, as you listen to the voices
Of love made easy and gracious ploys fulfilled,
And renew the heat of the water from time to time
From the tap marked 'Varm' (if you're listening in
                                        Stockholm),
And float the soap in play towards each other's
Crotches, in the softly dropping dark,
And chatter for only a sentence or two of what
Might be, and what might prevent it in a thoughtless world.

Greetings to you then, especially, and here
Is *Das Lied von der Erde.*

177   *Heptonstall February*

Today the moors unclench and clench
On a gift of warmth; the snow
Draws back one softened inch, but frost holds firm.
In our mid-afternoon new ice already
Glints, in the sun's very eye. A camera-eye
Would trace the loosened stream, and stop
On a rigid freeze: where suddenly grey
Spires, that were a waterfall, stab down
At the shrunken torrent.

                        None of these days
Will release themselves, the land
Not gentle into sympathy. This cold
Is well ignored by those who wait indoors
Inside their coloured windows, watching
The month increase and the land not change:
Let it come to the light and listen.

178   *Near Gun Hill*

Once drawn to promontories where the sea
Is grey and intemperate, with sheer juts
Of rock into rapacious, upheaved waters . . .
At Hartland Point in fog a bursting roar
Blares out on time and space from the lighthouse
And deafens its own echoes; while inland
Merely a sweet haze drapes the sunset fields.
Or at Rhossilli, or the Calf of Man:
A savagery interposes on the path
Of sun- or moonlight laid across that bleak
Table of restlessness, and breaks all thought.
Once drawn to this; and therefore not believing
Any disquiet on one rare windless day
Lying down and gazing on endless sands
On this eastern coast, line above line, and each
A deepening dried yellow to the edge,
With the last line the horizon: all a stave
Still innocent of anything's notation
– And to feel suddenly how the huge chords
Don't dramatise themselves, don't flaunt themselves
In obvious frenzies here, but lie and wait
While the first creature of the swarm climbs slowly
Unsheathing a black wing and tilts one reed.

In the spring of their hope you saw them crouching,
He outside in the sunshine and she inside,
And handling this bad cat back and forth, to and fro
Through the flap. And back through the flap.
They were trying to coax it to work the flap.

That summer the cat was not learning at all,
Though they pushed it persistently, head
First and tail last, towards each other
Through the yielding flap in the humid dark,
She inside, he outside, with fists full of moulted hairs.

And by the autumn still it had not learnt,
While the air was not kindly any more:
The flap on its hinges grated, he outside
Forcing hard the reluctant brute to her inside,
Who received it with aching hands.

It had to be winter next; it would not learn now.
It had never made it once of its own accord:
It had only ever let itself passively
Be jostled to and fro through the grinding hole,
To and fro, back and forth, she inside, he outside,

And both of them getting horribly impatient.

180 *Union Man*

His liquid lunches will not have unhoned
This lean man, upright at the bar
With the minutes of the last executive
In a thick buff wallet, listening precisely
And working through strategies. His brow
Is furrowed with niceties, his craft
Is the unravelment and intertwining
Of clauses in tense agreements. He gives
A week-end course in grievance and recompense,
And Monday, drives via home to all his high
Cabinets of cases, when the telephone
Clangs to the carpet as he stretches out far to a file
On a distant shelf, and listening precisely.
In a city where minds are slabbed with gold,
He builds a sheltering-wall of brick; and how
The commonwealth doth need such justices.

181 *The Leap*

One Xmas in the High Street, the Rotary Tree
On the traffic island by the underground Gentlemen's
Concealed a plenteous amplifier, bawling
The sound of music as if from down below.

Rotarians were shaking boxes for children
Too far away, too heathen, or too poor
To have this kind of Xmas; and two lovers
Looked out upon this scene from where they sat

– On a cushion of white noise which they could not hear –
At the cotton-wool-snow-dotted window of
A little formica restaurant, threading hands
And picking at green salads between interlacements.

234

That deep hum of noise from the near deep freeze
Lulled all the sounds around them, held them fast
From the clamours of the Xmas street, kept off
This world altogether, more than they would have guessed.

All they could know was a happy avenue
Stretching away in front of them, and on
Into uplands of opportunity; and they thought:
Of all the times, this time we have it right!

– When suddenly a sneaky thermostat
Cut the droning freezer out to the starkest stop;
And with a squirming chill down every back,
The whole room took a leap into a ghastly

Stillness, and vividness. Their hands disjoined,
And to their eyes came nervous, separate smiles,
Much less certain than before: that wicked cold
Went through their empty fingers to their hearts,

And froze out words. So when the shaken room
Relaxed, and as the seething copper urn
Spilled out once more its rasping twists of coffee
Into trays of passive cups, they had this instinct

Of a string having somehow snapped in the distant air
– Until the traffic moved, and the tree again
Stood and ritually glistened, and everyone
Went deaf as usual with the chime of coin.

Somewhere a bus drives on, on this chilling night
Of dusty April, between its termini,
The conductor winding his destinations
Backwards and forwards as if to obtain some
Renewal of the sense of quest; and these two
        Sit inside it all this time,
Holding hands and not noticing. She repeats,
'You would have wanted this child to be your own?'
And he gives her illusion no denial,
Having loved her enough, long since, to have felt
Exactly such a thing for about nine weeks
        When they met by the bandstand.

But truly he is thinking now, 'How can she
Be ever complete again, ever the same
As the woman of the past, when our pledges
Were engraved in deep letters and in our eyes
When we kissed by the boating-lake in the fog,
        And I could not bear to lose

The hand I capture now in this neutral way
Which *she* does not grasp?'
        – But let them travel on.

Give or take a variation of detail,
It could be happening almost anywhere,
Wherever a woman gives a man her news
        And he makes out he is pleased,

Yet not for one moment wants her happiness,
Preferring a slow gathering of regret,
Of self-doubt about her marriage, and a fear
That she may have spoilt her life when, instead, she –
But pregnant today, she feels magnanimous
        Towards all unregenerate

236

Lovers arrived out of the past, who have lost
Their cutting edge of novelty or nuisance:
Those old, superannuated cavaliers
Who send birthday presents through friends' addresses
Or make phone calls to the office, gentle bores
        Who will always minister

To the last shards of romance, her tiny crave
For a tremor of nostalgia now and then.
There is this sweet island in her consciousness
Where the trees gleam even now with untaken
Fruit from those evenings on the rustic bridges
        Making quips about moorhens,

Having schemes about beds in far-off cities;
And even now, she thinks, he would if he could,
He would pluck it if she let him, and suck, suck:
So he holds her hand, in London or Belgrade,
Allowing these assumptions to have their rein
        – Yet wherever they may be,

He is looking for the sudden prize: the chance
To re-start the process all over again
With another one; at forty or fifty,
To begin a brand-new journey through it all,
All over again (the new girl saying how
        Alien it would be, in

Her married or unmarried state, to even
Dream of bearing children, how she quite intends
To stay sterile for her career, for the sake
Of peace and quiet, or fulfilment through batiks,
While she takes the pill, and smokes, and wonders if
        This Jungian analyst

Can put her together, and whether she should
Consent to be chairperson of her local
Liberal Women's Group). How he longs for it
All to flood back, that poignant high adventure
Of plunging into young women still unsoiled
By cash and security . . .

He will therefore grip her patronising hand
Rather nominally, on whatever route
They ride today; and will outwardly maintain
A reverence for their past, and try to show
A nostalgia for it out of chivalry,
As the unborn child begins

To chafe inside her. – And she would not believe
That last night's yearning for the larger size of
Gherkins, in big glossy jars, which you notice
On the counters of downmarket sidestreet pubs,
Was a throwback to their first drink ever, at
The Hare and Hounds in Catford.

183   *In Praise of Nostalgia*

Condemn it as a *fainéant* indulgence;
But nations without it fix their constitutions,
Buy personnel carriers from Western powers,
And refine kinetic art.

Having nostalgia is having a proper respect
For small lights receding on a shore, without
Dismissing *all* pioneers who sternly steam off
Across the Forward Planner.

Not having it is licensing Zakki and Tobia
To patronise Nik and Germaine for their funny names
In 1998. Is saying, 'Look at these craptious
            Gears in these merdy old photes!'

When it's not as if the nostalgic were saying
'Revere them in their dignified garments, fragile
In the beautiful black-and-white past; from them
            We derive all truth.' We are not such fools.

One bad mistake, I agree, is reducing nostalgia
To wanton revivals of old detritus:
Hobbit socks and Whitelaw cardigans need not
            Come back again in my lifetime;

And one better form of nostalgia is a hatred
Of the arrogance of time ever passing: Adolf Hitler
Drank gallons of weak tea and ate cream cakes,
            And raved all night about the *future*;

He should have sat with the nostalgic, reminiscing
From evening round to dawn, and when dawn comes
One says, 'Do you remember how we sat last night
            Indulging our nostalgia? How sweet it was . . .'

Then didn't someone say nostalgia was not
A weakness, but a springboard? From where you stand,
With the warm past cheering you on, you dive away
            Into the coming minutes reassured

That they also will cheer you to recall them.
Don't listen to any injunction to 'Cut adrift,
Forget what you cannot change.' Think long enough
            About anything past, and it improves.

– My horror is of losing all regard for any
Caress, or meal, or music from yesterday. I would never
Willingly let it all go slipping like a splendid
           Orchestra out to sea. My dread

Is of being a forgetful old man at ninety
Hustled onwards, always onwards, turned right off
The dances of his youth (though he rarely danced them)
           And set there, stark upon the shore,

Amidst a rubbish from times-to-come: the trees
Casting polythene leaves, the calendar metric,
And each bit of flotsam swirling round his feet
           Singing, 'Hey! My name's *Tomorrow*! Bite me
                                              NOW!'

184   *A View of Sussex*

Our happy road is flanked by russet guards-
Of-honour, for November: tiny leaves
Flit at our wheels in suicidal pairs
As we drive powerfully south. You shake your head
Because you want to rearrange the hair
You won't let anybody see you comb
Except yourself. – And there, see how the lamp
Lights up those gables where the vine has turned
A dry vermilion round the 'Hawk and Prey',
Which flaps and creaks for the wind. We smell of air
As I grip hard on our receptionist's
Black ballpen, and write lies. But further in,
Along the corridors, the mantle of
The central heat comes down, a thrilling hush
Which deepens in our room. We drop our bags
Hard on a bench of wooden slats, we let
The tap drip and the light stay on, we start
Clutching the white stiff sheets to tear them back
As if we were ravening at new bread.

The buzz of a mechanical game played by working
Two handles, one on each side of a screen
Where you shift around an always-too-late white line
In the effort to stop a blip which flies very fast
Over a small dark firmament, you lose a point
If you don't contrive to intercept it; and gin,
And bubbles rising in the tonic, or clinging
To the side of the glass, expiring hopes:
An aerodrome building, converted not long back
Into a student lounge, with bar and cushions,
Double-glazed against the whining air, but somehow
The room is forced to admit the scream as it pierces
The level land outside, jet engines droning
On their high and undismissible register, dropping
Down fast to this haven of their firmament,
A sound striking suddenly through, as when you feel water
Reach inside a soaped ear.
                                    The runways were laid down
For a war predating mechanical games you can play

On buzzing screens, but resulting in radar,
And out across the acres of grass and tarmac
Stand air-force buildings of one and two storeys
Converted into a college for several hundred,
Made over into bedsits and lecture-rooms and that
Barrack is the library, with long open aisles
Of volumes for learning about learning.
                                    Sitting there
You can try intercepting an idea before it flicks past
(Without working a handle) but not for long now:
The engines will soon inherit the place again, the ideas
Expire, like all hopeful bubbles. For thirteen years
You could eat in the echoing refectory, run
A moderate lap on the games floor laid down inside
The hangar; but an unlettered wind wipes all

This land quite clean of learning, the students leave,
The last ministrants see them out.
                                        Eight years ago,
Ruth furrowed in that index for critical assistance
With the novels of D.H. Lawrence, and walked along
To a corner where they went to each other's arms
And her shoulder, for a moment, unbalanced a small row
Of volumes at 823. LAWR. And eight years ago,
They all fell back into place, in perfect order,
As he let Ruth go, not to be kissed again ever
By him, and watched her recede down the heartless
Perspective of the grass, farther off and farther still,
And go in for her Finals.
                                The ceiling of chandeliers
Above our student lounge makes a carapace against
The huge skies of this region, but the crude lid-lifters
Will prise it away, and we shall shiver
From more than nostalgia, and then relinquish it
To the fractured sky over the runways, allow
The Lawrence files to break open at their spines, pages
Flutter away into the slipstreams and vanish
In a distance which does not read. The flying blips
Fled past too fast, we were always too late.
                                        That ivy,
Which grew untrained up the wall of the Admin. block,
Rattles red against the brickwork, the colour it turned to
And stayed throughout last winter; a louder sound
Than any inside, where the rooms now scream with silence;
And there's the last bubble faintly expiring in
Our tonic water, like a lamp of Europe.
                                        Oh, but now
There is suddenly a triumphant jumping of feet
On the carpet up by the screen, because someone
Has deflected his final blip, and won! What a pity
It's a game and not real . . . One says about the real,
There are too many evils to prevent, or even
Notice them all, as you strive to work the hopeless

242

Handles you are offered, like using sardine-tin keys
For programming computers.
                              There was Ruth here once,
And the fall of her hair across the shaken spines
Of the Lawrence critics, and her lover's spine tilting
Towards her at 823. LAWR. He was one who read,
Like most of us, not wisely but too late,
And what should he have learnt?
                              And what have I?
– Hardly much more than one negative consolation:
There are too many evils, they race too fast, you lose
Much more than a point if you don't contrive to intercept them.

1980s

At first it looked as if the horse
    Came riderless, out of the green
Woods in the dropping night; and then
    We knew what we had really seen
Was Cheryl, draped with a green coat
    To match the dark and deepening shade
And make the white horse seem as if
    It strode alone across the glade.
– And had we stopped our borrowed car
    Ten yards uphill or ten yards down,
Or left its headlights on and caused
    Cheryl to switch her dazzled frown
And fix it on the trees that day,
    Not seeing us with fingers tightly
laced together on the gear-
    Stick knob – it might have been all right.
Instead, we chose the very point
    Where Cheryl (who had been advised
To give up riding for her health)
    Chose to emerge, and thus surprised
The two of us parked near the Mill,
    Facing the sunset. First she stared
At Polly, then she froze at me
    – My theory is she was prepared
To speak to us, then changed her mind –
    Firefly was not prepared to wait
On the last hundred yards of his
    Last outing – it was getting late,
So Cheryl did not rein him in,
    But let him stride on up the track
(And having summed up what she saw,
    Saw little point in looking back.)
And there were many interests
    A Cheryl of this life might find

In church, or bridge, or marquetry,
    To occupy an active mind;
And various were the causes which
    Resourceful Cheryl might have made
Her own: opposing the closed shop,
    Collecting old gold teeth in aid
Of pensioners or hospitals
    Or sewage systems, wearing a tray
Of flags to help the unemployed
    In the best nineteen-eighties way;
But Cheryl chose to ride instead,
    And lurking fate chose equally
To have her leave the twilight wood
    At just the point where she would see.
And so we knew that Cheryl knew
    About our meetings by the Mill,
And this was worse for being on
    A day she told us she was ill,
And now there were no lies to spin,
    And no excuses to invent,
As Cheryl had our number, and
    The shape of things was different.

187   *Inheritors*

The snow is at the same time as the owl;
When it drops down to the sill, the wings close,

First question: *Why should the owl*
Fly down each night to peer at our painted room?

Softly the snow-dots tumble from its back
As it stands on still claws and looks in,

Second question: *Why does the owl*
Stare in so long at our wine and velvet chairs?

Away from its nest, old feathers, suspicious gaze,
Away if you walk near the window, but always back,

Third question: *If one of us has summoned it, Which?*

– And so we sit, four men in a shared house,
In a particularly scarlet room,
Not easy as we snow down cards, four
After four on the shining table-top;

Not easy as our fingers claw them in;

Wondering what is meant by these visits
From two old interested eyes, not easy
Wondering also which of us might know.

188   *You'll See*

They all talked about growing into,
Growing into, growing into.
They said: You will grow into it.

– But it isn't mine,
And it's not for me.
– You will grow into it,
You'll see!

– But it hangs down below my knee,
It is too long for me.
– Oh it will fit you soon,
It will fit you splendidly.

249

– But I will sulk, and I will say
It is too long, it is no use,
No! I will sulk, and struggle,
And refuse!

– You will grow into it,
And love it,
And besides, we decided
You should have it.

No! – But wait –
Wait a moment . . . Do I see
It growing shorter at the knee?
Is it shrinking gradually?
Is it getting shorter?
Is it getting tighter?
Not loose and straggly,
Not long and baggy,
But neater and brighter,
Comfortable?

Oh now I *do* like it,
Oh now I'll go to the mirror and see
How wonderful it looks on me,
Yes – there – it's ideal!
Yes, its appeal
Will be universal,
And now I curse all
Those impulses which muttered 'Refuse!'
It's really beautiful after all,
I'll wear it today, next week, next year
– No one is going to interfere,
I'll wear it as long as I choose.

And then, much later, when it wears,
And it's ready for dumping under the stairs
When it doesn't actually really fit me
Any longer, then *I'll* pass it down,
I'll give it to someone else
When it doesn't fit me,
And then they'll have it,
They'll *have* to have it,
They'll have to love it,
They'll see, they'll see.

They'll have to grow into it like me!

189 *Clip*

Look how faded and worn the sun is, like old linen.
But it lights my neat young grandfather brightly
To the door of the little contraceptive shop;

Where his fancy has engaged with the yellowed sets
Of enveloped possibilities, their very formal
Old typography. Into an even further faded

Interior, he allows, as he pushes at the door,
An allocation of the ancient light
Discreetly, and vanishes from the lens, which holds

The window and the sunblinds only so long
As some graininess of image lets it seem
That dust is gathering on both shop and street

Even as I watch. This cuts to an unmade avenue,
A house, a sepia bedroom where high pots
Of flowering rubber plants, broad Chinese screens,

And beads low at a neckline entertain,
By being my grandmother's obviously, hopes
That I have been watching this film myself,

Not some interloping shadow, standing at
That young man's shoulder, a black care
Sitting behind the horseplay, about to expose it,

Like his near-fatal typhoid at twenty-three.

190   *Prophets of the Pier*

Well, once we told people's fortunes, but now
We sit in our robes and fish from the pier,
We fish from the pier; though they call to us
That the sea receded many a year
Ago, on our little camp stools we sit
And fling out our hooks at low green land where
Children walk by with their dogs through the grass,
And the slight summer breeze makes waves in it.

Well, we are wise and we are ready, when
The dyke they have built to hold back the brute
Sea shatters in the distance, for a full
Rampaging day there will then come waves not
Consisting of grass; and in pain and blood,
The children and dogs will be crying out
– And with our lines and hooks and prayers, we will
Fish from the pier in the horrible flood.

191   *Watershed*

I detected this change in the ways of my friends:
They had suddenly gone in for a decent shame
In their lunch-time conversations; no longer were they
Boasting of all their adulteries and grand lies.

Their talk had become decidedly more discreet.
They did not want to confess, and seek reassurance.
They did not stub out their cigarettes half way
And stumble out to make illicit phone calls,

And I said: This is really very seemly,
There are some of us who have found some strength at last,
This restaurant at lunch-time is no longer
A vista of private misery, a place

Where novice waiters are brought in to learn
How to come and steal away our untouched plates
With an unseen patience. And I thought it good
That my friends should have acquired some self-control.

But then, one day as the two of us were sitting
With nothing to say, and the band filled in
Our silence with its genteel sympathies,
I felt sad about all this; and began to search

The back of my mind to drag out some anecdote
Of hazard and betrayal to revive those dear
Dead days . . . And I found that I did not have one.
Then I saw that your hand, which I recalled would once

Have crawled to mine for comforting across
Whole Sohos of wine-stained tablecloths,
Had apparently forgotten my hand was there,
And was checking the bill, which we were halving,

As were all the other hands on all the other
Tables across the endless dry-eyed room;
Above which stood a clock with its own hand
Shifting neutrally one second on towards five past two.

192   *Dialogue of the Striving Soul and the Deprecating Self*

Soul: I release the worn black handle,
    And slap the last ball straight up
    To the top of the frame; where
    It pauses long enough, just,
    To shape the whole arcade into
    A tiny silver picture before
    It turns at last, and wanders
    Derisively down and across
    Not hitting any exciting coils
    Not bouncing any further red
    Numerals into lights increasing
    Speed missing all connections
    Dropping finally back into
    Its pit.
          My little score
    Shines out for one brief moment, and then goes dark.

Self: Ah, soul! You ought to realise how
    You did not remotely deserve
    Those encouraging lights and that
    Working handle when others
    Were fretting in long queues to get
    No turn in the end, or discovered
    That the chrome slit swallowed
    All their money and sent them down
    No balls at all, while the button
    Refused to return their coins. And of course,
    Over there all the time the real boys,
    With huge muscles and girls to praise them,
    And deep uproarious voices,
    Were playing the real game . . .
                    And don't think they
    Couldn't see you trying quietly to tilt the machine.

254

Stepping out from under mother's
Protection at five or fifty,
Up the ever-so-nasty wet
Miles of tarmac to the moor,
Bold to cross it though his short
Legs, he saw, were trembling,
He arrived at the wind-worsted heather
Out of reach of her voice, whether
Raised in anger or muted
In consolation. These were forbidden
Tracts, so remote from mother's suburb,
And what wonderful courage this was!

To have even started out was
Appalling audacity, loading
His belongings without her help,
Taking boots, map and compass
And creeping out to the door . . .
Could this truly be himself?
And could this invincible dawn be
Raining, as he set off, when she
Had predicted a sunny day with her?
It scared him. It soothed him knowing
How surely he would be creeping back
When the day was over.

And he could not tell if he might
Be prouder of having defied
Mother's warnings, or of guessing
How deeply he would defer again
To her, in the end . . . Down there below,

The voices of the crowd cried amazement
That mother's own particular
Weakling had gone so far;
And the little voice here at his side
Said the venturing out in dread
And the going back from fear
Were both attributable to her.

194   *An Orchard Path*

A guilty tremor in the chime of six
From his dishevelled mantelpiece . . . She waits
For the plaint of the express along the cutting,
Which she guesses the wind will let her hear,
Then she rises, in a calm of strict obedience,
And walks off obediently to be back,
Securely seated in her drawing-room,
As the doors of the carriages gape and slam.

– Though one day the train has left, she is running
And scarcely home before her lawyer husband
Is entering and handing his hat naively
To the discreet old fellow in the hall.
Catching her breath, she comes in from the garden
As if from the garden and nowhere else,
Dividing the curtains no more than her hair
Would be slightly rearranged by an innocent breeze.

– And later still, one day the whistle-call
Dies out, she hears it, over the summer fields,
And she does not move at all. She stands here still,
Though the train is already some way on,
And allocating other destinies.
The lawyer is destined to the empty house.
Her hair is neat. She smiles for the man in this room.
He stares at his prize incredulous and afraid.

195　*A Statue of Innocence*

or

Geological Time in the Department

(for John Betjeman)

Miss Frith was put on processing; that glue
And all those labels. Not seven months there,
And Mr Mortimer, who always said
'Miss Frith' and never 'Gill' or 'Gillian',
Right through the informal nineteen-sixties,
Rested one day his two hands on her hips
As she sat cross-leggéd on the high stool
At the labelling desk. She did not squirm,
She did not put the labels down; to be
A statue of innocence was her way
Of making Mr Mortimer redeem
His fingers, which (to be fair) he had not
Spread out all that widely.

　　　　　　　　　After ten months,
Miss Frith was briefly told by Miss Duveen
How Mr Langley, in the previous year,
Had twice put his arm round her shoulders in
The Lower Stack Room. No, it had not been
A question of her having felt some need
Of comforting, or of her wanting help
With the box-files; he had just come and put
His arm around her, and had no excuse
– An honesty for which he would obtain
A tick in the Eternal Register.

Five months went by. Then, Mr Mortimer
Suddenly kissed Miss Frith, full on the lips,
On the little-used back staircase between
The Processing Room and the Staff Canteen.

Five months! So things were speeding up. But times
Were frantic, what with the renovations,
And he never did anything else. All
Over the building lay the dusty planks,
The stepladders and dust-sheets, brought by bald
And jocular young white-coated builders,
Who painted and sang to small transistors.
They were apt to appear round any corner;
One could not really use that staircase now.

Miss Frith occasionally wondered what
Inscrutable inertia it was that kept
The silent Mr Langley three short yards
Away from her, at his metal table,
Through so many busy and humid days
Spent loathing the central heating. Of course,
She would not have welcomed an intrusion;
But she would have looked for *something*. 'In time,
Even the rocks,' she read, 'will change their shape.'

She doubted it. One day in May, Miss Frith
Lifted her eyes from all the labels on
The labelling desk, and put down her brush,
And observed that the dust in the still air
Was thinner than it had been. It was quiet,
The builders gone and the renovations
Finished till the next time. Now, suddenly,
With eyes less prone to notice than to gaze
(With dull eyes pleading for the world to change)
She saw that the traffic down there in the street,
Passing and crossing, on through day and dark
And never ceasing, was re-organized
Into an irreversible One Way.

Rain, said Nanny, Rain is to test our courage,
Dirt is to test our cleanliness,
Hunger our patience,
And night is to test our fear of darkness.
But rain is to test our courage.

That was because it rained all the time very hard
Where we lived as children,
In the house with the nineteen rooms of forbidden books
(To test how we could conquer the thirst to read)
And a few permitted books in the sitting rooms,
But Nanny in a book-lined room we might never enter,
In a turret above the lawn where the croquet hoops
Were feet deep in water for very much of the time.

But Courage, said Nanny, wellingtons on,
Backs up, chins up, and best foot forward
In a long line, holding tightly on to each other
– Out!

So the small but courageous band of us
Paddled hand-in-hand onwards,
Nanny first, me second,
Then the third and fourth, diminishing in size
To the very smallest who came infallibly last,
Head just above water.

And as we sadly struggled, the small cold hand
Of my youngest brother
Slipped out of the grasp of the one next above him in age.
And when that next one tired, her hand
Released the fingers of the sibling senior to her,
And the line fell gradually apart,
Leaving me
Waving frantically after Nanny, who was fár ahead
And had almost disappeared.

But *Courage!*

The call of Nanny rang distantly over
The widening waters in the dark,
And returned in echoes from the other shore.
The waterfowl answered in imitation and unison
To comfort each other

And Nanny's cry merged into theirs,
Growing fainter and fainter in the rain until
It became at last an everyday sound you hear
And think little about for very much of the time.

197   *The Pool*

To carry daylight to the pool I walk
Myself in that direction, throwing off
Its veil of grey with my eyes, hurling back
Tall hillsides with each step, causing enough
Space on it for the sky. But as the sky
Glides up and stops in front of me, I stop
And look – Somehow my head is only
A blur itself on the water's edge, my face
Is darkened by the half-light of this place
. . . You could remove me just as easily.

I could change nature with no greater power
Than a short walk, and a switching of my gaze;
But I see now that my shape is nothing more
Than a shadow on this world, and its brief day dies.
I go back to a room where there is room
For just a mirror – another mirror
In which I make no difference. This one is deep,
And in it, stones and earth will not retreat
For movements of the head, or of the feet.
Nothing can alter there. And nothing keep.

198   *Near Miss*

They would call me soon. And still I stood
At some window on the cold side of the house,
Somewhere between this and non-existence,
Letting the evening rotate towards me,
Fixing my gaze on nothing at all.

All the life in the place had left suddenly,
And gone out to the terrace. But I stayed one
With the objects in this room, in their graveyard poise
Of dresser, bed, and vase. Everything seemed
Too dull to be worth a judgement, first or last,

And too dead to be raised by voices; it felt
Too late already. If they had sent up
From down below to fetch me, *Come on, we're waiting!*
They would have found only a shape you could not
Prise out from the furniture and the shadows.

– So I quite surprised myself when I started
Running easily down stairs, round corners, and out
Through a door into the sun. And can't explain
The laughter, the groans of welcome, the shuffling up,
Or my head and shoulders in the photograph.

199   *Jogger*

The man on the liniment bottle is very young.
He is gaining rapid relief from muscular pains
Which must have set in early. I am rigorous
Like him, I know I am . . . But I do think,
Would my wrists ache if I rubbed my heavy legs
In the rigorous way required? Would I then need
To rub each rigorous wrist? And if so, how?

So how dignified, I think, that old Einstein
On the cough-drop tin, who stands up tall and straight,
And shakes his great grey sneezing head into
A starch-white handkerchief, trimly tucked
In a dignified black pocket. How easy,
Only to have to stretch one dignified
Hand to a tin for one all-solving jube!

200   *Doorway*

Where it stood by the roadside, the frame for a view,
It made the step from one weed-patch to the next
A metaphor. If I chose to walk across
This threshold to a mansion never built,
Could I manage to come back? Having left the road
To stroll into the fields, I saw this lintel
Presenting its challenge. And what it said was, *Walk*

Through this door, you are going to walk through,
After which you will not be the same. I had thought,
Was I always on a journey to that place?
– And now, was I always travelling to where
I am to-night, by a fire toning down to grey
Its image in those glasses, beside the girl
Asleep in the opposite chair? To such a stop?

To-night is six months onwards from that voice
Which said, *You have reached a stage where you must walk through,*
And not expect to return to what you were.
I am here because I turned back from that view,
Shaking my head and smiling, walking on
To where this girl smiles, in apparent sleep,
And stretches. What she does first when she wakes

Is pick the glasses up, they suddenly
Shine scarlet from the curtains. *What were you thinking?*
She says, as she goes past. I shake my head,
And smile, watching the fire. She goes on past
Its dying coil, then I realize she has stopped
And turned at the doorway behind me, tilting
The glasses in her hand. And has said, *Walk through.*

201   *You Ask*

What do I want? What is it I want to do?
– I should like to have, at an invisible quay,
At a tangent to any moral problem,
A bloody great boat, equipped with everything,
And with one operatic step, leap aboard, and leave
The rest of you behind with your confusions,
And glide away into a singing distance
Where everything is wonderfully resolved . . .

And then, one unexpected day, sail back
With another persona, yes, like someone
Else altogether, and nothing like myself,
As an unknown *deus ex machina*, making
Everyone stop and listen and behave,
Striking clarity into your souls at last, at last!
– And then pull off my mask and sing it out:
It was me! It was me! This is what I had to do!

She was terrified at the green shine of the sea
Between the planks of the pier,

So she held the stick hard and gnashed its crimson cloud
That fuzzed like a head of hair.

The brightness fell too soon, and the circling horses
Reared up as The Band Played On

With eyes of terror also, but painted like that,
While the girl shook on the dread

-fully quivering pier . . . And the only other
Thing she could find was a steel

Arm on a big, square, lit machine, she grabbed at it
And clanged it down. It went with

A lunge and a clatter that sent a row of discs
Insensately whirling; then

They slowed, and fixed her two passion fruit and a skull,
Which satisfied her for now.

When she turned away, the sunlight seemed perfectly
Natural, the coast restored

To an easy glistening, and the sea below
Was back to a friendly flop

-ping at the stanchions of the pier. She could breathe once more,
And gave out a little smile

As the gaps in the planks closed up. And no such thing
Would scare her again, for hours.

I

Crossing the end of Lancaster Grove
Is the Chinese girl, looking back at her huge man;
And she does not see the Scirocco swinging round,
Does not even see it missing her,
Only hears him roar, with an anger tired
From telling her so many times before:
'Can't you watch where you're bloody going!'
She smiles to admit her inattention,
Or show her indifference. In the man's hand
A cat-basket swings about, in the basket,
Immune to all occasions, a ginger cat
Sits, bemused and sociable.

II

In another hour, I put down the telephone
And go out to buy some socks. 'Not short-
And-flimsy,' I say, '*or* long-and-rough.'
'So medium wool,' says Henry the outfitter,
Who can outfit anyone. 'Try these. – Yes, sir?'
Behind me: 'Have you any denim shoes?'
Asks Lindsay Anderson. 'Only these,' says Henry,
Who has left me for a second with the socks.
'Only *those?*' says Lindsay Anderson. 'The trouble is
One is getting so conservative.'
'We are,' says Henry with authority,
'Expecting some more in.'

The facing mirrors showed two rooms
Which rhymed and balanced beautifully,
So everything we wore and ate
Shone doubly clear for you and me.

In the next image after that
Life seemed the same in every way:
Green bottles and white tablecloths
And cutlery as clean as day;

But in the third, things looked a mite
Less brilliant than in the first two . . .
A sort of mist was falling on
The features of a dwindling view,

And by the time our gaze had gone
Searching down to rooms eight and nine,
The world seemed darker, and confused,
Its outlines harder to define,

Its faces tinier. There, instead
Of warmth and clarity and bright
Colours for everything, we saw
A shadow land, a listless light

Which neither of us understood:
A place so closed and small and black
It nearly hurt, smiling, gripping
Our glasses harder, coming back.

205 *A View of Nowhere*

Our long thin legs exaggerate our steps
As we prance and stalk up the dunes lugging huge
Transistors. We are mechanical toys
Wound up and pointed over nowhere, blue
Windcheaters, canvas shoes, obedient
Creatures who would not guess how much we *are*
Our elementary times. Did all those beards
And bowlers and high collars ever guess
How they posed for their own bourgeois age?

The old serene sun of late afternoon
Draws out our shadows. Suddenly you hear
Our music turning quaint, collectable,
And see our clothes draped on museum stands . . .
In a moment we ourselves will be gone too,
Along the sepia roads of this July,
Not guessing how the sea outlasts it all,
Pushing back at us today more signatures
Of what we are: torn sea-birds on our sand.

206 *Lieder*

(for Peter Porter)

Horseman, horseman galloping with the wind! Look at me, look at me, I am the beautiful daughter of the King of the Hobgoblins. If you look at me but once I will gallop at your side, and lead you down, down into the caverns of the Hobgoblins.

The poet sings: Although I am forbidden your company, although you write me whole pages, whole books, whole libraries of cruel rejection, I shall still come and play my piccolo under your casement. Remember, only timid young ladies obey their mothers.

The young man says: You may think I am like a kite on your string, that I will obey every tug of your heartless fingers. Beware, beware! One day I shall refuse your bidding and flop down into the mud.

The poet sings: I love my cat, and I love you. My cat is small and warm, and so are you. My cat plays with me and has sharp claws, and so do you.

The young peasant is very lazy, but his beloved is very short in stature. I will take up my shears, he says, and cut and cut at the grass until I can see you, my dear. What wonders, O what wonders love will accomplish!

She says: If you are a butterfly, I shall be a net. If you are a rose, I shall be a pair of secateurs. If you are some crisps, I shall be a wrapper, and you will be ready salted. I am a most determined young woman.

The poet, starving and penniless, sings for the King. O what gifts, O what glories, says the King. They are worth more than all the banquets and all the gold in the world – and turns the poet out into the snow at the palace gate.

207   Theatre

Oh look, a dog walking along by himself!
I can tell he wants me to believe he has
A destination.

When I dragged the curtains aside, they became
A fourth wall enclosing his performance of
A purpose, strolling

Across the stage of the street not sniffing, not
Diverted by anything. And see, a cat
Which connives at this

Dog's desire to seem busy, therefore just sits
And knows he will be safe. What fine perception!
The dog exits, left,

And he is now in the past, the cat and I
Have entered the present where nothing happens,
And three large blue cars

Driving past is not dramatic, only part
Of everyday life. Except that in that house
A curtain opens,

And a face cranes out with crude astonishment
At three glossy cars! They cross his empty stage,
They want him to think

They had a destination and a purpose,
And at the corner a policeman has connived
At their busy wish.

We might try hard, but this other face and I
Cannot see the same production. Entranced, he
Stands there gazing, but

For me events of tables and chairs inside
The room behind me are more amazing now.
Let the play go on

In the eye of this other beholder, I
Shall finish with it and pull my curtains, sad
At so many walls.

208   *A Fear of Wilderness*

They leap without letting on they intend to,
These cats. Assuming they always do land
In amenable safety, they cling to
Your lap with four paws cold from the darkness.
You shiver at the ice they bring in them.

But slowly your legs regain a heat,
Their claws retract, and the vacillating tail
Has finished; the four feet now turning warm.
What had been once, outside the door, a fear
Of wilderness is now a comfortable

Interesting glow, of cities seen from trains
You are neither entering nor pausing in.
You pat and patronize, they settle down
To a steady breathing. In the yellowed light
The two of you are rational animals.

209   *Entering My Fifty-third Year*

Another animal lounges on my table,
With none of my guilts or aspirations.
He has been poisoned with boiler-fumes, had
Ear-mites and eczema, undergone a short
Paralysis of his hindquarters and survived.
Last year he used up one of his lives in causing
A twenty-ton lorry to swerve into a ditch.
Have I done as much for the environment?
In a moment he will probably leave me
And go over to the garden of the Grapes,
Where people who do not know him from Adam
Will feed him with bacon scratchings and ploughman's cheese.
Would they do as much for me? They do it for him
Because he is definable, they know what he is
And the little things he likes. Today I am as many
Cards as there are in the pack and weeks in the year,
And they would not know where to have me: a merman
Stranded between the tempests of youth and the dried-up
Plateau of walking-frame and electric blanket.
If they found out, what would they make of seven books
Where the life not coded in poems is hidden in blurbs,
And a foot (of Achilles, or Oedipus?) twisted

On a Norwegian mountain and creasing me now
As I lope a birthday mile on a corrugated beach?
I crunch over empty shells in my swimming trunks,
Past forbidden nudists rejoicing in the comfort
That the undressed self may be itself and find
Great spiritual solutions and repose . . .
What is that, they might just ask? It has two legs
Quite suited to a kilt, up to the knees,
But beyond that only girth and ungainliness,
And not-of-the-newest. I limp, and ask myself
How much longer has this machine? It prolongs
Its life with meticulous arrangements, hating to leave
A chair not parallel with the table, or find
The Co-op coffee granules on the wrong shelf;
But it grows slower with its diligence.
It listens less and less when people answer
The questions it poses, they might not have been speaking.
The issues it sorely wants to understand
Might be happening elsewhere. Last night, having had
A dream of death, it groped downstairs and ravaged
The biscuits by torchlight at four a.m., as usual.
It hopes it works them off with exercise.
– Today I am still running after the slim one
Who was never there in the past, but some time might be,
Pursuing the true self in this trampled shell:
Inside a man half-a-stone too heavy is a man
So light, and lightheartedly serious, he really finds
Life is both profound and easy; not this tired struggle
In the effort to grasp the *scherzo con espressione*
Which the cat has played without trying all his days.

Sir, at the window of the study where
His prayer-books blocked the walls, grabbed for his bell
And the clapper was missing; so he shook
A silence at the playground. Many years
Before it could be technically so,
The sound had gone and left only the vision:

The vision of a bell vainly swinging
At a lordly wrist while our little world
Played on regardless of his stare. *Inside,
Inside!* he had to shout. And we all trooped
Inside to our places, mine being under
A secular picture somewhere near the back.

Picture the wind and rain in tantrums,
And me enjoying lovely hours of learning
In that school of life. Miss Wyke's bright-coloured chalks
Are poised at the blackboard writing truths, the room
Basks in a lime-green shade on sunny days
When the blind is down. And I feel my elbow

Nudging Miss Wyke's cool shoulder as she bends down
To read what I have written, all her red ticks
Fall lavishly across my splendid pages.
And then there come the long, long holidays,
All lustrous on lawn and sundial, where I wish
The shadow spun much faster than it did:

I am yearning for the shadow of Miss Wyke
To bring maturer wisdoms in September.
In my secret exercise-book I make
The summer hours more sweet, Miss Wyke draw near
By invoking her grace in fictions, in tales
Where I find the bell-notes are scarcely needed.

About this time I find inside myself
A social conscience in the shape of marbles
Cadged out of Barbara, who said she liked me.
They touch with glassy kisses and are gone,
And I mourn in the alley's red-and-white globe
The transience of gain, the truth of loss.

– Today I gained the top of the hill and saw
The school, in the haze of distance tinier
Than houses in Monopoly. Barbara
Could be the figure I picked up and set
On the doll's house swing in the recreation
Ground alongside. Night blotted out the scene,

A night in which I find Miss Wyke in dreams
Among her books and music, in Sir's room now.
She asks me to say sorry to Barbara,
And run life sensibly, without a bell.
The fields and towns I see in her unstained windows
Are much more like real worlds. I read her books.

211 *Fire Drill*

Now we all troop out, now we all troop out
Along the arrows on the notices;

But it's not for real, they told us in advance
There was going to be an exercise.

The hooter blares on down long corridors
And over into portakabins. Here

Is a word half-finished on a typewriter,
There, a comb stopped in half-done hair. Miss West,

Never seen full-length before, is standing up
And out from behind her desk, Mr Vince

Hasn't rescued the word-processor from the flames,
But he has saved some important-looking memos.

What would we do, we say, if it were true,
And not a practice! Leaving our coats inside,

We pour out, as instructed, from the main doors
And the side doors; and all protocol has gone.

On the equal grass today's warm sun and breeze
Flow round our unusual outdoor laughter,

And anyone talks to anyone. Back inside,
In the empty spaces, nothing can be the same.

We shall go back with a sense of changing,
To rooms where the sun falls in a different place.

– But we can't go back, they want a photograph.
They want a photograph and had not told us.

Stand still – like that – stand still, *stand still!*
There is going to be a tremendous flash.

'. . . this cheating device of buying and selling.'

– G. Winstanley

   Not having else to do, the boss strolls out
From behind his dark glass panel to keep an eye
On things in general. That hulking lout
Of an assistant has been told to see
What the customer says that they should rectify
On his electric typewriter – which he
Maintains has never functioned. Can they deny
The small print in his small green guarantee?

   The boss is sighing, though it could be fuming.
Will this bugger get *something* right today!
Can he *tell* when someone thinks they'll try to swing
Repairs for their own misuse? This bloody fool
Might let a slippery customer get away
With murder . . . Has he learnt to spot the cool
Attempt to pull a fast one? Will he say
'You have not read this clause. Or kept this rule.'?

   You don't *have* to be mad to work here, but
It helps – to stanch the bleeding misery;
Helps to allay the darkness of the pit
Carved in you by mad customers with lies
And surly tempers; helps calm the agony
Of sour resentment in the ferret eyes
Which turn as the boss crawls surreptitiously
Out from his hole, to fume and supervise.

This is the coin
spinning in air
to decide who wins the toss.

This is the thumb that flicked the coin
spinning in air
to decide who wins the toss.

This is the hand that owns the thumb
that flicked the coin
spinning in air
to decide who wins the toss.

This is the brain that controls the hand
that owns the thumb
that flicked the coin
spinning in air
to decide who wins the toss.

And this, over here, is the twelfth man,
who lent the coin
as a method of being noticed for something
if not for his part in the game.

It is the custom here that the loser of the toss
keeps the coin as a consolation
for the brutality of Fate.

The owner of this coin did not know of the custom,
or he would not have lent for the purpose
a rare doubloon
of the Emperor Paronomasia IV.

As it spins, he watches it, trying to seem unaffected,
thinking, Will I ever get it back?

The situation is complicated by the fact
that the doubloons of the Emperor Paronomasia IV
have two heads.

214   *Box*

It was really remarkable
You should ring after all these years . . .
I was on the brink of a quite
Momentous decision, I mean
A momentous *gaffe*, in my life;
And your call dragged me back from it
Like suddenly finding a room
Where I stood there at the window
And was just preparing to jump!

You cannot explain why you got
In touch? Well – *telepathy*, yes?
What else sent your hand racing out
To a telephone down in Strood
To release this bit of your past
Like a small, crated holy ghost
In Leeds? Your desire to explore
What things your past might be doing
By ringing it up was so *right*.

And there could be more out here, yes?
If you phoned me a second time?
Just dying for that little nudge
To enter the present and bring
New life – and old fascinations –
To a friend it recalled so well
(Who had clearly remembered *it*?)!
I am just like I was, you know,
Except this tiny bit older . . .

Aren't you awfully glad you rang?

215   *Watermark*

The lovely Anita, in earrings already
At twelve, in the nineteen-forties, looks out today
Through a Speak Here perspex veil in a Barclay's Bank.
With her awesome self-possession, she was equal
To any approach; and strolled the – respectable – streets
Surrounded by gallants who furnished heavy aid
Against strangers who dared a look at one precious gilt lobe.

Our middle age should have altered a lot of things
– The shy boy level now with the beautiful doll,
One broke and the other plain. But where life's ledger
Builds columns of meticulous disenchantment,
Anita still sits tight at the clasp, making sure
That its cheques and balances add up to a dead stop
On all extravagant longings; a tarnished bell
Calling gallant support against those who might grasp the gold.

A slip road slopes off from the arterial road,
Running parallel to it for a bit,
Then veers inland and comes between two rows
Of passive terraced houses, fitted out
With concreted front gardens whose wooden gates
Will open to a thumb pressed on a latch.
A gate jars on one step, the letter box
Is clacked three times, as if this is arranged.
When she opens it, a banister offers
A post to drop a coat on, and there is heard
A cinema organ in the kitchen,
Braying a ballad on a wireless set.

The hall is tiny, and she makes a smile
Providing the back-facing sitting-room
Where, if the crimson curtains drew apart,
A line of dazzling washing, the purged wear
Of the past week, would slice the square of lawn
Diagonally into two triangles;
But as the sun is bright, the curtains hide it.
She moves as she is moved, where she is moved,
Half-stumbling downwards, falling sprawled across,
In cotton dress and apron, the settee
Below the biscuit barrel. Now the runner
On the sideboard shifts a fraction, being brushed.

It reaches five-and-twenty to eleven
On this quiet weekday, and the mid-morning post
Spreads a brief shade across the door . . . She stands
Out of sight to re-open it, and make
A quick farewell, and close it, and turn alone.
She turns towards the empty banister.

She wonders if it ever took place at all.
None of the furniture is stained or scratched,
The settee on its castors has not moved
As much as an inch. In a beam of the sun,
The dust still goes across and up and down
Behind her in the sitting-room. In the hall,

The letter on her mat is not picked up.
She thinks about stooping to pick it up,
Then knows she cannot stoop but only stand,
Stand shaking as she grips the banisters
So tightly that her trembled hands turn white
And her wrists go thin with the horror. No one will know.
Anything that was here is cleared away,
As surely as the stains on the clean clothes
Strung out on all the washing lines. As yet
There are no radio phone-ins she might try
Blurting the worst to, to be mollified
By solace from the airwaves. And besides,

She is not on the phone.

217   *The Exit of Dr Fitzsimmon*

In the seventeenth hour of the symposium
The trolley came slowly round the door.

The deconstruction of syllabuses paused
For the gathering up of cups.

Each one sublimed the lust for liberty
With a courteous device:

There were those who helped the lady by handing over
A teacup lopsidedly couched inside
Another one, in a spillage of grey tea.

And others pulled down sugar-bowls from ledges,
Or fingered spoons from between the legs of chairs.

But the Rev. Dr Fitzsimmon, as the dinner lady
Applied all her dutiful strength to the door to drag out

Her tiers of rattling crocks,
Leapt up to serve her, his papers stuffed
Unconsciously under his left arm.

And with his right arm Dr Fitzsimmon
– From the outer side, on the landing – held the door
Most graciously extended, so the lady and her cargo
Might trundle on through.

Cups and saucers gone,
The meeting went back to its dry labyrinth
With Dr Fitzsimmon gone, undoubtedly escorting

The dinner lady on through other doors
Further off down the long, long passages, swing doors, main
        doors,
But every one of them leading him ultimately on
To the great Front Door of the Polytechnic
And the Car Park beyond:

An ingenious man,
A chivalrous man,
A free and exultant man driving home to his wife

In his Renault 14.

Once again driving along a motorway
To a reading perhaps, or on holiday;
But this time accompanied by the slim,
Much older figure of a woman nearly
Loved many years ago, now on a whim
Called up and taken out for a clearly
Mistaken trip into nostalgia: this
Doesn't work, our fifty-year-old kiss

Isn't much of a physical recollection . . .
We come to an A road, and an intersection
Gives us a kind of mini-roundabout,
A circular hump of concrete, hard and white,
With three roads to choose from; but we are in doubt
Which road is the correct one, and are quite
Surprised to see that a fourth road has been closed
By planting grass on it. Still, we have nosed

Into what we guess to be the proper
Route, and we do not pause to stop a
Passing pedestrian dressed in red to ask
If we *are* pursuing the right track,
Though all at once it becomes a tiresome task
Avoiding the bumps and ruts. We can't turn back,
The road is no more than a narrow, hedged-in lane,
'Unadopted' possibly? And again,

Though we doubt if we have hit upon the right
Direction, we drive on, jolting, until we sight
A long, low, disinfected building, obviously
A very modern hospital, because
As we step out and slam the doors we see
A vestibule, with chairs, and corridors
Down which cream-uniformed nurses disappear
With files or clipboards in their hands; and hear

The muzak seeping its reassurance:
Nothing to test our patience and endurance,
Just a slow, gleaming harmony. Not afraid,
We go aside into a clinical
Ante-room where there are sinks, and laid
On spotless surfaces a finical
Array of ambiguous instruments . . . Along
A wall on metal tables sit three strong

White-coated women, very unattractive,
And one of them starts forward, an active,
Smiling and businesslike blonde who is the friend
I drove with – she who travelled *with* me!
In her hand is a kind of textile ball, a blend
Of gauze and other fabrics. And I can see
It's shaped like a rather large contraceptive,
Or a pair of underpants. I'm not receptive

To what appears to be her wild-eyed, rare
Desire to try it on me, somehow, somewhere . . .
The other women watch, and shift their haunches
To have a better view from where they sit,
And I realize I am dreaming, as she launches
Into a menacing harangue – oh not one bit
Am I enjoying any of this, struck down
With revulsion in my seat. The women frown,

But of the three I note the pleasantest,
And then conclude that I must do my best
With this dream and the challenge it is making.
I shout, 'Let's have that horrible device!'
My friend smiles now, yet she is taking
That panti-web of gauze away, and twice
I grab for it, and only the third time snatch
And hold the thing, and with it run and catch

The nicest of these cold Eumenides,
Who lets herself be caught; and then I seize
Myself and wrap up in this bunched-up gauze,
And take her with it. So the others can
Now fade into a background of moaned applause
For what we do. Waking, I hear a van
Which drones a plaint of sighs and happy tears:
A burst of rock as it engages gears.

219   *The Rain Diary*

For my geography project I would keep a rain diary, a record starting on 1st January of the days that year when it rained and approximately how much.

On 1st January there was no rain. On 2nd January there was no rain. It did not rain on 3rd or 4th either. Would I go back to school on 8th January with nothing to show? Only blank pages with the dates in blue-black italic and the expectation of punishment?

Amanda kept a sunshine diary. The sun shone all the time that New Year, every day was like the legendary 1st January 1942. I saw long shadows of bare trees in Amanda's garden revolving on the stiff white grass as the sun crawled low and bright round the Warwickshire sky. Amanda, day by day, logged her hours of sunshine in duffle coat and mittens, putting out her tongue to warm her finger tips.

Tiny planes inched over the blue from the aerodrome leaving lacy strips of vapour which crumbled into strung-out blurs. There was no rain on 5th, 6th or 7th. I gained a sense of what life in general would be like.

On 8th January I stood at 8.55 a.m. on the worn stone step of the school with my blank diary – and raindrops fell. But I had no time to write anything down, the bell was pounding in the school campanile and we could not be late. So I opened my rain diary and let the rain fall into it, stain it and crinkle it, as the others fled past me into school.

To which rain I added my own joyful tears, knowing that Amanda might have statistics but I had a concrete event.

220　*Looking at Her*

When he looked at her, he invariably felt
Like stretching his arms up, as if about to do
A long and lustrous yawn. Of course she knew
She had that effect; and whether she lounged or knelt,
Or walked or simply stood, he was never clear
If she was prepared and eager to let him bring
His hands down around her neck, and press her near
– Or would shake her head and permit him no such thing.

This was her talent, to stir both lust and doubt,
She did it the best of all feats she was able;
And therefore other women felt sure she bored
The men she attracted; since all of them, without
Her seeming to provoke them, of one accord
　Would yawn and thump their fists down on the table.

221　*On My Recent Birthday*

Yet another dentist chalks up a low opinion
Of my courage. I drive back between conifers
Up a lane past a pool where agile moorhens
Display the ability to walk, fly, paddle or dive.
The grown ones teach the young ones, or the young ones
Have it instinctively; but young humans
Will differ from their parents and disappoint them,
Displaying insouciance on the dentist's couch
When the family thing was cowardice; or vice versa.
This is our difference from the animals,
This tendency not to follow the family rules.
What father moorhen wins a Sandhurst sword
And lives to see his son retailing badges
To be worn by 'Bird-lovers Against the Bomb?'
The conifers drop their cones, plant life goes on
In a million pots and forests, following precedent

And nothing else at all. But the dentist's children
Slip through the teeth of their inheritance,
Make small unchippable moorhens in plasticine
In their pre-school playgroups. They cannot walk,
They cannot fly, or paddle, and under water
They stay down for ever. They have varied,
Like everything made by man, including man.

222   *Politics*

Lighting the cigarettes I need not have smoked,
I almost burnt my beard; but also found
My eyes went squinting down towards the flame,
And the page, or face, or room on the farther side
Slid out of focus into broken halves.
That was my fault entirely; but is it mine
If that girl with the Abbey National plastic bag
Is standing there, on a strip of grass between
Dual carriageways? She is ruining
My focus of this scene as a unified
View of pollution where, on the farther side,
One car in two is a speeding panda
With its blue nipple flashing to smash the pickets.

I fix my attention on the alarming Law:
The girl is on its side by standing there;
She puts an unconscious flaw and distraction
In front of my perceptions – am I to blame
If she's rather too attractive for the view?
Old men may want their youth back, but old nations
Pine for the liberties of middle-age,
The mortgage paid off, the authority . . .
In Baker Street, Sherlock Holmes smoked a pipe,
Which keeps the flame much farther from the face.
Will someone please guide that girl to safety
And clear my field of vision, before the smoke
Rolls down my throat and blinds the eyes with fears?

It takes only three to look the same way
And you have an Incident. If I look as well,
That makes a fourth and Something Has Happened,
An ambulance jumps the lights and the Police
Belt out of white vans howling down our ears
Like clods of curdled metal; for nothing more
Than four people chancing suddenly to turn
At the sight of a girl's hair spiking out of
Her head like a surly palm tree.
                              But then the streets
Are filled with randomness, what happens there
Seems always sudden and deplorable.
Walking the streets I see too easily
A confluence of the worst in us, beyond
Arranging into calm or tenderness.
The streets are only there to hurry through;
Although, as I turn away, an art student looks
At a hoarding framing the scene and says, 'That's great!'
'That's aesthetic!'
                  His camera is out,
And two days later he stands up holding
A transparency to the light, the world improved
In his celluloid frame. He smiles at it, he sees
The misery transfigured, here they are,
The hoarding, the ambulance, the Police, and the palms
On the head of the passing girl, all now arranged
Into one aesthetic greatness; and there is nothing
Less like a question in his shining eyes.

The three-year-old who will not go to bed
Tugs Gunga's tail, and Gunga patiently
Permits him to, because he understands.
An animal *knows* when it is children.

Eight o'clock now, in the drawing room
Of a house of proconsular maxims, built
In Hampshire in memory of the hills;
The lights of the town could be any town's.

She can no longer see to write, or hear
To think, so the elderly lady
Turns on the light above the wicker chair,
And licks her letter down, and turns to watch.

Watching her grandchild and the darkening fields,
She thinks, *He knows, he knows*: inside the cat
Is a small child psychotherapist resolving
To stay where he is; it makes things easier.

The mould of things seems perfectly secure:
The animals can tell when it is men;
The old man in the bedroom winds up the clock
Which tells him what time it is in Simla;

The daughter in the kitchen daintily
Prepares an England to receive them all;
The pile of 45s in Mary's room
Is not seen as something doing any harm.

225 *Profoundest Love*

She gave him sand from the Tyrrhenian Sea,
He sent her a present of sand from the shores of Lake Erie.

He dropped some grains of her sand on the edge of the lake,
But kept the others, it helped him remember her.
She mingled a bit of his sand with the verge of the sea,
But retained some grains in a tiny box because
They reminded her of him.

And this was happening everywhere in the world,
Whole deserts exchanged between Asia and Africa,
And people everywhere swopping seedlings and saplings,
Whole forests exchanged between Finland and Brazil.

Cat-lovers transplanted whiskers from their cats:
'My cat has your cat's whisker and yours mine.'
We think of each other much more often that way.

I stood by the motorway watching the sand trucks pass,
I saw huge lorries transporting uprooted trees,
I saw vets' ambulances speeding with mad blue lights
– The whiskers for the transplants.
My name is Vladimir Nikolaich:
Back indoors I switch on a radio I cannot understand,
I am in High Wycombe, the news is in English here.
My Rosemary knows no Russian, I love her so much,
And she is in Kharkov switching on the radio
And comprehending nothing in the least

– Except that we exchanged for one another,
And think of each other very much indeed.
Ours was an act of the profoundest love.

226 *Mares*

The pink dog darts about on the edge of the sideboard.
The water rises eagerly to his feet.
It will fill the polished horn of the gramophone,
Submerging the strings of the salon orchestra
In their antique love song. The tenor is singing, 'Turn
The garden tap off, love, poor Spot will drown.'

Commander of a pirate underground train,
A prominent liberal journalist guides it
Up the tunnel. In the illumined coaches,
The passengers undress for hard-porn video
And electro-convulsions. On an escalator,
An inspector points and shouts, 'We'll get you, you bastard!'

Nothing wrong with the great capacious bed,
Or with the three schoolgirls all snuggling up;
And no jealousy of the smallest one, with glasses,
When I see her next morning by the fruit machine;
She is only cutting a loose thread off the sweater
Of a Pakistani nuclear physicist.

If I went a day earlier than I plan to,
They wouldn't shoot me on the hotel steps;
If I arranged another hotel altogether,
Or took an earlier flight, they still might not;
If I went by sea, not air, that might be safer.
All the hotels are my former Oxford college.

Petronella sidles up smiling to tell me
How the old flea-pit has suddenly re-opened,
A stone's throw from the crematorium.
We ought to queue early, I like Petronella,
Her lips are flecked with urticaria,
They love her at the crematorium.

A fabulous welcome: met at the station
By an orchestra of centaurs in dinner jackets.
'We'd like to give you the honour' – the first violin –
'Of conducting us in some items.' 'But I've never –'
'Oh yes you have!' – 'But I'm unable –' 'Please,
Here's the baton. You know *La Boutique Fantasque.*'

The woman has been working hard on relaxation
In front of the cameras. Against all custom,
She lights and draws on a black and white cigarette.
The smoke through her teeth fills up, blanks out, the screen.
We only hear an antique voice, proclaiming.
The water rises eagerly to her feet.

227   *The Boyhood of Raleigh*

But the end of it all was a shuffling line of ten thousand
Stretched out at the airport, everyone in search
Of a difference not too discomposing:
A compatible sort of bathing, docile fauna
Trotting up to nuzzle on the hotel steps,
A wheel of chance where every player wins . . .
'And when we were there it felt easy to be there,
And now we are back it feels truthful to say
"I don't feel I'm back" or "I don't feel I ever went",
The place was an illusion. We were not illusions ourselves,
We made the links between what you call "different" places,
Which are more the same because we have left our impression,
Which modifies the place as one wave modifies a beach,
Or "like" another English changes your own.
We sit with the arm of our traveller's tale extended,
Reciting the fictions of distance, we tip up our bags
And find the fool's gold of unchangeable coins,
The centimes, the bani, and here in the bottom
An unused token for a locker in Central Station,
We'll use it next time. And the children are amazed,

The boys want to go when they are adults, or when they have
    passports,
They have sat long enough being just themselves
On this side of the sea, can't they be it on the other side as well?
"Look at this!" they would like to say, holding up
The plunders of the gift shop. "You see, you see!
It proves we have been there and thought of you.
We weren't alarmed by the difference at all.
It was so immense we have brought back part of it
To be found nowhere else but there (and Victoria Station):
A Duty Free ballpoint pen with a toucan's head!"
What one boy thought and wrote in the room beyond
The gift shop and the green channel was
A distant recollection, of himself. All his words
Lay silent in the books, the forests continued
To grow without him, and the plundered chests of coins
Closed their lids as if he had never brought any back.
The wheel had turned and turned and stopped there.
He had gone no farther than his heart had sent him
On its regular missions of circulation.

228   *Through Binoculars*

Between forgetting one hypochondria
And registering the next, there comes
An interval of an hour or two called *Health*,
When the world leaps into clarity and enter
A yacht, for example, over from left to right,
Red sails in the sunshine, and down there a family
With eight bright globes shaken out of a portable rack
For a game of *boule* on the beach, or I veer across
To a distant bearded man of sixty plus
Who gets a nymphet, honestly, nuzzling his forearm
– And no relation! (He will not curse if the wind
Sweeps his windbreak down.) In other words,

Short of censoriousness or pure despair,
There comes a sunnier spell called *Tolerance*,
Where I share, on this luminous oval afternoon,
The painter's way with a single shaft of light
Down on details which have shaken out themselves
Into patterns I might even see as *Hope*.
Now he stands, only a nose's length away,
The solicitor, dumping a weekend anorak
To race his green ball to the water's edge,
So his labrador, pacing him, has no need
To taste the sting of salt retrieving it.
I feel virtually happy enough to speak.

229 *Continuation*

Now suddenly noticed, a little way ahead,
The figure stands in the middle of the road
Not moving apparently, its back turned,
Its arms out of sight.

                                    And this is daylight,
So I smile at feeling all the more disturbed,
And at wanting to prove that it must be harmless.

I shall walk so as to be heard inside the hood
The figure wears, not to scare it in turn
By approaching too quickly from behind;
And set my feet more deliberately down
On the frosty ground, tap my stick more distinctly.
When I glance up for the comfort of the sun,
A seabird flies and cries over the blue,
Neck stretched in anguish . . .

                                    She or he might be ill,

And fixed in this rigidity by some thought
Too terrible to confront or to speak out.
There is a woman in the way it stands,
And a question of what words ought to be said.
Will she require to be coaxed back carefully,
And seen to her gate and doorway, and left
With a clumsy sense of some duty half-performed?
– Then brooded over in the coming days,
Whenever I pass the curtains which never move,
And the darkness behind them after dark?

. . . I have overtaken her now, and catch
A face alive enough, but raw and frozen,
Which turns as mine turns, to acknowledge me;
But her eyes go frowning back to an open book:
One hand grips its spine, while the other writes
Black line after line of writing, covering all
The space on every leaf, she is half-way
To filling it.
        In the seconds as I pass,
She has seen that I have seen it, so we both smile;
But nothing is asked or given, nothing spoken,
Except a glance to recognize that we heard
And saw one another, and were not surprised,
And had rendered ourselves both natural after all,
To a road, and a winter afternoon.
                             She frowns;
And writes. We continue as we were.

230   *In January*

In the salt-marshes, under a near black
Sky of storm or twilight, the whole day
Dark on the creeks where the wind drives wavelets back
Against the filling tide, I have lost my way

On a path leading nowhere, my only guide
The light half-way up a television mast
Five miles across the waste; and if I tried,
I could imagine hearing, under this vast

Raw silence of reeds and waters, the deep drone
Of generators, gathering up the power
To send its message out; and, stopped alone
By this channel's edge, revisit a lost hour

At a restaurant table, in a vanished place
(An organ chiming in the hushed cave below)
When three sat smiling in an alcove space
And saw their futures, thirty years ago . . .

And ten years earlier, learn each adverb clause
Written out in the spring by those in dread
Of School Certificate; without much cause
For fearing death as long as they had read

The good green textbooks. Further back, next to me,
Her pencils in a leather pouch, her dress
A blur of gentle yellow, is a she
Who smiles with such a sidelong vividness

I can even touch her hand. And further still,
I walk up between desks rising in tiers,
And see the old imperial pictures fill
The walls of the same room, lit by gasoliers

– My father's now. Then suddenly return
To the path over the marshes, and the light
On the meccano mast, which tries to burn
As strongly as a fixed star, secure and bright

Against the black of nightfall; and provides
Small quizzes for our lounges, puppets that grin
To tame the evening's terrors. England hides
Its head in its small comforts . . . Seeing in

– Alone and lost and darkling – this New Year,
I stare round at the dark miles of this nation,
And through the winter silence only hear
The loveless droning of its generation.

231   *Sea Pictures*

1

A man is bicycling along the sands,
Predicting the firm stretches where his wheels
Will not sink down; he listens to their hiss
As all the waves of the sea push towards him
In amenable ripples. He rode here down a lane
Where September offered all colours of blackberry
At the same time; at the dunes he lifted up
His vehicle over the gorse; and on the beach,
He set it down and pedalled off westwards.
He notices the boat far out, its windows,
Its smoke, and the man and woman on the sundeck.
When the boy turned and lashed out with his spade

2

At his aggravating sister, what could they do
But condemn him to stay and guard the clothes?
So the rest of the family, sister included,
Who would, in the boy's opinion, not have suffered
The same indignity had she swung the spade,
Make tracks towards the distant recession of waters,

Ignoring the tears which are flooding down over
His abolished castle. And then, double spy, Sod's Law,
He is stung by a wasp, and his older brother
Has to sprint back and see why he is roaring.
He comforts him; and picks up his dropped spade.
There was once a woman absolutely averse

3

To having her name romantically inscribed
On the sands, it was better to have it called
Romantically over the waters. And this dread
Of having even the letters of that word
Dispersed by the tide was one of her variants
Of the fear of death. But the elder of the two boys
Hasn't heard of such reluctance, he takes the spade
The smaller one is bored with, seeing it builds
No castles by itself, and begins to write
Some initials on a wide, firm, yellow stretch
Twenty yards or so away from the family clothes.
'The broughams of legitimate love' which the classic

4

Novelist saw, are out this afternoon,
Creatures of slow and polished habit, getting
The best of the warmth of mid-September where
A line of them has poised itself sedately
Along the clifftop, windscreens to the sun
Which glints as well on countless points far out
On the surface of the not-too-restless sea,
Towards which in the distance a family
Of discontented people slowly treks.
At rightangles to them, behind them, a man
Will cross in one hour's time on a bicycle.
Two grandparents from one brougham see the two boys

297

5

As they gaze down from a clifftop rail the Council
Is still allowed to paint; and notice too
The boat almost stationary in the water
Half-way up to the horizon, though they can't see
The man still on the sundeck. In their boot
Are the blackberries taken from where they parked
In a safe straight lane, turned on their hazard lights,
Went round and checked the handles of every door,
And picked with plastic bags along the hedges,
While the dog sat mutely up in its barred-off space
And imagined human reasons for doing this.
In a cabin of the ferry, the woman lets

6

The door close behind her, having come back down
From the sundeck leaving the man; and she gives
This worried frown to herself in the mirror,
And goes hard at the problem of her hair,
All fraught and fixed and clenched by the attentions
Of only a slight breeze, with a honey-coloured
Comb. It needs to be coaxed, she needs to be coaxed,
But the engine beat is steady, the sea quiet,
And she balances easily. She is happy
With the spray that rinses her window, and decides
To take the camera with her when she goes.
'They are unloading coal at that small seaport

7

'Exactly – *there*!' The man has entered, starting
An uneasy conversation, and they both look
Through the window at an old tub releasing
An irregular cargo of brownish stuff
In rumbling slopes and screes as it creaks and stirs

In the harbour waters; holidaymakers watch.
'They say that coal has come from India,'
Unloading in the profound September sun
Which day by day seems more impervious
To the onset of autumn, as the woman's hair
Seems impervious to the corrections of her comb.
A sign made of coloured bulbs is saying 'Arnold's',

8

The name of an *Amusements* coffee bar
With machines which wink and flash, and thrust out tokens
Exchangeable for refreshments. Girls stand round
In leather, smoking Marlboro cigarettes;
Approaching from the quayside one hears the beat
Thumping out in the heavy haze; and Arnold stands
At a screeching urn not letting his poker-stare
Relax above the dull glass cups he fills
With cappuccino, sliding them across
To boys with mousey forelocks who eff and blind
So the leathery girls can't fail to overhear.
Plugged into his radio, Arnold, late one night

9

Heard something he would struggle to describe
For years: this heavenly voice with a colossal
Orchestra behind it, singing, it sounded like
Paradise, he would give his right arm to know
What it was that woman sang, he could hear, like,
The sea in it. Arnold, a fixture here,
Travelled far when the voice on the radio sang
On that long-ago night when the light was out
Above the rabies notice on the quay,
And the quay was deserted, and the harbour
Filling with ripples from Scandinavia.
A fly neglects its hindlegs but cleans its forelegs

10

On a burst éclair in one of Arnold's stands,
In the window fronting onto the quay where coal
Came on shore to the detriment of honour.
For a 10p coin in a slot, a painted donkey
Will jerk and shake to persuade a child to smile,
And elsewhere Arnold has arranged for aged
Citizens, senior and vulnerable,
And none of them the owners of broughams of love,
To have bingo played on them. Everyone
Gets something at Arnold's, and Arnold is content
Notwithstanding the cry of the singing in the night.
Back on deck the woman tries to remember where

11

She rode along on a high bus above amazing
-ly wide unvisited beaches, with roaring winds
And breakers all the summer, and free of footprints,
And tries to think why it is the selfsame spaces
Should feel forbidden now, you could not visit
To draw initials or ride a bicycle,
Or paddle through a dangerous undertow.
It wasn't the Black Sea coast or the Indian Ocean,
But somewhere nearer, though certainly not so near
As the littorals blessed by the patron saint
Of seacoast adulteries, St Lascivia.
When you go out through the archipelago

12

The first of the islands are amply inhabited,
With councils and roads and elaborate traffic signs.
And then the small towns are large villages,
And the villages dwindle down to sociable clusters
Of one or two small red houses, though even now

In these you sometimes spot a post-box bearing
The logo of the royal mail. Then finally,
By which time it is dark even on their sundeck,
The lights are from single cabins on single rocks
With one boat tethered in a cranny, the last
Places of all they might remember you.
'Tell me about them later, I'd like to take

13

'A photograph of that man on the bicycle.
And what was the boy's game writing those initials?'
'It wasn't a game, and don't take a photograph.
I wanted to tell you how I felt just like Arnold
When I was staying on the Black Sea coast:
In an adjacent room of the hotel,
The cleaners were making the beds up and a radio
Was transmitting an opera. Through the open door
The baritone was filling the corridor,
A resonant, yearning, echoing baritone,
And at once I knew I should never forget the sound.
A dog was lying on the esplanade,

14

'And I had the sense, standing there by the window,
Of being at the edge of a still from an Eastern
European film, and not real. And I knew this feeling
Would be an always reachable memory;
Especially as I couldn't exactly tell
If the dog on the esplanade were alive or dead.
Some men were now approaching with what looked like
A sack, to pick it up. Yet when I joined
The woman at her own window on the next floor
Five minutes later, dog and men were gone,
And she hadn't seen any of this at all.'
'Why don't you want me to take a photograph?'

15

'Because too many photographs are a problem;
All those quotidian dull remembrancers.
Myself, I keep a cache of a special few
In a hidden envelope somewhere. There is one
Of myself in the middle distance jogging
Along a wide yellow beach, and another
Of a jumble of roughly teddy-bear-shaped
Concrete blocks, sea-defences at Constanţa,
Both examples being taken on sunny days
When no wasp was stinging and, in general, Sod
Was happy to suspend his evil Law.'
Writing images for people to come across

16

Is like swearing to attract attention, but more
Effective because more people notice it;
And when you have overheard an image it makes
A deeper difference. I couldn't get away
From the images of the dog and the baritone
Romantically affirming in unknown music,
With all the power of long experience,
That love was a province of maturity
(Anton Walbrook playing Hoffmann in *The Tales of*,
For example), not a hobby for adolescents.
It kept me listening, watching at my window.
Somewhere I read that Freud said, 'Civilization

17

'Is the postponement of gratification';
And for that reason I have put off learning
To swim until my sixties. I shall jog,
Which is rarely gratifying at the time,
Only later, when one still can run upstairs

In one's fifties, in that arsehole of the year,
The month of March. So, leaving the bicycle
Padlocked on a sandbank, I jog; and as I reach
The initials, waiting to be smeared out flat
By one repetition of the tide, I disagree
That writing them, the boy was up to a 'game'.
A man is jogging along the sands,

18

Predicting the firm stretches, which you can't tell
By their colour, only a dry and level look,
And by footsteps which barely mar the surface,
Though left by whole families. Sometimes the yellow sand
Looks hard, but it has still retained the water:
Don't plunge into that mushiness, or the going
Will get heavy-hearted, and your chest-bone ache
With a sinister burning as you plod on, and on.
Sand-patterns of corrugation are tough on
The soles of the feet, avoid those. And never try
To run much on loose sand, you simply won't.
Above the beaches of the Antrim coast

19

You could ride on high buses once, past cemeteries
Where plastic domes placed over tombstone wreaths
Protected them from the wind, and gaze far down
Across gaping bays of rock and untrodden sand
Where in recent years to leave a car might be
To have it detonated; fair enough.
And the idea of the North Antrim coast remained
As a reachable memory, kept safe somewhere
In a hidden envelope of the mind,
Not a photograph. To bring it out would be
Like replying at last to a standing invitation
Issued forty years before and never answered.
'If someone was feeling ill, or just confidential

20

'About the special one malaise which sent them
To the end of the archipelago, to the last
And smallest of twenty thousand solitudes,
They could still return.' And now the slow still moon
Was in silver pieces in the ferry's wake,
So they stacked up their conscientious chairs and went
Downstairs to the cabin and felt less landlocked
Than before, and were suddenly lovers.
'You should have let me take some photographs
Of the archipelago gradually turning
Into isolated seagull rocks,' she turned and said.
In their deep freeze the gathered blackberries make

21

The sexagenarians' equivalent
(Plucking them, hoarding them, discussing them)
Of the fruits once cherished by those who made
Libations at the shrine of St Lascivia.
She it is protects women who live on seacoasts
And feel a surge of forces wherever they face,
And know, where they live, they cannot be canutes;
These seacoast adulteries being most usual
When one participant lives by the sea (the woman)
And the man visits regularly from town.
[Their love involves this kind of fantasy.]
It has been known for two people living

22

In the same seaport to have an illicit liaison,
But St Lascivia does not hear their prayers.
They say she listens to the prayings of
The many others (if not the atheists,
Who get more done by hoping) who have to wait

For visitors from the city: that she keep
The crucial letters until the midday post
(Which doesn't get so much scrutiny), that she cause
The husbands' trains to be late if *they* are late home,
And have the restaurant's name and price erased
From the tell-tale credit card account.
I can remember nineteen forty-eight

23

As the year of walking the promenade at Eastbourne
On evening after evening, leaving aside
Their holiday and my parents to explore
With a sudden half-enjoyable loneliness,
The fantasy darkness under Beachy Head,
Where the sound of the band fades down and the bandstand lights
Are compressed into a clutter of distant stars.
Passing the neon signs: *Electric Lifts*
On modest small hotels, my mother (still able
To walk, and run, and even play tennis) wondered
Why electric lifts were considered such a boast.
I read *The Insect Play*, and in the bathroom

24

Mirror did not look like a butterfly:
Less colourful, less fragile, more permanent,
And happy in retrospect not to live in an age
Where people gaze into mirrors of butterflies
Reflecting only themselves, and never coal
Crashing down onto quaysides to carry power
To rooms where potted rubber plants are nourished
By hunger on a Coromandel coast.
'The boy was not playing a game with those initials,
But moving towards maturity, showing in sand
The postponement of gratification.'
At Mahabalipuram, remembering

305

25

Louis MacNeice, the cows of sea-worn stone
Smile out at the sea, an extraordinary blue
With a freshness going out and on for ever,
But crashing back against a sudden shelving
Downwards of yellow sands in a crumbling bank
Beside the shrine, where they will sell you moonstones.
And the mile on mile passed parallel to the blue
In the bus back to the city held me close,
Scanning down to the Indian Ocean past sunburnt grass,
My first tropical coast, at fifty-seven,
Not to be jogged along or trifled with.
Someone had written in studs on the road in front

26

Of the great rock-carvings, the initials of
The strongest political faction to emerge
From the feuds after the death of MGR.
The letters were stamped into the carriageway:
DMK. The coaches driving across them
Made no difference, the sun glanced over them,
Beggars begged over them, and they were not erased.
On a wall, a rival face, Miss Jayalalitha
(Called 'this film siren' by her enemies),
Who wept at the cortège of her dead lover.
She beat the Congress (I) into third place.
If I had to reveal the truth about the coal

27

Slipped into the little port, it was scab coal
Imported to beat the miners, and the year
Was nineteen eighty-four when the ferry passed
Along the coastline carrying them away,
The man and the woman becoming lovers

Somewhere beyond an archipelago.
She tugged her hair free, only half-listening,
But did take in the moral of the coal
As someone might have taken from a lover
Suez, or Vietnam, or the Falklands War;
And then resumed a lover's fantasies.
Here he is, writing initials on the beach,

28

And as he makes the furrows and smells the damp,
He yearns, which is what you do when you are mature.
This boy is using the sand as the first page
Of the very first poem he will ever write,
And what if it is only a *concrete* poem,
Or even a *language* poem, that is enough.
He has created something to show he feels,
And with the heart he draws around them *what*
He feels. But for decent reticence he does it
Twenty yards away from the clothes and his stung brother,
Who is not looking, weeping in the sand.
'After seeing the place where the dog might have been,

29

'And wondering if there had ever *been* a dog,
I went into a strip-lit marble bathroom
Done in cold green, all elegantly Spartan,
Befitting a place where Ovid yearned for Corinna.
The sound of the opera might just have stopped,
Though I can hear it now, and see the sunlight,
And the shadows of the men on the esplanade.
I felt unreal because I was somewhere else,
On a foreign coast where foreigners stared far out
Into the deep prospect of Central Asia.
I wished I had thought to bring a camera.
If you stand on a day of sea-mist and look across

307

30

Any strait dividing two of the Scilly Isles,
You can believe the one you are looking at
Is very far away . . . separated from you
By a wide sea of rocks and ravaging currents;
It is a *trompe l'oeil*. And in front of the man
Who bicycles along the Norfolk coast
Is the half-sunken wreck of a Second World War block ship,
A sight providing a similar illusion:
It seems miles off, but you can stroll out to it
And not see the incoming tide surround you,
Like a curtain hem let down by the horizon.
'I wonder what an Arctic coast is like,

31

'And how you know where the sea-edge (a remote
Conception of tides in a hunter's mind) ever is.
In landlocked countries the sea must be an idea
Culled from pictures, still ones or in motion,
A long, long way from Arnold's coral reefs;
Where languages have hardly any words
For "undertow" or "sea-mist" and can't translate
"Its melancholy, long, withdrawing roar".'
'You'd need to imagine the impossible, just as I
See you daily when you are nowhere near, and not
So close it seems a madness to be apart.'
Walking towards him down a long boulevard,

32

She arrives as they do in those dreams when you
Are an unseen being observing everyone,
And she walks right past him because it never makes
Any sense to think they could be in the selfsame street.
His thoughts have set her moving, staged an image

Of a glamorous and intricate machine
Gliding certainly and dangerously towards him
– And into the room where she becomes a presence
Like an incoming tide rewriting her,
Instead of erasing her like her initials
(Which are studded indelibly in his mind).
One day, nostalgically, in a hidden

33

Envelope, a man came across a photograph
Of his grandparents paddling from Margate to Ramsgate
Hand-in-hand with his father, the grandmother's left hand
Hanging on to a spade, while grandfather, farthest out,
Exhorts the trio forward through the ripples.
He knew his grandfather was a photographer
By those sepia pictures in the envelope
Hidden in a personal drawer; and yet he must
Have that day leased the camera to someone else
To take this picture; there has to be another
To capture those ancient people, and that girl.
In nineteen-o-seven you were not supposed

34

To move an inch, a fraction, especially ladies:
Photographs were a posed phenomenon,
And these three relations strolling the tideline foam
Eighty years ago had managed to hold the pose,
The boy's disconsolate look, grandfather's look,
And the movement of their ankles and their shins
Through the ridges of the incoming wet.
So they all slosh through a gentle undertow
Out of their early century, moving on
To assume their immortality somewhere else;
And grandfather gets a picture of the girl.
The grandmother's face in all these photographs

309

35

Is the indulgence of her husband's whim
Of trapping into a box the garden scenes,
The family groups, the walkers breasting tapes,
And the impending sea storms, lots of those,
Even though the very moment a lens cap
Is back in place, and the camera stored away,
The sunlit poses are turning sepia.
Photographs watch and watch the changes caused
By time, and trace them happening as surely
As the hour hand on the clock can be seen to move
If you follow it with sufficient concentration.
One night in a landlocked country, the owner of

36

A camera waits for the orange light to gleam
To tell him he can use the flash. He stands
In a city in a distant mountain province
Where the sea is rarely invoked in metaphor,
But where his inherited disposition
(A grandfather's whim) removes a lens cap in
A snow-filled street, and a woman in furs, in seconds,
Turns round on the ice, and balances, and smiles in the dark:
A set of images dangerous to put
In a hidden envelope found in the morning post;
And the smile and the darkness are both permanent.
The woman on the sundeck would have taken

37

A photograph of the single bicycle's tracks,
Inexplicable to walking families,
Who might grasp footprints or even horses' hoofs,
But can't see people ever *cycling* here,
Let alone applying the brakes to stop

And watch a ferry pass, as the man does now,
A prince at a ruined castle and some initials
Attaching to a girl by Lake Balaton,
Remembering a dog on a Black Sea strand
Unchained by death, and pausing here for breath
Before he jogs towards the one seagull rock.
When they stop looking, the man and the woman

38

With their boot full of blackberries on the clifftop,
Whose living dog gazes out between the bars,
The cyclist stops, with less than the certainty
Of someone who has cycled before today,
And more with the insecurity of someone
Who has rarely achieved a balance on his ride,
And is glad to be getting one foot firmly down
On the sand, and the other down beside it, and lean
On the handles of the vehicle, and keep
The twangling instrument upright while he stares,
While he stares far out to sea at the fixed clouds.
He is *all the daughters of his father's house*

39

And all the . . . He sees boys who write initials
Where only the waves will come across them
Grow into lovers bargaining on sundecks,
Losing their lens caps in Hungarian snow,
And turning round from clifftops to where the broughams
Have changed into hearses. Now I've reached the end
Of its interlacing tracks, I hold the bicycle
Cleverly upright with one steadying hand,
And space my feet for balance, and watch the sea:
The clouds, having settled where to rest, will not
Be moving again for the rest of the still day.
The waters have become an off-blue curtain

Let down by the horizon, and behind
This fabric something impels it, sways it . . .
The tide smooths down its shifting folds and layers
To touch me only as a small grey hem
Criss-crossing against the wheel I point at it,
And turning over into colourless,
Amenable ripples; but the wider air,
A huger, superseding element,
Fills everything with its roar, I can't make out
One wave or breeze to listen to for itself
In the general outcry, where I now observe
The boat sail out of sight, to vast applause.

232 *Observation Car*

At last they arranged it so that you just couldn't see
Out of any train window. You had to focus
On the back of the seat in front, or on the floor,
Or on the obligatory food, wheeled up on trolleys
To where they had strapped you in; though a favoured few
Could end up riding at the rear of the train
In the Observation Car, from where the receding lines
Added ever-increasing length to the two sides
Of an angle wedging acutely into the past.
How fast that terrain seemed, and interesting,
Though it vanished before you guessed it had ever been:
You saw your bridges after you had crossed them,
You learned what was before you saw it coming,
And everyone pointed and said, 'The amazing things
We were missing all that time! If we had known,
We might have stopped the train and got out to enjoy them.'
– In this assuming they were better off
Than the others, sitting boxed in their airline seats
And observing nothing. When occasionally

Someone tried to complain to the guardian who came
Down the gangway cancelling tickets, he would say,
'You are fortunate to have seats, either there or here,
In the midst of such a good metaphor for life.'

233 *September Days*

When I tap on the barometer, its needle
Flicks upward; but the year is rendering down.
It has grown too used to itself to last for long,
And has to be content with doing gracefully
The things it can't avoid. I look up,

And those clouds block the sun for hardly a minute
More than they did a week ago, in the summer;
And when they move, the scene can seem to be
As juvescent as ever. But when I move
Through this gap in the hedge, I start some pheasants

Going off like motor-horns, sweeping away
Across an autumn haze of wheat-dust, lifted
From the cut fields by a high wind forcing
The grass and poppies into crestfallen curtsies.
Each day the month comes back with its shining face

A little more austere, with its shadows
Slightly longer and colder to step aside from
Into something like warm sunlight. The crops uncut
Are moving their heads now, like an applauding
Audience expecting someone to take a bow.

There is only me in this landscape. There was only me
This morning, in the brightness of the beach,
And I thought I still had strength to run against
Those droves of white sand raised by the same wind . . .
Should I bow, in winter's direction, like the grass?

I am waiting at the bus stop back to school,
But how on earth – ? Nothing has ever changed,
Not the street, not the curtains in the houses . . .
This is the last hour of the holiday
Before the bell, an hour holding as much
Of freedom as I shall ever know. Somehow
I sense I shall never regain the sun
That shone on my breakfast things, back in that room
Five minutes ago. And what is she thinking,
My mother, as she clears them away? Does she want
Me to grow up or not to? What are her thoughts
As I leave her and, waving, she shuts the door?
What is there growing in the day for her?
By standing here I commit myself to worlds
Where no one will be proud of me with no reason.

Now the bus looms from the skyline, reaching me
With a top deck front seat vacant: Jupiter
Could sit up here 'gazing down from heaven's height'
– Though that was last term's book. By the Plaza,
It takes a wide turn, passes the Hospital, drops
A few of us at the Library, and drives on.
I look back for one face (still there!); and now
I'm walking the wooded lane again to school.
And why do I now take my place with the others,
Still noticing the grain of the table, scored
Into rivers with compass points, all coloured blue,
While someone circles with this term's Shakespeare?
Of course I know already which play this is,
Its lines having thronged in my head most of the night . . .
If I open it when it comes, I commit myself.

How is it that I recognize the stains
On the old green cover, as it hangs in mid-air
Between him and me? I am waiting, watching
For the morning to start in the old, usual way:
For someone to start the jokes about the things
We might go in for: marriages, mistresses,
Ministries, either in Government or Church.
By ten o'clock we will have exorcised
The future I dream this in, and forgotten it.
Now the play glides towards me, and a voice
Is urging, whispering, 'Have it, hold it, feel
The weight of it, it's light, you'd not believe . . .'
So I take it. And the volume, like a rock,
Weighs my hand down, as it did last night before
I committed myself to forty years of sleep.

235   *What Lovers do in Novels*

What lovers do in novels, day on day,
With changing amounts of patience, is wait and yearn.
When they can, they write letters, when they can,
They try to eat a little, or try to sleep.
And all the time they are reading other novels:

Novels which recount the techniques and agonies
Of waiting and yearning, and occasionally in ways
That bring hope.
                        For example, here's a chapter
Where a lover sighs and lays a novel down,
Still open, on the leather arm of a chair,

And thinks (leaning deeply back, he thinks):
I have read through summer and autumn without
Consolation, nothing happens that I desire;
And yet I shall read along the shelf to where
My sorrow is found exactly, and understood;

Is found and rewarded, counted and repaid.
If I am hungry, if I cannot sleep,
If the telephone needs me, I shall still read on.
There has been a raggedness about my life
That a true and tidy fiction would trim back.

There is bound to be one novel which does all this.

236   *All Best*

I go with the grain of foreign courtesies
By writing, to somebody met only twice,
I remain, your impassioned eternal lover
Or *My soul is yours each minute of day and night.*
Inevitably, a laughing answer comes:
'No, no! It is all wrong. I tell you, please,
The words we are using here, and you will find
The nearest words in English to say it right.'

So for months all my letters begin and end
With ever more misjudged felicities,
Still striving to please correspondents for whom
I love you until death is no stronger than
Good morning, and for whom not to say,
In concluding the simplest thank-you letter,
I touch you all over, always, in my thoughts
Is tantamount to insult. It does not work.

I watch the leaves turn colour, at different speeds,
And start another letter wondering
Should I go back to intriguing understatement?
The kind I used once, coaxing long threads of hair
From between a pillow and the incomparable
Shoulders which trapped them, so as to release
A head and lips for a more than thank-you kiss
– When I only had strength enough for *kind regards*?

316

237 April Light

Slowly the tree falls, and we lean back
On our axes watching it, in the film,
Leaning on arm-rests in the Odeon.
The trunk and riven stump will kill nobody
In the good April daylight we had then.
So when the man with the name my friend had
Thirty years ago, and a credible address,
Dies today in the *Guardian*, struck by a falling tree,
This is fiction, it can't *be* him, it's a common name,
And trees fall commonly in reported storms.
So I don't go to the telephone, and I don't start
To write at last the letter I never wrote
When neglect was slowly cutting away at friendship.
I laugh at the idea, at the superstition,
And lean back in my chair, watching the light
Fall on a spring day killingly like winter.

238 A World of Pre-emptions

The time had arrived, a hermit thought, to be sociable for a while, so the anchorite's existence would feel more of a deprivation when he resumed it.

On the outskirts of the town, apparently, was a new café, which advertised home-made flapjack on a leaflet left in his cave-mouth. One sultry day the hermit decided to hang up his silence, as a dog might its arse-hole, on a hook; and take his savings of £5.90 (a note and small change); and go down to see what the place was like.

His foot on the mat inside the door rang a bell, but the waitress did not look up, only coughed over the confectionery on her counter (she was beautiful to the hermit and he did not mind). Before he could sign to her, or speak, she brought him flapjack and lemonade as if she had already known his needs.

Two silent men in a corner might have played dominoes had there been any to play; but they seemed content not to, not wanting to vie with one another even in the maths of chance.

And wonderful! – there was no canned music, so the hermit was not distracted from the incidental colours and sounds: the heliotrope blouse of a woman stepping across to the Ladies; the clang of a roller-towel tugged down in its metal case moments later.

The waitress had had her ears pierced two days before; but all she had in them were two small brass rings, not the gleaming figments for which she had given herself to the operation. The hermit noticed and admired them; for him they were enough.

He watched the bubbles rising in his drink, and the legs rising in the skirt of the waitress. How he would deserve another decade of celibacy after observations like these!

Half an hour passed, and the sky clouded. The two men had left, carrying the quietness between them elsewhere, perhaps to the Central Station and a train to a distant village. The woman in the heliotrope blouse had left.

The waitress was clearing food into fridges and freezers and larders in a manner suggesting that closing time was near. The hermit's social moves would have to come soon.

A dry electric storm began outside. Thunder clapped and lightning forked, but there was a positive *coitus interruptus* of rain, which was unleashing elsewhere without drastic effect. The town was not prepared for rain, so the authorities had diverted it accordingly.

The hermit approached the counter with a short prepared speech. The light had turned the deepest blue. The windows were inky with the ulterior motives of the storm.

The hermit looked at the waitress and she at him. They stared at each other with what he thought was the level, summatory gaze which can reach down into glands and gonads and start dynasties.

He wanted her to charge him, so he could be sociable about the transaction, hear his voice communicating with her so that his knowledge of all he was denying himself might be refreshed. And then the waitress just said, 'Ninety pence.'

'Ninety pence.' And because the hermit had the right money, there was no call even to say, 'I'm sorry I've nothing smaller.' He was without any speech of sociable information to give.

And he realised that this was a world of pre-emptions, where all desires were painlessly limited and fed before you even knew you had them. Every move received its countermove even before the game had been devised and marketed.

When he had decided to be a hermit, there had been no rock and no cave on the map; and yet, when he arrived in the town an agent found one to sell him, at a price.

There had been no café until the morning he felt the need to be sociable and found the leaflet in front of his cave.

As he left, hearing the doormat ring his departure, the waitress was unleashing the venetian blinds with a clatter, and shutting in the café lights for the night.

When the last blind was down and the last light gathered in, she pressed *Stop* and *Reject*, removed the cassette of the Music of the Spheres, and put it back for another ten years in the cardboard sweet box on the shelf marked 'Universal Fruits'.

239   *A Dream of Launceston*

(*for Charles Causley*)

So clear and safe and small,
on the nearest horn of
about twenty-seven

319

steady-breathing fellows
who have me cornered in
a field in North Cornwall

with their overbearing
friendliness (is it that?)
the ladybird allows

a petticoat of wing
and then recovers it.
And then: one pink-and-blue

nose lifts, and a deep note
rides out over the grass
to tremble the yellows

of the low primroses . . .
And 'Shoo' I say, and 'Shoo!'
in my nine-year-old voice

each time the dream comes back.
They do not shoo, and I
will not grow up, at all.

Reading the numbers on
the twitching ears as if
nothing more happened next,

I crave the freedom of
that tiny elegance
to flaunt itself, and fly.

Today's choice for surgery glides past
With a wave and a request: 'Brass handles, please!'
The surgeon's lips will smile inside his mask,
The anaesthetist's hat is a perky white
Like a fast food chef's.
                              Late in the afternoon
He glides back, waking, as the January
Darkness renders us our long clean room
In coloured windows: blue sisters read
Our records, and a witness nurse stares down
At the red pills shaken in the dice-cup.

With the supper done, we shuffle up our chairs
To allow a space: including in the deal
One other player, to be entertained
Because he is too close for discomfort,
And far too ordinary to fend off
With superstition.
                              Still he has not won
When the ceiling lights dim out and the pictures fade,
And we return to bed, passing the table
Where the coloured pieces of the Monster
Puzzle lie half-unsolved in the half-dark.

241   *Crossings*

In hospital with the National Health, I see
A newspaper obituary for J.W. ('Jack')
Martin, Kent and England, easily our most
Impressive sporting Old Boy; and I'm intrigued
To find it's by Roy Fuller, friend from another
Sphere altogether. My south-east London school
Had just two famous sons, J.W.
Martin and Lord (John) Vaizey; though far back,
In the 1920s, Montague Summers taught there:
'A fine, distinguished man,' one master said,
Not gauging the sum of his reputation . . .

I see Jack Martin up at Whitefoot Lane,
The school sports ground, position a sly Point
Four feet from the Ist XI Captain
During Old Boys v. School; and duly bounce
First ball of the over, blithely, easily,
From pitch to bat to hand. Silenced, I stand
At the Debating Society that same week,
Thinking to make a case against the public
Funding of medicine, as left-wing Vaizey
Rises up blithely from the floor to place
A vigilant Point of Information . . .

242   *Tristis*

Though the room is lucid again, she actually dares
To hang around demanding to be a Muse.
No more than a gleam, a glitter, a scintillating
Wheel set alight by a hateful, hidden spark
– Does she think to inspire by being *that*?

Or by being the way the perspective in a street
Turns nonsensical? By jangling the print on a page
To a seething mix which hustles the book aside,
And forces me to sweat until her writhing
Steadies, and slowly settles, and switches off?

She always comes for free, she's saying, why don't
I pay her creative attention? I owe her that much.
And one day I'll miss her, she wheedles, this could be
The very last chance.
                                    I am tired. But you want it? I'll give it,
Your due recognition. Don't go. Stay and hear what you are:

A whore from the stews behind the ordered screen
Of everyday appearance, a short-time fix
Of dirty grey confusions, a half-hour drab
With a tawdry veil that shimmers.
                                              Now you've taken
Your pound of spirit, feed and don't come back.

243   *Secrets from and with*

'Whirlpool closed for repairs'

At least we were seasick among friends

He who controls the photocopier controls the polytechnic

Religious Hats (a cigarette card series)

Amuse yourself sandpapering the new cathedral

Like musical chairs but adding a new chair every time
      the phonograph stops

Terminal, man. Your data stop here

Did you see that prostitute in a helmet going past
    the window?

The cows are chewing clockwise so we *must* be in the
    northern hemisphere

Can you tell me who lost the losers' race?

Moments of Hideous Indiscretion (a cigarette card series)

He was *disgusting*, Marie Lloyd said he was *disgusting*

And rose again on the third day the organ of the
    Granada Tooting

You've changed, you talk in noun clauses all the time

The last moral maxim going out of the other ear

Grow your beard up to your nose, pull your hat down over
    your eyes, shut your mouth and abstain as if
      you were voting

Are you a Gentleman, or a Player? – I am a Quantity
    Surveyor

Varieties of Post-coital Triste (a cigarette card series)

If you are on your death-bed, why are you doing a handstand?
    – To see the answer printed upside down.

244 *A Brighton*

'Brighton': not far, a lie or an excuse
Like dental checks or grandmothers' funerals.
'Did you have a nice day at Brighton?' asks the master
Receiving a boy's forged note about his cold.
The question is South-London-rhetorical,
A euphemism coined for the blind eye.

In Denver and Kanpur they have no Brighton,
No brief escapes to the fictitious sea.
The lovers say, 'If only there were in our lives
A Brighton, willing as an invented friend,
So people could allow that we went to the station
And saw the ticket clerk practise his knowing smile.'

245 *War-thoughts*

> now that I have returned and that war-thoughts
> Have left their places vacant, in their rooms
> Come thronging soft and delicate desires . . .
>
> *Much Ado About Nothing*

This is the day when our brave boys are safely returning. The flowers and the bunting, which drapes every street, have been sponsored by Chambers of Commerce to fête their home-coming, whose victory has rendered our pride and rejoicing complete. Our boys, too, feel proud – of the courage they showed for the nation with sheath-knives and missiles. Their honour will not be put down. Their honour is sacred. Such honour has been our salvation. The military virtues are back in town: our boys will have fought with a far cleaner spirit than others, and not once succumbed to strange vices in soft, scarlet rooms, in foreign bordellos frequented unknown to their mothers. Our boys will have sent them back postcards of classical tombs and Renaissance chantries.

Their war was our video game. Their privations were set out in graphics that whirled on the screen, while mandarins from Defence, with their charts and statistics, were showing in detail the world that our boys would have seen. When our boys turn the corner and enter the square in procession, their feet will stamp once and be still, the line come to a stop. The scaling of fifes and bombardment of side-drums will lessen, our hearts miss their beat as the rifle-butts drop with one crash to the ground. They will stand up erect (no one falters) while wreaths of respect are laid over the previous dead; and then march off again, to break up and disperse to their quarters, where some of our boys will crawl gratefully off to their bed.

But others will flourish their swords in the thirsty environs of bar and casino and dance-hall, and shout battle-songs; at bus-stops at midnight will curse – and be cursed by – civilians not proud of our boys for redressing their wrongs. Their officers, though, will lie stretched out in exquisite arbours, enhancing their peace with anthologies of trees; and tonight will assume elaborate masks for the dancing; and go in for drawing up battlefield strategies of love; and each delicate move of love's quarries will show on their sigint computers precisely. Thus, turning up for the Governor's Reception, one young blood, the bravest, will know where to find the best beauty and come at the spoils of his war.

246   *The Automatic Days*

The Days of Hope and Love

Monday morning in the spring, no customers,
And beginning another automatic week,
The Manager, all humorously formal:
'Ladies, I'd like you to meet Beverley!'
– And Beverley shyly walking in and nodding
To Tamsin and Mrs Gurnard, who have worked here
Six months and seven years respectively;
Beverley having been trained upstairs for her role,
Its courtesy and vigilance, told what

To wear and how to wear it, told to look neat
And above all to always smile. And all those things
She learned at school she might as well forget.

In the middle of this floor, most of the day,
Mrs Gurnard sits in a nine-inch-higher-up
Enclosure with her cash desk and credit slips,
From this panoptical vantage being able
To see down lines of dresses in all directions,
And watch the furrowed looks of customers
Holding the garments up against themselves
To wonder how they might look in daylight,
And scanning the length of their bodies to the floor,
And looking in vain for mirrors to flatter them.
She has to keep an eye on everything.
To Beverley Tamsin says, 'Mrs G.'s all right.'

But on Beverley's second day, Tamsin says,
'You think you can laugh and joke with her, and then
She goes all prim and chilly; serious.
Like, she was telling me the Manager
Has this funny way of pronouncing "suppliers",
He says it "supplars". And I laughed and that,
And went on sorting this pile of dresses, when
She turns and says, "You're not at a jumble sale,"
– All sudden and sharp, with a funny look – "You're *not*
At a *jumble* sale." But mostly she's all right.'
They both look covertly at Mrs Gurnard
Where she smiles and hands back someone's credit card.

And what should portend love and hope, the spring,
Does indeed bring the Financial New Year,
And the stocktaking for everyone, closing earlier
The first three afternoons of the previous week;
Which Tamsin finds a bother. Tamsin thinks,
'When it's sold you know it's gone; so why trouble
To count it before you sell it? Tomorrow,

You sell some more, the number's different.
Next week they buy in new stuff for the Sale . . .
I don't like the Manager's jokes, his great long lists
On clipboards, Mrs Gurnard going spare.'
You have to give them time to understand.

The Day of the Asterisk

The music stops in mid-bar on the PA,
So all the customers realise there was music
And wonder what comes now. 'Will Mrs Gurnard
Come to the Manager's office, will Mrs Gurnard
Come to the Manager's office. Thank you.' Click,
And the music starts again. Therefore she swivels
Round to tell Tamsin to stay with the cash desk,
And strides off smiling* down a glade of coats
To do the thing for which she has been thanked.
The customers themselves feel thanked for suffering
A remission of the music which they hardly
Knew they were hearing. Tomorrow is the Sale.

*She smiles at the girl on the cosmetics,
Penned in among the scents and paints and creams,
Who returns her a tanned and haggard look
Expensively reproaching anyone
Who passes, and will not be beautiful.
She smiles through the caféteria swing doors,
And she smiles at Trevor with his green agreements,
Imprisoned by some thirty capering screens.
At any second, somewhere in the world,
You can push a flat square button and get the sound
Of an audience screaming with happiness.
She pushes the bell for the Manager's happy smile.

Identity

Next day she wears a square blue disc which says:
MARY GURNARD
ASSISTANT MANAGERESS
A few inquisitive customers contrive
To read it, then look up and fit the name
To the face, or *vice versa*. More customers
Interrupt what she's doing with enquiries;
It must be the disc, or something in the way
She stands, or gives instructions to younger people,
Or just seems older ... Beverley's little disc
Says only BEVERLEY, Tamsin's TAMSIN.
Mrs Gurnard now walks faster everywhere,
Effect of being promoted to be old.

From now on she is one of eleven 'A.M.s',
Men and women; and nearly all the time
The shop is in focus for her. But customers
Are a *problem*, or watching them is; one of
Her big responsibilities the moment
She enters. Being a customer herself
Does not feel natural any more, you go
To other shops, and watch; or wonder who
Is customer and who Security.
Some of the staff are Security as well.
Beverley has a dream that, except for her,
All customers and staff are Security.

Forms of Summer

The eyes of the naked dummy, just shiny-smooth
Head and trunk and legs, no arms as yet,
Which stare over Trevor's shoulder as he humps it
Past other dismembered, hollow legs at
The hosiery counter, posing on small
Balletic, stuck-down toes, are eyes which frown

Reproaching everyone, any way they look.
In their store-room, all the dummies stare like that,
A gallery of smoothness and reproach.
As it passes her, it reproaches Beverley.
It catches her eye and she doesn't like it.
She likes it better when they give it arms.

He is taking it down to the Summer Window.
It will sit there, legs apart, with a traumatised gaze
Through the glass at shoppers passing in the Precinct.
It will be dressed for Summer, and for Sports.
As he turns a corner, almost bumping in-
to Tamsin flinching back against a wall,
He calls out, 'Be like that!' quick, as, a, flash . . .
Someone else carries down arms, and clothes,
To make a woman of it. The sun shines in
On the soft pavane of dust through the display
Of badminton equipment, where she remains
Looking healthy and distraught for seven weeks.

Behaviour of Lifts

The lift-door opens. Trevor, with a trolley,
Grins as he shifts it to let Tamsin in.
She crams between the trolley and the closing
Doors, which have tried to trap her, but draw back
With mechanical respect. At last she is inside,
And down it goes, slowly, the two of them hearing
The music, watching one number go out
And another shine, as they pass groups of faces
On floors where it does not stop. In their silence,
Trevor sees the silver crucifix which lies
On the broad plain of skin above, between, her breasts.
The Ground Floor arrives . . . 'Can you press the Open
Doors?'

Going up again it misses a floor and opens
Where nobody is needing to get out;
So there are smiles. Or opens two floors higher,
And is empty to a deputation waiting
As if to receive a visitor, people who say
They are going Down, not Up. The arrow says Up,
The bell has chimed it open, it will not close
Until someone leaps in, yelping, and stabs a button
And leaps out fast, and it works! But through the glass
They see the serenaded vacancy
Refusing to move, insisting it stays and waits.
Then it opens again, like a future, like a grave.

Oral Contact with a Duck

Rise up a brief metal escalator, see
Mrs Gurnard dash into a cubicle,
And dab some powder on her face, and touch
A spot not there this morning, and snatch her bag,
And lift her coat from an alcove and hurry out
Through the suddenly dropping swathe of heat
At the glass doors opening onto the Precinct,
Where, among the concrete pots of late summer flowers,
Goodbody's have put some lime-green litter-bins:
'A Message from Goodbody's: KEEP OUR PRECINCT TIDY!'
– At entirely their own expense. Mrs Gurnard
Drops into one a wrapper from a mint,

And then she goes on with her sandwiches,
And enters the Park by an almost unknown gate,
A small pedestrian gate too narrow
For cars or even horses, used by few,
Where she does not pause to read, on a notice board,
The Regulations, giving opening times
And things not allowed in the Park: no dropping
Of litter, no giving of political speeches,
No playing of musical instruments, no groups

Of more than six persons to play any game
Except on the authorised pitches. She is alone
On this cloudy lunch hour, free of the Summer Skirts,

And a duck walks up towards her, hopefully,
With the arcane, superior look of a species
Not often spotted in the Park, a fowl
Flown in from somewhere else and followed by
A mate in a plumage not to be described
Without a bird book. She undoes her coat,
And the duck appears to scrutinise the disc
She is wearing under it, with her name and role
Punched out in capitals. She calls, and stretches,
And holds out a piece of torn-off buttered crust
To the duck, which stands and . . . stands and . . . Mrs
                                    Gurnard
Speculates, 'Can you sniff if you have a beak?'

As the duck stands pondering, and Mrs Gurnard
Speaks to it quietly, trying it with the bread,
She seems to sense a moment of inanition,
A second of being mesmerised to nothing . . .
Her stare, as she stares, middle-aged, at the bird
Is like the preoccupation of a child,
Or the acquiescence of senility
In things coming harmlessly close to hand:
A somewhat low point of human consciousness,
A chilly moment when being alive (for her)
Is only being alive to focus clearly
The sniffing beak, and eye, of a strange duck.

The Clearances

The Early Autumn Clearance begins next week,
And no one feels ready for it. 'Back to
School!' still challenges in the window. Tamsin yawns,
While all day long the artificial flowers,

In their most perfectly arranged cascades,
Are spilling out from baskets on golden strings;
Or bogus foliage, standing in wooden troughs
Of artificial soil (each swathe and frond
Of bracken, every stalk and tendril, false),
Is wavering slightly, as the counter fans
Bend slow and cagey faces sightlessly
From side to side, droning all afternoon.

And what floods in when the Clearance opens
Are impotent- and violent-looking people
In anoraks, men and women, with plastic bags,
Who saunter through the glades of Goodbody's
Automatically. Here they are, pressing at
Pink mattresses with the spread-out fingers of
One loose hand; and there they go, turning up
Price labels on bath towels and dropping them,
The newness of everything turns them shabby,
Imperfect persons puzzled by perfect things.
They cannot live up to what they see, and if
They bought it, it would start to live down to them.

Beverley

Beverley has for a moment the madness
Of seeing every happening as unique:
A shot of Tamsin rearranging skirts
With a squeal of hangers, or a nun lifting
A frying pan slowly in the Kitchen Ware
And turning it over, scanning her blurred face
In the shiny base of it. Beverley looks away,
But wants to faint as she sees Mrs Gurnard
Stroll past the TV screens all smiles at Trevor,
And each screen flooding with a farewell crimson
As a jocular cartoon worm wriggles off
Into the sunset, doffing his hat: THE END.

Some of the thoughts that come can be so awful,
She has to go through the China, and past
The Furniture into the Garden Goods, and down
To an extreme hushed corner where older
Assistants render slow help with Sewing Aids,
And out through a green and white Exit. In the Precinct,
She could be any other assistant escaped
For lunch; except it's twenty-five past three . . .
Will she walk up and down to breathe, or just
Walk on not knowing where she might end, until
She looks all wrong down at the bus station
In her working skirt, among shoppers with plastic bags?

Somewhere Else

One Sunday Trevor has asked Tamsin out
For a drive, in the wet, down waterlogged lanes
And narrow open roads over prairie fields
Of sugar beet; and they are lost, with the dusk
Coming on. At a lonely intersection,
Near to a wooden sign they cannot read,
He stops without warning, and an unseen car
Is blaring at them, a front-seat passenger
Is turning to snarl. NO THROUGH ROAD TO THE BASE
Is what the sign says: lights in Amusement Rooms
Shine distantly over chained swings. The heating cools
Too quickly, their windows fog, they can't see out.

Whatever Trevor wanted to make of it,
Whatever Tamsin wondered about, or feared
(What *had* she agreed by coming out at all?)
The day makes the decisions. Water-drops
Run very fast, opaquely, down the windscreen;
And somehow he cannot move his left hand farther
Across than the gear-stick, which, in the deepest thought,
He joggles to and fro. As the land withdraws,
He draws, in the steam on the glass, a nose and eyes

334

With his forefinger; and one eye runs a tear.
They look out through the face at the looming dark,
And talk about Work between the silences.

The Last of Autumn

On a slack Monday morning (in her dream)
Mrs Gurnard comes in and sees a customer
Paying coins into Tamsin's outstretched fingers.
Tamsin's fingers turn them over onto her palm,
And they transform into toads. Not only that,
But the customer is wearing the Manager's hat
With a square blue disc on it: BEAT THE XMAS RUSH,
And is some peculiar kind of reptile.
Tamsin is also stroking him, or it.
'You are not supposed to stroke a customer,'
She tells Tamsin. Tamsin makes a sign.
Trevor and Beverley only stand and laugh.

On a slack Monday morning, Mrs Gurnard,
Having had a 'frightful night', comes in and sees,
And focuses, only the rain dribbling down
On the windows; she thinks every droplet carries,
Like a shell on its downward racing back,
A small aborted Precinct. And all around,
Xmas is starting up: this year's diaries
(Cheaper since March, and August) all replaced
By next year's; near the typewriters, new shelves
Of gift-packed stationery in pastel boxes;
Mistletoe wrappers round adhesive tape;
Small snowman price tags added to Artist's Pads.

The Sunshine Coffee Lounge

The caféteria has doors made to swing,
Like the doors of a Wild West saloon in a film,
Spectacular to burst through and bellow while

The camera has them swinging shut behind.
A trickle of Xmas customers comes in:
Two women with each other, a short woman
Leading a child not wishing to be led,
A red-bearded man, two Security
With shoulder flashes, and three sixth-form boys.
The cashier slides onto her plastic seat,
The kitchen echoes to a sudden shriek
Of badinage, and the filtered coffee drips.

And the customer with the red beard goes along
The row of pastries, shut into compartments
Which you open by lifting vertical perspex lids.
An eerie glow of striplight is enough
To give his eyes a leer, a ghastly look
As he gazes in, very slow and indecisive,
-to the recesses of a range of trays,
As if there were nothing more melancholic
Than these flat plains of pure confectionery,
And nothing worse than to place some on a plate
With a pair of aluminium tongs, and get
It rung up by a silent, sad cashier.

In the Snow

November: Tamsin, helping to window-dress,
Lifts a large cardboard Santa Claus into a window,
A two-dimensional figure of a bare-
legged blonde in Santa's red hood and gown,
The traditional elderly bringer of gifts
Updated to please an age not given
To reverence for age, but certain to esteem
The gift of sex. She rides a little sleigh,
And she'll be down your flue in a week or two.
Anyone passing might be forgiven
For doing a double-take thinking she was real.
'Her legs must get cold, in the snow like that!'

The reindeer pulling her could not be real,
But the plainclothes Security at Xmas are.
'You need them then more than any other time,'
Says Mrs Gurnard, quoting the Manager.
They go round in the guise of men-in-the-street,
In fur-collared coats, or jeans and anoraks,
Choosing their gifts with young Security wives.
They examine three-piece suites, watch demonstrations,
And ask about the price of foreign soaps
On the cosmetics. They watch the assistants
Most carefully when they go home at Xmas,
Hands deep in pockets clutching children's shoes.

In the Tinsel

Now it's the time for carols, carols, carols,
Incessantly resounding on the PA,
Only pausing to notify lost children
Taken howling to the playroom and left to swim
In seas of coloured balls. Half of the screens
Show Xmas videos of Seasonal Offers;
Snow is falling in them. A tiger walks
To and fro on his hindlegs the length of the Ground Floor,
And draws attention to the Toys Department
With a sandwich board concealing his lack
Of credible features. Mrs Gurnard turns
A young tramp, sleeping, out of the photo booth,

And Tamsin is in the tinsel. In her dream,
She has stolen it from the Interest Rates display
In the Building Society Xmas window,
And draped it round and round her as she walks
Glittering, as she glides, up the Precinct
Like a distraught one of the recent dead
Who make their way half-dazed through the studio
Mists of the hereafter in a film about
People from a wrecked airship touching down

(So they come to learn) in heaven. And Tamsin is
The youngest one, who never should have died.
It's right her boyfriend joins her at the end.

The Automatic Days

And they finally arrived at the grey pit
Between the Xmas rush and the New Year Sales;
Which you could fall into and not be thought of,
And lie there gazing up at a paper bell
Tangled round with bows of artificial silk,
Looking frayed and stained in the draught from the swing doors,
While the days did not draw in and would not draw out,
And the sunsets came cold and frail. Going through
PINE MIRRORS: HUGE REDUCTIONS, Beverley's face
Is reduced to a summary of the months
Since spring; she shakes her hair across its learnt
Grimaces, will she stop for the New Year?

Next day she stops at a particular
Pine Mirror, a line rather hard to sell,
And fixes in it a special rigid stare.
Far away behind her in slow miniature,
She sees Mrs Gurnard and Tamsin listening
While Trevor tells a joke, automatic days
Are passing while she stands there. Everyone
Knows of the moment when you choose between
Yourself and the mirror they give you. Beverley,
Seeing all of Goodbody's waiting for her to move,
Pushes her hair back and controls her lips;
Braces her spirit and walks right on through.

247   *Graveside*

Our faces show we disapprove profoundly.
He should never have brought us all to this

On a summer's day. Or any other day.
It is as if he were setting out to shock.
He could have found other ways of reminding us.

– Though for all his nerve, we remain superior,
Outnumbering him, and still in a position
To discuss this rare disaster.
                                        If we all put
Our heads together, surely we could devise
Some precautions to take against it, soon!

248   *A Pride*

In a cold October twilight, down towards
An estuary beach of mud and stones,
Three lifelong friends lurch and scramble over banks
Of red soil fallen from cliffs which one afternoon,
Fifty years ago, broke and carried the whole of a church,
Its churchyard, and half a road to the shores below.

They plunge headlong on crumbling cakes of earth
Where tipped-out garbage has mingled with the rubble,
And grass and painful gorse grown over it;
And sometimes they can't keep upright, and have to slide
On their arses with their hands thrown out to grab
At the fragile vegetation. But finally

They arrive at the river, and slither on the stones
– Which turn out to be nothing more than heavy
Medallions of mud shaped by the lapping tides . . .
The scum of the water nudges at their shoes,
And why did they come here, dangerously treading
The remains of fifty years? It is getting dark,

And they have to lug their bodies up again,
Up all that distance to the eroding edge
Of the cliff again, in unspoken competition,
With care to avoid the crevasses under the grass.

There is, and there has been, no kind of point or pleasure
For legs or lungs or spirits in any of this,

Though when they can breathe at the top, looking down across
The tracks by which they ascended, there is a pride
In their sweating faces. And yet, by themselves,
With no one else at the end of the day to admire them,
Or even convert them to symbols, why did they want
To do it, they ask? – After all, it was getting dark.

249   *Two Prospects of Adolescence*

(i)

My shoes left neatly side by side alone,
My socks peeled down and draped over a rock,
My trousers rolled in even folds, each fold
(As I was always taught it ought to be)
The exact breadth of a turn-up . . .

I kept them all in sight from the shoreline,
Where I steadied myself on the sand's hard corrugations
And confronted the North Sea with my book.
The wind felt at my feet and at my shin-hairs
As I waited for the sea to catch me up . . .

And I stood it out in ankle-deep ripples, reading
Of the party that echoed in Auerbach's cellar,
And Gretchen growing in the dreams of Faust;
While my friends, up in the dunes, trembled in trances
That dared the flagrance of lovers in Pompeii . . .

(ii)

I am remembering by re-reading you:
We are dancing together over my diary's page,
And we are dangerously breakable!

Oh we would shatter into ruins if
We went any closer, the polite and maladroit boy
And the circling girl . . .
                    It's late, I close the book
On my squandering of all that innocence.
How it could have prepared me . . . Why did I never see
That the fear and inexperience provided
Premonitions of a truth it took so much
More living to recognise: all there ever was
Was breaking?
                    I am longing in the dark
To recover the feel of those intact gyrations,
Your fingers resting on my shoulder and scarcely
Touching it, my right hand at your waist,
My left hand neat in your clammy and clean hand.

250   *A Walk by Moonlight*

I cross the side of the Square at a safe walk,
And shall soon be passing the solitary guard
At the Palace. Up beyond him, one in a dark
Leather jacket stands; and waits. I am assured
By his noncommittal look that I have been seen.
This is ten seconds after nine-thirteen.

Keeping to one of the two permitted routes,
I am thirty yards from where he leans on the tall
Palace railings, when he devalues his cigarettes
By lighting one. TRAIASCA PARTIDUL
COMUNIST ROMAN, say the letters of the sign
On the Central Committee, opposite. Two lights shine

From its huge grey rectangle. One is a bright
Slant of yellow from the door, which strangely stands
Wide open, and the second is a late
Lamp lit in a fourth-storey window, a light which sends

The message that Someone is working up there,
At nine-fifteen above Republic Square!

And are they suspicious of me, walking up
The pavement towards them? Because the man
Now approaches the soldier (whose trained grip
Doesn't slacken for a second on his gun). . .
Could it be that I become the subject of
The muttered conversation these two have?

Now I've passed, but their faces are still watching the only one
To disturb them for some while; and though their voices
Talk freely, they still talk quietly. When I look in
-to the clockmakers' window I see other faces
Saying it's nine-sixteen and all is well.
I'm two minutes away from the hotel.

*   *   *

Now that I'm back I have enjoyed my outing.
The clerk at the desk is ready with my key.
When I enter the lift, which has been waiting
While I've been out, I get its night and day
Rattle of muzak; and I hope the door
Will open, at the hush of the fourth floor.

Yes, my shirt hangs on the mirror, where it was,
And my notepad hasn't moved. On the counterpane
Are my dictionary and tablets.
                                 I'll watch the news
With *Telejurnal*; after which the screen
Will give me the Inspector, the good Roman,
To-night, and no doubt for some nights to come. . .

*   *   *

If anyone is listening, I'm at home.

Bucharest 1987

342

1990s

251 *The Last Stone*

Moving from hope to hope like stepping-stones,
One day the eyes and feet discovered
That the next step was too huge, they'd reached the last
Stone possible to reach and would stand there always,
Exhausted by that very last lunge forward
Onto its narrow, dry security;
And there would be nothing left to do, but stand
With your shoes having, so far, kept out all the water;
But with your expensive threadbare trousers threaded
By a rising wind, and your little jacket round you
Not enough to keep the cold out; and try, and try,
To hope, to *hope*, you could retain your balance;
This being only half-way across the river . . .

252 *Barto*

Beyond the door the green arrow pointed at,
Was one of the dankest human corridors:
Cold, short; one lightbulb swinging unshaded
In a draught from an unseen direction;
No telling what was paint and what was stain;
No guessing what might be roped up inside
The scruffy baskets pushed into that alcove,
Or what the liquid spilt from them might be;
A half-world not to stand mesmerised in,
But no going back to the door of entry
And the first warm place.
                                    There is another door,
Leading out to sounds which might be traffic
Or might be the sea at the foot of a cliff,
And that is where the draught is coming from,
An invitation to an ultimate cold . . .
I comb my hair, make sure my back is straight,
And press the tired flesh of my face to smile
As I do not Push Bar to Open.

All those perfect white dots are perfectly still,
Like bits applied by a brush until I look
And see them flap and fidget separately,
Rise up, veer round, resettle. The marsh down there
Is also painted, until I look and find
That all its turrets of green, the gorse, the samphire
And all the fawn tufts of grass, shake negative heads.
I swear the clouds haven't moved all afternoon,
But unless the background sky has shifted . . .
I look, and under any kind of calm,
Each hand that restrains on an arm or calms on a forehead,
Is a perpetual restlessness, a hurrying
Towards the end; which only consciousness
Can be terrified of and want to put a stop to.

254   *On the Death of Margaret Lockwood*

All the old picture girls are dying,
The proud posed queens
Of the magazines under the cushions,
The black-and-white touched up
Ladies of all the Annuals.
Soft millions of dots
In a thousand photographs
Have smiled past one final gazer.

I like to think he too
Begged heads to turn
And face him and lips to smile,
And found his avid eyes
Distracted by useless words
In the printed captions:
And for a second, thought
Of having second thoughts.

Several layers of paint never did
Turn the wall in the scullery the matching
Deep green Dad wanted, in the end
It was always pale and peculiar again.
One night there was a hole leading through to a space
Going on and on like the one in the hospital,
With the endless shelves I was told I came from.
On better nights it became the carpeted
Avenue in the basement of the store
Past the springy double beds and the sofas,
And ended where it narrowed between mirrors
Hung both sides head-high down a dimmer stretch
Where people turned their heads all the way along.
I followed it, it changed to an arcade
With tatty lawn-strips of an artificial
Deep green grass. At a counter we stood around,
With a kind of cruel and watchful aunt in charge,
The ping pong balls sprayed up in different colours
From out of a fountain, looking something like
The constituent planets in a diagram
Of the unsplit atom. They dropped if you were lucky
To end up in the small nets you presented
On the ends of bamboo sticks, nets made
Of a tearable fabric like an Xmas
Stocking in a shop, or a big girl's stocking:
You won a money prize for six balls safely
Caught in your net. I would stand for half-an-hour
Or as long as my pennies lasted, but I lost
My money in the end. I always finished
With my net nearly empty, and the woman sent me
Away from her counter to a deep green wall,
Or not a wall, a hole or door which opened
Onto a corridor like the hospital's,
The endless one with all the endless shelves
Where I, they told me whenever I asked,
Had been a dot slowly growing a long long time.

347

On Monday the automatic *Mind the Gap*,
Which sounds out with a sudden hectoring roar,
Didn't speak. 'Don't they care,' said some grey-haired chap
I thought I'd seen on stage at the Cottesloe,
'If we all go plunging down?' His two old feet
Were dithering humorously, but even so
He minded, having heard it the week before.

On Tuesday it did speak, and so I dropped
A glance at my own feet, for safety's sake;
And saw where the left one lifted up and stepped
Across a lighted depth which offered me
(The only passenger leaving for the street)
First option on its bright infinity . . .
I took my time – it was my time to take

And no one else's after all – and thought:
Those footlight bulbs shining beneath this train
Cry out for a performance. Therefore I brought
My right foot over, at the same leaden rate,
With sweating grace and flourish to complete
A great dramatic solo, of the sort
You don't need help with;

                       though I'll appreciate

Company when I use that stop again.

257 *Three Places*

In the first I thought I was assuming
The substance of air and it was easy.
I was breaking into atoms and I was smiling.
I couldn't tell if they had given me

A room for this without or with a window,
I was facing a wall and couldn't turn round.
I was turning into air, and could make a sound
With my lips or in my throat; but who would know?

In the second I was somewhere on my back,
But recovered enough to realise it was a shelf,
And I was an object displayed on it. And a crack
Of rectangular light showed me my self
As a thing which might, at a nod or sigh,
Be shuffled into one piece and slid away
Into whatever slot of night or day
Was available to store or burn me in.

In the third it's different. Because I am whole
And moving at last – up a steep green
Corridor at the end of which my goal
Is a roomful of windows, and set between
The windows, chairs; and no flat shelves where I
Could watch my self spread out. If I find the strength
In my hollow shell, I'll climb the length
Of this polished cliff. And sit to watch the sky.

258   *Exercise*

When I suddenly made out I was near to the edge,
I could balance still, and not shake or shiver,
But I couldn't tell with mind or hand or foot
How near it was; or for that matter
If what I took for the brink was in fact the brink;
Or on the other hand whether
An opening-out of the sky around me
Made it *seem* like the brink.

And naturally I knew this was all pretend,
But I couldn't remember how many or how few
Imagined yards I'd left before I would take
One step too many, and fall down over or through
Crash and finish the game.
I had to be sure it was true
That the path behind could lead me down again.
I had to find voice enough to *Stop the Game!*

259   *Repairs*

On Monday the scaffolding went down
Like propelling pencil leads
On the rough cloth of the lawn.

On Tuesday it went up like a framework
Of medical attention round the house.
A water-hose dripped nourishment on the bricks.

Today I feel retained inside it
Like a structure too piecemeal, too frail
To stand up by itself.

I need to believe it was worth all
Their fixing in place of tubes and bolts
And planks and pulleys, that everything

Will be better for the work than it was before.
They come to dismantle it to-morrow.
I need to believe I shall still be here.

So whose are those postcards, typewriters, sunglasses?
And who piled some last-year's newspapers like that,
Not thinking that he might not be coming back?

To move through such belongings as one alive
And feel I am a dead man who left them just
As they are lying now, seems ridiculous . . .

But why doesn't the sun on the table give my hand
A shadow when it riffles these letters, which
Are all addressed to him? And when I look,

It ought to give my whole body a shadow too.
I should understand why the shapes of all these objects
Are so clear they shine; but I don't. Could it be because

I am crying at them? Otherwise, how explain
The ridiculous optical delusion of
My shadow suddenly slanting out from somewhere

And claiming them for its inheritance?

261   *Inertia Reel*

Waking after the nightmare of a too-high urinal

Dawn: a new day waiting, terrified, to be auditioned

I shave, forgetting I have a beard. I dress, not remembering I meant
to slop around in pyjamas. I have a super ego, but is its memory going?

First Steps in Hypochondria (a Correspondence Course)

Ah, a brisk morning walk! Feeling good, but a bit like a newly-
sharpened pencil: a little less left than yesterday

And no real appetite for lunch. I'm offered another nymphet but I'm full up already

Hypochondria Lesson Three: not the strength in your fourth toe you had at forty

Eat All You Want and Still Look Anorexic (a Correspondence Course)

So the afternoon stretches insensibly on, past the hour of my birth in a climatic and economic depression

And tea-time already! Not ready for it, nostalgic about lunch, the oil-cloth on the table, the glass cruet won at hoop-la, the savoury mince

In the newspaper: Barnacles make trusty pets

Hypochondria Lesson Eight: Never stir weak tea, let your toast cool a little, *always* boil lettuce before eating

Sunset: rehearsal for what might just come right *to-morrow* evening

Send for your barnacle today (meaning: Pay us to unload our vagrant crustacea on *you)*

How to relate to your bedclothes (a Correspondence Course)

In the newspaper: Scientists have proved that the time we spend asleep thinking we are awake and the time awake thinking we are asleep cancel each other out

Last thought at night before sleep overcomes my dread of it: Oh, I shall survive; but it will take a second lifetime

The way those waves are processing
Towards me this afternoon, their ceremonial
   Sets of uncurling crests . . . Is the sea attempting
  Some sort of tedious message? It seems that all
    It offers is some maxim like *To me*
All things must return or *Watch this space*
   Which opens for you – so enticingly:
   You're bound to enter it and feel at ease . . .

Is it ever going to halt those blue
Monotonous arrivals? From where I stand,
   Half-a-mile away, is it trying to wash through
The tops of that rim of pine trees, where the land
   Makes one final gesture, and the heath declines
Down into the dunes? There's a village on the left,
   And some ploughland slopes off up some contour lines
To the right, and a slow, persistent, deft

And ritual patience of the sea licks, licks at
This whole scene, starting with the trees – in vain,
   As if it's lost its touch. I'm thinking that
I have no time at all now for its plain
   Repetitions of the old siren pledge
To win and keep me.
               Though the whole long day
   Is setting with that sun, each field and hedge
Looks green and living still, as I stride away.

The boy, an only child, is taken out
To tea with some cousins. They are a family
Of five exuberant girls; and they dance and shout
In the absolute conviction that you are better
For being five than if you are merely one.
To be a singleton can't be much fun,
So the five of them dance round him mockingly;
And in forty years' time all six receive a letter.

Forty years later, somebody will write
With news for all of these people; but that can wait.
The boy wears a brand-new sailor-suit, the spite
Of the five capering cousins is taken out
On its trim blue smartness: one of them dips a spoon
In the gooseberry jam-pot, and very soon
His trousers are smeared with pips, and a huge great
Blob runs down his collar, all this without

Any protest from their mother, the boy's aunt,
Who is used to such behaviour in her brood
(How can you punish every jape and taunt?)
But upright on the upright piano stands
A sepia photograph of Aunt Caroline,
Indomitable, single and fifty-nine,
Who knows how these girls will not come to much good,
And that the devil finds work for idle hands.

In minutes the boy is close to resentful tears,
He retreats into a corner, the girls pursue;
Aunt Caroline lives on for forty years,
Or, to be precise, she dies at ninety-six.
His parents are enraged, but his mother won't
Presume or dare to utter the word *Don't*
To her sister's children. Aunt Caroline, too,
Would simply watch and ponder these bullying tricks

If she were there. Back home, the stricken boy
Vows never to go back, never to speak, at all,
To these cousins, who so thoroughly enjoy
Being five in the family that they must ridicule
Less fortunate children. Aunt Caroline is poor,
And thrifty; and behind her bedroom door
Has a mirror, fitted loosely to the wall,
Where she stores unspent pound notes. The space is full

By the time she dies, she has had few bills to pay,
So the sum went on increasing. Other hands
Came to count it in the end, hands that knew the way
The law must apportion each intestate pound;
And eventually the solicitor's tidings drop
Onto various family doormats. At the top
The letter says: *In re Miss Caroline Sands,*
Deceased: We beg to inform you we have found

The estate of the above to be valued, net,
At two thousand pounds, most of it cash concealed
At 94, The Crescent. If you kindly let
Us know the names of those to receive due shares
We should be much obliged. The angry boy
Is a married man today; and he learns with joy
The import of this letter, which has revealed
A most amazing justice; and who cares

That he was mocked, nearly forty years ago,
By that spiteful mob for being an only child!
Each branch of this cousinhood will soon know
What share of the two thousand to expect,
And in one large and noisy family,
When they see that the cash will be shared out equally
Between branches, not individuals, a wild
Delight will change to curses. 'Is this a fact,'

One girl exclaims, 'that because I am one of five,
I receive only sixty pounds of this hidden hoard,
While in the post for that one child will arrive
A letter and a cheque for over three
Hundred quid? It isn't fair, it's a disgrace!
That stupid boy, with green jam on his face,
Will be getting five times my share? This is absurd.
We'll write to this solicitor instantly . . .'

But next day she, 'phones the boy, to say that she'd
Love to see him, with her sisters, to celebrate . . .

*   *   *

The boy remembers the last time, and is afraid.
Their mockery still hurts him, and the lack
Of kindness in people. Still . . .
                              Though he made that vow

Not to visit them ever again, well *now*
– *No!* He cannot change his mind. It's much too late.
They are planning some strange revenge . . . He will not go back.

My mother says, *That bonfire's still alight*,
But I can't tell where she's pointing. *On the right*,
Can't you see it now?

                And then I catch one spark
At the far end by the plane tree, in a dark
Recess of the undertrimmed garden where
She does sometimes light fires. So I lean and stare
Through the room the light paints on the window pane
As she holds back the lace curtain, and some rain
– Or sleet, or snow – blurs the garden with sharp spots
Drumming down on the glass. And I shift some pots
On the unsteady scullery table, hoping for
A clearer view as she moves off through the door:
I can't have raked it over properly,
She murmurs guiltily; to herself not me.

But though they went on creeping back into
Our after-supper talk in the room we knew
As 'the kitchen', no one ever thought to go
And make the fires safe; our pre-war radio
Detained us, with its post-war comedies.
While out there in the garden, under the trees,
The flames were obstinately burning on,
My mother was reminding us that one
Small spark could fire a city, she had no doubt
That someone should have gone and stamped them out;
And all loose ends were living wires, they'd kill
If you forgot, and touched them.

                    But with no will
To act herself she left us reassured
That most fires died out of their own accord.

265   *Lost*

Would they play it on the wireless if we asked?
Would they know it? Would they have it in the archives?
Would they think it worth playing a lost old tune?
Aren't we too old to ask? Aren't they too young to see the point?

The scarred and scratched, the rutted, bakelite
Of a million 78s around the world,
Reduced to a nostalgic cackle-crackle,
Its voices out of pre-electric time,
Is everywhere waiting requests from the nearly dead:
Can't you play something for us?
Having come so far we are immutable now,
We are going to stay immutable until death,
And we'd love to hear that lost old tune again.
Can't you play it for us, on the very last gramophone
Equipped to play 78s?

A girl went down to the actually dead
To enquire about her lost virginity:
The dead are a great Lost Property Office
From which no postcards about things handed in
Are ever mailed out. But the girl went down
Because there are more virgins even now
Than there are ex-virgins among the dead,
And she believed such girls might have an answer.

When she came back up she was still an ex-virgin,
But she carried in her hands some precious discs
The dead had given her, made of bakelite
– There are things the dead will yield up if the living
Go and ask them with a genuine respect.
'Give them those,' the dead had said, 'and they can put them
In their archives to be played when they get requests,
When they get those enquiries after the lost old tunes
From those who remember, or have read about,
The innocence of popular music, lost
Midway between the Somme and the Wall Street crash.'

266   *Anniversaries*

With the old pre-electric telephones
The crackle was louder,
The scraping of cosmic sandpaper more violent.
When your voice came through from Yucatan
It sounded authentic; for months
I hoarded your tiny atmospheric phrases.
I like to believe you hoarded mine
Like the last shilling in the tin.

Now that you come through every day,
And you're almost 'in the room',
I don't credit one clear breathing word;
After an hour has passed I remember
Virtually nothing. Unless
They give us that sandpaper back again,
I'll imagine you spending me in Yucatan
Like the last million in the tin.

267   *Lucky Thirteen*

Don't call, just come. Come into the room,
Hang your shirt over the mirror and 'feel free'.
I put the telephone down in that corner,
Underneath my nightdress. The air-conditioning?
Noisy, probably safe; but I'll play some rock.
Sit down in one chair and hold conversation
To start. Any more, *write it down, write it down!*
. . . Prepare yourself to wake quickly if you sleep,
And I hope you not talk in your sleep.
From here you will see the sun rise over
The Heroes' Monument. If it does,
And you stay long enough for that, it will be
The first times we ever kiss in daylight.

268   *Experience near Porlock*

A cry, a crash, and a vengeful shout
From the street below; and I have written:
The mountains had to start somewhere, so why not
Immediately rising out of flat fields
Where the sheep need no stamina for grazing?
I saw them do this from the train on Thursday;
And the next afternoon I saw from a window
The train I travelled on the day before
As it wormed across my picture without me,
A pleasantly far-off giant insect.
I watched it, it used up no stamina
When I grazed on it, so I slipped myself back
Inside it, and dreamed I still travelled as I lay
On the grass of a foothill under the mountains

The day after that, the day which was yesterday.
I could see the train from there as well, see the window
From which I saw the train, and from that third place
The two were in a calmly vanishing past
I was dying to hold on to. – But then came today,
With an evening too dark to see very much at all,
Only dream about it in the vanishing
Room behind the window; and only write
   A drunk has finished the dreams in his bottle
   And smashed it to bits on the pavement.

269   *Mark and Melinda Prepare the Luggage*

You two, please take us back now we understand.
Take us back now we speak the language more like our own.
Take us back now our questions aren't simple-minded.
Take us back now we don't want just the phrasebook answers.

We didn't believe in you in your two dimensions,
We might believe in you now you've grown the third.
Let's all take a plane to where life is so much freer,
Where there'll be a little restaurant we can't speak

For the thump of the rock band, and as we leave
We'll be ordered to enjoy our days, some place
Where the crucifixes advertise Coca-Cola.
– Perhaps we'll take a plane to Budapest

So Mark can stand again on the Erzsébet Bridge
In the fumes of the traffic he taught us the words for
When there wasn't much of it; and stroll round the boutiques
Behind the Lenin Boulevard that was.

And Melinda, let's go back to Keleti Station,
Buy some tickets at the window, stand and punch them
In the little machine on the wall of the yellow tram
Past the cemetery where János Kadar lies,

Past the flat where József Antall is living now.

270   *January to April*

So we've come through, to a cold plain stretch
Without commitments; and might as well
Go for new beginnings because there's nothing much
To do except begin. Besides, this spell
Of shining January sunsets looks as clear
As our first, clean diary pages of the year

. . . Except that the prospect is suddenly stained
By a squire with a shotgun, warning me to keep
My nose out of his business. Beyond him stand
His shooting party, angry and kneedeep
In root-crops blasted by frosts; from near and far
They glower in fury at my intruding car

For giving out a warning to the prey
Their beaters wanted to scare up from the ground.
Their attitudes suggest a wasted day,
And their smiles are threatening: I feel I've found
Where the heart of England beats to fortify
Its old solid bones and veins, and I can't deny

That I'm pleased to have upset a project whose business
Was impersonal slaughter; though it manages
Few corpses today, and they like me even less
On account of that. To-night, strange images
Of death, by remote control, will fill their screens,
And armchair switches bring them warmer scenes . . .

This February is mild, and yet last night
The temperature fell, and further cattle-stuff
Was ruined. In its longer, colder light
There's no one to intercept me if I make off
Down the same track today, through fragile snow
Where mud and guns delayed me weeks ago.

The squire has gone, leaving the game to me,
And my walk is a way of meditating on
The questions left behind by his memory:
Is mankind worse with the missile than the gun?
Does it work more evil with remote control?
And at how many removes will the whole

Moral issue vanish completely? Farther on,
A hare sprints across my path, turns round and looks,
And waits like a dog, a prey for anyone . . .
I could teach it to be moral and read books.
As fast as I could teach the squire's young friends
Not to fire if they saw it. When the short month ends

And March arrives, the winter still holds out.
It's the worst time, flaunting every day the dream
Of a spring which it denies. Yet who can doubt
That its coming will seem banal? New girls will scream
With the old enjoyments, while their elders sit
And give up trying to make sense of it

− Someone tell them it's all useless, that the world will
Never change, merely pass through frost and blood
From the snowdrop to the ridiculous daffodil
Every year; pushing flowers up through the mud
Of death's green season from a hope which tries
To appease the bones and the smashed weaponries . . .

And where the daffodil surfaces again
In the squire's fields, and demands some celebration,
I stop my car today in the April rain,
And see it only as a distillation
Of the palest hope earth could ever seek and find
In a war which left so few whole bones behind . . .

1991

271   *In Moslodina*

'If we never learn much from history it is because
"we" are always different people.'

In the Tourist Hotel somebody leaves a tap
Running too long. The first drip to fall on me
Strikes at my left thigh; the second stays
Poised over the armchair, then suddenly
Runs, and drops several inches farther up;
The third and fourth I catch in two ashtrays.

Forgetting my own bath, I rush to get
Dressed and raise Cain, cursing a world with too
Many forgetful fools in it, and surely far
More than there used to be? Plus, a huge new
Tribe of the unknowing, happy to let
Some others tell them what their memories are.

The drips fill tumblers, vases. Through the dead
Door of the room upstairs a national song
Booms to drown my knocking. Girls in folkloric dress
Light candles on T.V. . . . I watch a long
Dark, cross-shaped patch on the ceiling form, and spread:
A continent of sheer forgetfulness.

I've always had this dread of growing old
In untidiness: a worn tobacco pouch;
The edges of a table cloth rubbed and frayed
Into tassels; accumulators; a deep drawer
Full of tram maps and busted pipes; a couch
Where a dusty cushion pictures an esplanade
In faded Devon; all my grandfather's store.
Long after he was dead and his goods were sold

(But mostly chucked away) those hoarded treasures
Seemed what it meant to live on to his age,
And I, too, would end with the same cruel
And pointless load of close-at-hand bric-à-brac
Stuck round *me*, like the toys fixed in the cage
Of a tamed songbird. Dud capsules of lighter fuel,
Old tins, ancient Pelicans, today brings back
The dread-full sight of them, an old man's pleasures

(And his failures) – I can feel his presence
In the junk in my own room. So now I'm able
To picture myself his age, I'll up and set
The VCR, spread brand-new books among
The dustless disks on my working-table,
And fight back with Order; hoping to forget
That because this is my life, my style, the young
May see it as my trash, my obsolescence.

273 *The White Lady*

(in memoriam George MacBeth)

I found your door, and touched your bell
    The same day my friend died.
I said, 'I've come to buy your love
    Because I'm terrified.'

The terror was of death itself,
    For his, and my own sake;
Whoever knows how much more love
    One faltering heart can take?

– And terror, too, at what I'd done
    By taxi-ing to you,
When sorrowing for a dead man was
    The tribute that seemed due.

I grieved for one whom my friend loved,
    The last who understood
Words were his blood and sinews but
    Her body was his food . . .

Had I dredged up some craven lust
    From younger, darker years
To smother up with sweat and sperm
    A night that called for tears?

But – 'You make love to me,' I said,
    'My friend has died, and rests,
A shrunken thing, in wasted bones . . .
    I'll pay you for your breasts,

'And lips, and hairs, and supple hands,
    And tongue that raises me
And licks away the feel of death's
    Putrescent infamy.'

You said, 'You pay me for my tits
   And my hands to work you mad,
And, like, I'll pay you back your friend
   With things would make him glad

'If he could know you cried for him
   So hard you came to find
A girl to rub away the ash
   That settled on your mind.'

And you, blonde stranger, knelt your nine-
   teen years above my pain,
And crying with me paid me back
   My old friend's life again

– Because, I crept back to my room,
   Your softly-punished child,
And in last summer's photographs
   I *swear* he knew; and smiled.

274   *The Telescope*

But these days, like gazing down it the wrong way:
Thus, a hotel corridor focuses a street
Where a hub-cap fills most of a small door
With an aluminium circle, as complete
As a big ship constructed in a yard; which looms
To block the sky above the dying town
That built it. The row of shops and curtained rooms
Is blocked out by this container, soon launching down
To the seas of a One Way system; but now two
White-bloused and black-haired visions cross the floor
Halfway down the passage, and start a new,
A likelier flash of interest . . . I can't stay

– And I'm leaning on a long cylinder of straw
An hour later, someone's machine-made feed
For the winter; it pierces through my shirt
And stirs my skin. That onward track must lead
To the sea, though first there's a restful skyline
With a soft swell of wheat on it . . . I watch
A dragonfly drop and settle, and define
The colour blue on a grey stony patch
Of the path, where one journey of tractor wheels
Has laid two ruts, suggesting a harm and hurt
Which feet don't inflict. And very soon this feels
Like a place where you can't be exactly sure

How you ever came. So I move on, still in hope
Of finding the sea; until at last I stand
By the edge of a tidal lake from where I see
Over there a metal sign stuck in the sand,
Forbidding something – though whatever its intent,
It seems to be saluting the marching skin
Of the water, a parade of ripples sent
Forward, forward by the afternoon breeze in
Perpetual advance to a climax somewhere,
Some high point of ocean . . . Attainably
Close, would you think? Like the breast of wheat? Like the hair
Of the girls who walked in the tiny telescope?

275   *The Advantages of Small Town Life*

Where the cultivation of sameness is the law,
A variant sub-clause like you can provide
The difference everybody can enjoy.
It's fame to be a bedtime conversation
In three thousand five hundred blue heavens.

You have curious little habits they chat about,
And encourage: a barman's right hand
Goes up to the grenadine when you enter their pub,
His left to the Worcester sauce. Your green moustache
Is charisma in ten thousand memories.

You're an amiable chap, and such a deep one!
Most of your telephone calls are from ministers,
The operators say so; your light's on late
And a rumour spreads: He's at work on a scheme
For harnessing the force of unwanted erections.

Your presence is power, your absence is power,
Your unexpected return is a thunderbolt.
They know about your postcards from Novi Sad.
With a daily walk they can time things by,
You can miss out once, and their eggs will be boiled to brick.

For years you can cash their illusions about you
For the D-marks of licence. To be different means
To feel envied, to feel free, they are less than you,
You are noticed everywhere. And at any time
Their deputation with Tsornoffs will know where to find you.

276   *Principal Boy*

At her very first entrance she outshines   All the sycophants
        and spivs   She strides with tall ease on a stage that
        looks manageable now   Its agoraphobic wastes seem
        amenable to reason

We see there's a bold young man to the rescue who is
        also   A daring resourceful girl   She can act like a
        tough brave boy and be dashing and strong   But will
        never never surely be loutish or rough

So she's Brother and Sister at once and can   Remember the little
      things and be Mother as well   But she's handsome
      Brother entirely courting the Princess   And for all of
      the time whenever she speaks and sings

Her role is supposed to have nothing to do with sex   You
      may only purely admire her no other emotion   It is
      not to be even a distant aseptic love   You could
      never forget a kiss and yet never desire her

If a sultan or vizier shouts or a genie shows bottle   She
      looks scared like a woman but that is only
      pretence   She's gallant and good in every turmoil or
      scrape   It's just that she doesn't want to seem
      superhuman

Supremely she disentangles the threads in all the plotting   If
      there's villainy in the way she propels it aside   We
      walk with her unharmed through the thickets of
      childhood fear   We always knew she was destined to
      win the day

And then at last yes the walls lift and fold back and she
      shows us   The hills and the sun when the whole dim
      scene is transformed   She is puffing us up for the
      world outside the Exits   Where we have to face up to
      the Fact That Life Has Begun

We remember and worship her legs in the homegoing
      tram   She is out there imperishable somewhere in the
      dark   She is watching and waving and smiling and
      saying   'Be strong! Shall you look on my works you
      meek ones and despair?'

I have to call it something like despair,
Forgetting the name of somebody who came
Across a room and very suddenly
Set herself down in an opposite chair
And placed her two stockinged feet on the arm
Of my own chair at twenty-five past three

Thirty years ago! Because, I could tell she guessed
No one else would be watching, the window only showed
The rooftops and part of the sky, which we could see
Had turned a dark blue, darker than the rest,
And I missed the chance she offered . . . I recall it snowed,
With the flakes failing to settle, just timidly

Wafting over the brickwork of the grey
Terraced streets which rose up slowly from the river
Like an adjunct of its mist. – And I think I know
That the town could be found once more, that dark blue day
And those grey streets reappear, if I could ever
Call up her name; which would persuade the snow

To fall again, and the room to still be there
With its window onto rooftops, and cloudy light
Shining into a narrow space where two people meet
Thirty years ago, each stuck in a deep armchair
Pretending to guess if the snow might fall all night
– And the man would settle for stroking the woman's feet.

278 *February*

Once there was half-term, now it's only
Four pale little lunar weeks without a focus:
Days to tread water in, fill the pending tray
Of an ante-room month, and gather weeds
For the obsequies of the Old Financial Year.

I have heard old wise men in the country say,
'But there's always one day the sun'll give you
A hint of spring in the middle of February!'
– Wrong as usual. I shall relax and enjoy it
In the inevitable wake of winter.
You tell me that the days are drawing out?
Like freezing poultices.

279 *To Delay*

(*for Stephen Spender*)

The searching for empty seats
The listening hard to announcements
The skitter of electronic signboards
Through place and place and place
The re-reading of paperbacks
The purchase of useless gifts
The faces masked with boredom
Wired into walkmen
In the rip-off bars

– And the consequent need
For long explanations
For cancelling rests
And abrupting meals
And ending shorter encounters
With briefer kisses
And using up limited time
In moving on fast to the next things
Much too rapidly done

– But sooner that than being left alone
At the very end when everyone else has gone
With their baggage and passports and children
All checked and accounted for
And too many seats to choose from
The overpriced restaurant shut
The sweeper's broom at your ankles
The public address switched off
The signboards finally blank

280   *Bastard*

Into a suddenly sunny spring dawn
A bastard creeps out through a crack in some
Until-then immaculate-looking woodwork.

He inhales the air and smiles, and everything
Looks good to him. And so he takes a few
Experimental paces, trying out

His legs and wondering what clothes to wear:
A city suit? Some jeans and a baseball cap?
Or an 'I ♡ my building society' T-shirt?

Because he plans to walk into an Organisation,
To stir things up inside an Organisation.
He is going to Go For It and get others Going,

And he's past Reception already, and up
In an express lift to a penthouse suite already,
And they have an office waiting for him already,

And his first dictated letters on a screen.
In the other offices, behind their hands,
They are talking about him, quite a lot,

They are saying, 'How did that bastard get that job?
I'd like to know where the hell he came from!
I'd like to see his qualifications for doing

What he does.' – All talk, and he knows it, it's safer
To talk than to act, the smaller bastards
Know the truth of that from long experience,

They've learnt to carry on and keep their heads down
To protect their own bit of woodwork.
                                        So all goes well,
With the faxes slithering out from other bastards

In other penthouse suites all round the world,
And the graph turning upwards on the wall-chart in
The Bastard's Conference Room, the spread-sheets glowing

With the marvellous figures the Bastard envisages;
And his desk is clear and shiny, and people's smiles
Are amiable and innocent, or seem so.

Or seem so . . . In his deep suspicious brain
The Bastard worries occasionally that their lips
May be smiling, smiling for him, but not their eyes.

Still, for now, things go splendidly, the Bastard is seen
On 'State of the Art' and 'Man of the Week', and has
A 'Room of my Own' and a 'Holiday of my Choice'.

– And then one day a casual conversation
Stops short when he enters a room without warning
And another day the people do not stop

When he comes round the door, but self-consciously keep
    talking
With knowing looks, and ever-widening smiles.
The Bastard pretends he hasn't noticed, but

He goes back to his office and he thinks
'Those bastards could be ganging up on me . . .
I must watch that little bastard with the haircut.'

The Bastard is full of fear and fantasy,
And the fantasy that made his world for him
Becomes a fantastic fear of losing it:

His mirror tells him always to guard his flanks,
And never leave his knife-drawer open when
He turns his back on even his secretary

– But he does have courage. It tells him to have it out
Face-to-face with his team of Assistant Bastards
And find out what the hell is going on.

Oh no, they'll never tell him half the story,
Oh yes, they'll sit and talk behind their hands,
But he can still fire the lot; or he thinks he can.

Today they are gathered round a table, with vellum pads
Which some of them are writing or doodling on,
And some are self-confidently leaving quite untouched.

It's the ones who pick up no pencils and take no
Notes who are the most dangerous. They know
The result they want without fidgeting about it;

Especially the little bastard with the haircut.
He speaks in code but it's clear what he's implying:
The Bastard is letting the Organisation down,

It ought to do better; and all the smallest bastards,
The shareholders' democracy, have been stirred
To demand a different bastard at the top.

This year they're eager for a different scene,
This year they're after a man with a different style,
This year they'd like a bastard with a haircut.

The Bastard's hand is turning clammy on
His thoroughly doodled vellum pad,
The sky is blue for other bastards now.

He sees what is coming next, and he'll speak out first.
He rises from the table, he looks at them
With steady eyes, and steady eyes look back,

Though the lips are smiling. 'I've seen your game!' he shouts,
'I've sussed it out – you're just a lot of *bastards*,
A lot of dirty, crooked, scheming *bastards!*'

When the door slams hard behind him they look at each other
And shake their heads with humane and pitying smiles.
'Poor bastard,' one compassionately murmurs.

The haircut says, 'It wasn't easy, but
It had to be.' And a third: 'I'm so relieved
It's over and we can breathe.' And a grinning fourth

In a flak jacket moves into the Bastard's chair
As the sun sets golden, and the immaculate walls
Begin to look like very porous woodwork.

281   *Adlestrop Now*

The name, as I drove west that day,
Flashed from a hedgerow. Since the sign showed
Only two miles, having time enough
I took the little winding road

Along to the village. First I passed
A wood, and then a field where straw
Burnt black, and near a notice-board   .
Which said 'Neighbourhood Watch', I saw

Two well-trained citizens staring hard
At me, and at my number-plate.
Alarms clung to cottage walls, and locks
Guarded each wild-rose porch and gate,

And after a brief stay, I thought
I'd go. I had no wish to stir
Rumour in all those covered nests
Of Oxfordshire and Gloucestershire.

282   *Ballad Form Again*

Seated one day in the sauna,
    Hands on my steaming knees,
Counted my two feet, got it right,
    Thought, What do I do with these?

Numbered my human failings,
    Pardoned them one by one,
Took a shower and dried myself,
    Walked out into the sun

– Snatched for my dark, dark glasses
    Moment I hit the light;
Find shade a little easier,
    Can't take the world too bright.

Strolled through the City Centre,
    Followed the One Way signs
To the Consumer Precinct,
    Saw the new clothes designs,

Saw the new architecture
    In the new eclectic style:
Post-modern Bauhaus Gothic.
    Looked at the gargoyles smil-

Ing on the old church pinnacles
    As the sky turned grey then black,
Folded my dark, dark glasses,
    Thought of turning back

But pressed on, with my umbrella,
    As the hail began to pelt:
More climatic experience
    Under my belt . . .

For shelter, was there a tea-room
    Or a library to be found?
No – only the hypermarkets
    Gleaming all around.

Trod carelessly in the gutter,
  Water gushed over me;
Thought, Forces of Nature as usual,
  Behaving amorally.

My feet being wet in my footwear,
  I decided to call it quits,
So I lowered my umbrella,
  Collected my few wits,

And checked the number of gargoyles
  – Thirteen vindictive elves!
Thought, Don't take the piss out of gargoyles,
  They do it for themselves.

Headed back home, determined
  Not to go out again
To waste the good of a sauna
  Walking in lousy rain.

Thought, Shoes which let in water
  Should be junked for sterner stuff;
And the same goes for the ballad form:
  Enough is enough.

SAATCHI AND SAATCHI:
FIRST OVER THE WALL

– West Berlin
graffito, 1989

In the Amusement Arcade was a small glass case
Containing a wooden bird with a beak that smiled.
For a one-pound-coin you could turn a handle and
It flapped and flapped its coloured wooden wings.
This was like the freedom given to the East
To wear our coloured wings and flap for coins.

*   *   *

There are the black wings of death
That frighten us into living,
And there are the coloured wings of death
That brighten us into forgetting.

The flap of the first wings almost touches us.
Because they come to remind us we are mortal,
The moments we hear them we know we are still alive.
When we hear them passing over we know we are free.

But under the other, coloured wings of death
We hear and feel nothing to pain or alarm us:
They flatter and soothe and leave us unfree.
They would like us to believe they were wings of life.

They are wings of death which sing with the liberty
Of clockwork nightingales. They cool our skins
With air-conditioned breezes. They sing 'It is freedom
To choose us.' And they are leaving us unfree.

To say they do not matter is not to be free,
And to say 'I find them amusing' is not to be free,

And to watch them with a superior look but still
Stay watching is not to be free.

The black wings never change, you can recognise them
Always. But the coloured wings sometimes acquire
Transparency, they pose as natural,
Or they shift and alter like kaleidoscopes.

The black wings of death can never be defeated,
But you can do something about those coloured wings:
You can cut them by understanding what they are.
You can cut them with your indifference or your contempt.

You can cut them along the seams and through the stitches,
And tear them apart and let in the surrounding air;
Though to start this you need to be a bit free already,
Not a wooden bird yourself, flapping wings for money.

If you are free you will know where to find some scissors.

284 *Sonnet of a Gentleman*

How often have I courteously uncrossed
My legs to let someone in a tram pass by,
Only to kick him on the shins, thus lost
The whole point of the gesture! Some of my
Best efforts go for nothing . . . In a louts' age
A gentleman seems an anomaly,
Apt to incur bewilderment, even rage,
When his decency goes wrong.
                                        But truthfully,
To be gracious, charming, courtly, open doors
For ladies, raise one's hat, use fountain-pens
Rather than biros – all this is a cause
Requiring no apologia or defence,
And in my heart of hearts I know I *am*
Helpful, and needed; like the city tram.

Ground.   Plug, in an orange
                    Socket, turns a tape. Girl clerks
                         Proffer pens and smiles.

Mezzanine.   Use-less hall space; glass
                    Restaurant doors, sheets over
                         The band's bright weapons.

First.   Still you can't see sky.
                    A Person from Porlock: *Am*
                         I disturbing you?

Second.   With signs, a 'Plan of
                    Evacuation'. Useful!
                         Blue plug-socket here.

Third.   Miniature ferns
                    In a chipped bowl; one glass door,
                         Out of two, missing.

Fourth.   Green ashtray grained like
                    A breakwater. Carpets, clean.
                         Laurel in a pot.

Fifth.   Sky. A cloud looks through
                    Lace drapes; lift-buttons bleached and
                         Hollowed by fingers.

Sixth.   Two old men in hats,
                    Awkward with a lift arrived
                         Too soon. Carpets? Stained.

Seventh.   A wall clock wrenched out;
                    A rose in a jar wilting
                         Faster than its leaves.

Eighth.   The band-leader's room.
                 I know, seeing him go there
                      (All his summer life).

Ninth.   The last drone and gulp
                 Of the slow lift. I tread on
                      Carpets that fly air.

Roof Terrace.   What you feel, here you
                 Feel it: scared; free; bigger than
                      Tree, cart, ball, church, plums.

286   *Incorrect*

'Why must I pack and leave before noon today?'

'At Passport Control you used the ablative;
At Customs you opened your suitcase from left to right;
You summoned a taxi using the wrong fingers.
You did not pick up your key from the counter correctly
At Hotel Reception; you blinked in the lift; you did not
Remark on the arrangement of the bedside lamps.
Outside your window was a view of the marshalling yards
– You looked at it before teatime.
You went for a walk and did not pass the Statue;
Your failure to smile at them enough in the Gardens
Defamed the fun-hats of our Neo-Greens.
You went in to dinner promptly on the hour;
You dipped your spoon over-deeply in the soup;
You chewed the bread as if it was made of crumbs;
You cut your steak with unseemly emphasis;
You chose your dessert with unsuitable approval;
You sipped your coffee repeatedly moving your lips.
No doubt if we had watched you with greater attention
We would have found other rules infringed or neglected.
If we had monitored your mind when you slept,

383

We might have recorded inappropriate nightmares,
The wrong hobgoblins appearing in your dreams,
More shiftings of your blanket than were needed,
And a temptation to under- or oversleep
By numerous seconds.
                              Were you really not aware
Of any of these regulations before you came?
Did you not even trouble to open the Tourist Guide?
These are some of the reasons why you must leave by noon. . .
These are some of the reasons why you must never come back.'
'So what can I do, please tell me, to atone?
May none of these transgressions be forgiven?'

'You can do nothing. Things have gone too far. Besides,
Atonement has been abolished, and forgiveness
Is therefore redundant.
                              But – we make this clear –
Of course we shall be willing to overlook these crimes,
Of course we can permit you to stay as long as you wish,
Of course you may return whenever you like
– If you nod your head firmly, once, now. At the specified
            angle.'

287   *Vladimir*

Into the men's staff room of the second school
I taught in, in foggy nineteen fifty-five,
Through a term-ful of dripping days, with spiders' webs
Full of frost from October onwards on the bushes
In the gardens of the Council estate, would burst
At morning break, in drill suit, our P.E. man,
His whistle bouncing on his burly chest,
Shouting *Vladimir! My name is Vladimir!*
In a jarring deep bass voice I hate to think of
– That being a line recalled from a forgotten
B-feature film about Russian submarines

In the North Atlantic, threatening our liberty
To vote for Eden and commercial telly.
He'd fling the door wide open, bound in for coffee,
And boom out *Vladimir! My name is Vladimir!*
– Every bloody day. First we joined in, and then
It stopped being funny, and it never had been,
Though he kept it up well into January,
So giving himself a new nickname with the boys.

That same year, Mr, Sir, and (later) Lord
William Penney gave the world the British bomb,
On the Monte Bello islands; fall-out fell
Thirteen thousand miles away while our P.E. man
Felled fifteen maddened men with his stale joke
Which no one, from the start, had been amused by.
But – *Vladimir! My name is Vladimir!*. . .
If you could corner Plato – Aristotle –
Cicero – Thomas Aquinas – Goethe – Tolstoy –
And put it to them at some moment when,
Exhausted by high matters, they might *just*
Bend their minds to a small quixotic proposition,
I rather hope those sages might agree
That that man's joke (for which he got no knighthood,
No peerage either) had a slight moral edge
On what Lord Penney did, in that same year,
To keep fictitious Vladimir away;
And was a kinder gift to our mad world
Than all the cancers in the Indian Ocean.

The height-of-summer forests replete with surprise,
The very woodpeckers crying 'God bless our souls!'
– And our surprise, to burst out in the train
To the sunlight of a plain between rainclouds,
A space of streams and rocky villages
– And step down at the village where Herr Rasmusson
Took guests in a cabin bedroom beside the fields
On the Co-op gherkin farm he was manager of.

It was rain all night nevertheless,
But rain as one of the natural sounds
That partners any deep and healing silence,
And never infringes it. It drenched Herr Rasmusson's
Green lake of gherkin plants; but after breakfast
– Of sweet cold fish and onions and tomatoes
And crispbreads and butter and berry jam and coffee–
We sat and talked in English, discussed the gherkins

– And the sun came out! 'This is good, this is good,'
Said Herr Rasmusson. 'Now our chance to take the crop.'
'If it rain too big,' said Mrs Rasmusson,
'All the gherkins grow too fast, and in the wet
We cannot pick them, they grow into – "Marrows"?
The trucks that come to take them will *not* take them,
They are too big, no use collecting them
For the factory bottles.' 'Yes,' said Herr Rasmusson.

'If it rain too small, they not grow up enough
And we sit round lazy, my husband and myself,
My mother – "Mormor" – our son and all our workers,
We play draughts and wait.' 'Yes,' said Herr Rasmusson,
Looking out at the sun. And Mrs Rasmusson:
'The summer started dry, they were too small,
Now it rain too big, it never stop, we drown.'
'But it shine now,' said her husband, 'and we work. You too?'

We put on his recommended gloves because our hands
Would be grazed and torn by the plants, they could draw blood,
And we crossed the track to where the great leaves grew,
Sun-stained and -spotted, like huge maple leaves,
Cupping pure liquid ounces of rolling rain
That ran down in oily drops as you bent, and pushed
The undergrowth aside to get at the gherkins
On their prickly stalks of blotting-paper green.

You had to judge: If a gherkin was too large,
You plucked it all the same, but you threw it into
A separate bag for the uncollectables.
And if it was too small, and clung to its flower,
You left it to be picked in two days' time.
You looked for the happy medium, tried to see it
In a bottle of thirty in a downtown bar
– And carried it carefully to a wicker basket.

Where I crouched, the foliage swathed me, soaked my socks,
And my eagerness dragged the plants out of the soil
They had nearly grown out of anyway;
The best part was my cool, fastidious judgement.
When I stood, the sun hit me! Only we three
– My wife, young son and I – were exhausted already,
And easing our backs, a few dozen gherkins only
Having passed through our hands, strained and sore inside
                                              the gloves.

Herr Rasmusson, Mrs Rasmusson and Mormor,
And their workers old and young in Co-op sweatshirts,
Were away in a working line that had long outstripped us,
And were nearly up by then to the rocky horizon;
They had filled most of Mormor's woven baskets.
In about an hour we only filled one basket,
Though our cautious gherkins were all the proper size.
We stood and smiled, at a task only quarter-done.

We had tickets for the 11.10 to Oslo.
Herr Rasmusson came down from the top of the field:
'It is enough? You have done hard work for us,
You make many bottles!' His generous broad hand
Of thanks and leavetaking wore no protective glove,
His smiling jaw was stubbly with blond prickles.
We strolled away proud and happy in his praises,
Our own ungloved six hands all joined together.

– Except for our two outer hands, which lugged our cases.

289   *The Cities*

    I was born in one of London's various cities,
And travelled through others that I never could
Explore except from an upper-deck front seat,
In the time I was a nineteen-thirties child.

    Grown up from that, I learned to use the maps
Of more of them; but forgot to understand
What my own city told me, that outdated place
I thought I had left behind. When I go back now,

    I can feel inside myself something waiting, hidden
By time and the Red Routes and the roundabouts,
By the deaths of faces I grew up among
And lost the strength to know.
                    I like to think

    – Or fear to think it – that one day my city will
Disclose itself, its faces reclaim their focus,
Its culverted rivers flood the hypermarkets,
The cinema organs rise through the motorways.

Thing about girls was, they were everywhere!
They lived above furniture shops, alighted on
Your field of vision in recreation grounds,
And licked ice-creams by corner-shop entrances,
And sat in groups in the very same seats each day
Of the first bus home the moment school came out.
They could be the daughters of plumbers, or officers
In local government, or sit two rows in front
In the Regal, and you'd never seen *them* before.
There could be girl cousins with them, or friends who'd come
From a distant town, and you thought, *Please don't go back!*

Women are different, though, living with local
Government officers, married to plumbers, leaving
Cars on rainy superstore parking places,
With hardened furrows set in their twenty
-Nine year old faces; complicit in mortgages,
With futures on too-fragile salary scales.
I believe that women have never been girls at all,
Just women from the start, kept somewhere else
When the streets were full of girls from everywhere
– And finally released to do away
With girls for their lack of brutal obviousness,
Girls for their courage in being unusual,
Girls for their cheek in being their younger selves.

291   *Three 'O' Poems*

1.   *A Defence of Reading*

O in the spring the legs were out,
    And they were smooth and trim,
And every eye that saw them felt
    They must be out for him.

O in the spring the legs were out,
      And they were cold and pure,
And chastised the ambitions of
      The eyes that felt so sure

– But they declined to play the game
      The proud legs had begun,
And they could stare down anything
      Faster than legs could run.

Therefore the summer saw the legs
      Give up their cold disguise,
And sun themselves to frazzles for
      The catching of the eyes;

And thus it was the bolder eyes
      Could stare down easily
The flimsy ramparts of the legs,
      And have their victory,

Have it, have it and tire of it
      Much sooner than they thought,
And spend the autumn brooding on
      The truth the legs had taught:

That love is not as hard-won or
      As worthwhile as it looks,
And those that tell you differently
      Have only stared at books.

2.   *Ars Poetica*

O here we go a-gathering
      The samphire from the crannies,
Inside the little baskets woven
      For us by our grannies.

Two hundred feet below, the rocks,
    And up above, the spaces,
And here the wind that thumps us while
    The rain runs down our faces.

Yet still we edge down clutching
    Special clippers to collect it,
Hoping to find it hanging out
    Where no one would expect it,

Looking to catch it unawares,
    All richly green, and blooming
Within our fingers' nimble grasp,
    Before it sees us coming.

If gathering rosebuds should be quite
    A profitable doddle,
And nuts in May might sell O.K.,
    Our samphire brings in sod-all;

But following daily such a dread-
    ful trade to earn a living,
With every second on that cliff
    So cruel and unforgiving,

Is fine – as long as no one comes
    And asks us what we do there . . .
We'd have to say, Without our toil,
    Just who would know it grew there?

3.   *Against Mathematics*

O Sod sits up there on his bench,
    And when things are just awful,
Throws down some extra lumps of mud
    Pretending that it's lawful.

But though Sod's Law is petty, and
    Productive of frustrations,
In its odd way it does permit
    Of kindly deviations:

Where mathematics says *Man dies*
    Like all the other fauna,
Sod's quirky Law says *Live some more,*
    There's trouble round the corner.

Old Sod is sly but jocular
    – Plain fact and not a rumour –
But Maths by definition works
    Without a sense of humour;

And whereas Sod chucks mud with no
    Fixed rules for hour or season,
Maths functions logically by
    The ruthless clock of reason.

There is no mercy ever for
    The ones who starve in attics,
Victims of the inexorable
    Laws of mathematics,

But Sod at least has idle days
    When he provides some quarter
– And makes a happier study for
    Your able son; or daughter.

292 *Teashop '92*

O superfluous sprays of light on an esplanade!
The winter urn is cooling, the girl is closing:
I'm sorry, she says, *We are closing now.*

– But the customer asks about tea with such hope-less charm
That the girl is not resentful she cannot
Go home quite yet; perhaps go home any more.

This one can charm the birds down from the trees
So they thud to the ground in dozens, and the girl
Is second by second feeling wingless

– And she drops down behind the counter, behind
The fridge of coloured ices, small plastic skips
Full of scraped-at choices of lime, or tangerine,

Or rum-and-raisin. It drones while he drums his fingers
(Little finger up to thumb) and smiles and smiles.
The girl lies there and thinks, *Do I have a choice?*

With my head against the cartons of UHT?
With my eyes trapped by shelves lined by newspapers
Full of photographs of terrors I hadn't really

Ever noticed 'til this moment, one leg straight out,
One leg bent under, one thin arm free to move?
Could I lie here and hope he leaves, and closes

The door? she wonders. *I shall know if he's gone*
When the bell rings. Or should I push
The panic button, fast, for living help?

Or should I serve him? Over the sea, the sun
Goes through the bottom-line horizon, far away,
Below three colour-choices of January cloud.

293   *A Witness*

Did something drop down and move out over the shore,
Just now? In front of, then lost to sight in, the mist?
The colours in the perspective tell me nothing.
Did something occur that the light would not yield up?

– That was the final question of the day,
The seascape as usual resigned to dull entropy,
No spaced-out clouds forming up into glowing processions,
No cinematic gloriousness and hope.

– It might for a moment have been something falling there.
The day had begun, and was ending, blank. But at four-
Fifteen was there an unobserved low-tide success?
An Icarus landing on sand, getting up and running?

294   *Throwback*

Ridiculous no one told them they could stop:
At the extreme end of a corridor
Was the ballroom of what was a Grand Hotel,
Sold and left to the weather to shut it down.
I could curiously hear as we walked along it
(I and somebody else who might have been
Any one, I suppose, of a number of friends)
Certain amplified sounds. more amplified by echoes.
Turning out to be music. Surely it couldn't be
An orchestra still at it? It could be the wind?

But there, when we walked in over the fallen door
And across the plaster fallen from the ceiling
(As on one night of my early adolescence,
When I followed, at her suggestion, Dolores O'Leary,
Her real name, on VE-night, in Sportsbank Hall
As a flying bomb had left it) were a bride and a groom
Still dancing, still dressed in their wedding stuff.
To see them now, circling round, looking over
Each other's shoulders, didn't seem quite right.
Nor did their calling to me by *my* real name.

295   *Mosquito*

Fancy this in October, the last
Mosquito of summer left buzzing alone,
Its last fling in my room on the sixth floor
Of a tower block hotel; marooned like one
In his seventh decade with only the past
To look forward to, as the one sure

Topic he can buzz round with some old chum.
'I had a good bloody summer,' it seems to say,
'With waiter and bellman, and that prim peach
Who keeps the consultant's books across the way.'
And for one last sally it swoops and bites my thumb.
So I bite mine back at it, and reach

For a folded newspaper; all the same aware
How much I resemble it, my own small spites
And hopeless needs reduced to the last fling
Of one who doles out charm in sexless bites
To check-out girls and bank clerks as if to swear,
'Oh man, I buzz and suck like anything!'

How nice looking up, some cloudy afternoon,
To see that what has fallen suddenly
Is twilight, and an earlier chance to draw
The curtains while you have the energy.

Now everything falls, go down with it and give
Yourself to the gravity, putting up a show
Of warming wistfulness with the last leaves.
Fall hard, and stay there, waiting for the snow.

The nights are drawing in, nothing wrong with that.
The poet says: *Darkness cures what day inflicts.*
It is as normal to welcome winter back
As to loathe the spring. Popular interdicts

May forbid that preference, but snow walks are like
Illicit love with no one else betrayed;
Are like the joy, as you step out through the white,
Of the first alligator in the first everglade.

Harden your skin, then, for the rigorous spell
Between October and the April days
When the clocks go wrong again. Live for the thought
Of the bracing dark and the heavenly displays,

On frosty nights, of dotty groups of stars
You may sit and try to specify all night
– As if there were no tomorrow to dissolve
Their shining in dull anywheres of light.

297   *Sevens for Gavin Ewart*

(1916–1995)

Something Audenesque for a conclusion?
  In dignified, indented, limestone lines?
But in Wystan's geology hills were permanent,
  Whereas human geography constantly changes,
That being its only constancy. We reach plateaux in life
  When friends seem likely always to be there,
Changeless features in the landscape. And then –

There are places in poetry where nothing seems
Appropriate to write after the sudden dash
  Suggesting an interruption, or a shock:
The words halt dumbstruck in the mind, in blankness
  Of a sort you never showed. You had six days left.
Sat upright in a chair in the too-warm ward,
  You were checking proofs: 'I'm not on my last legs –

'I've work to do,' you affirmed, with the stern expression
  Reserved for the moments when you took exception
To some shabby behaviour or rotten rhyming.
  That look could be unexpected, the touchstone suddenly
Revealed that made you mentor as well as friend,
  Our example of someone never speechless in verse,
Never letting words fail you, or work remain unfinished –

Like your final quatrain, done on a day when 'not much
Poetry was coming', and putting the old and their carers
  Firmly in their place with rueful sentiments
Adapting Lewis Carroll. Seventy-nine
  Is 21 years longer than the average
Male could expect to live when I was 11
  (The NHS, we believed). Poets don't, these days –

Another wise thought of yours – need to push their careers
    By dying young. But cell and virus and blood-clot
Might have waited in some cases until four score
    (You had six years of the Second War, and then
Two decades of silence). And surely given us,
    For a little longer, your memory: of the famous
Far younger than we saw them, and of course –

    The legendary dead. E.g., Mr Yeats arriving
Late for *Sweeney Agonistes* in an attic theatre,
    Treading fatefully up the stairs to stand in the doorway
In cloak and hat as if he was some part
    Of the performance. Our memories, Gavin,
Will retain your own appearances at parties,
    Standing, as you preferred, in some quieter corner –

Forever Ewart's! The last time we talked at one,
    It was prosody, *New Verse*, and the Café Royal
We discussed, not conglomerate managers twitching
    The strings on which their puppets dance for cake . . .
With disgraceful energy you assured me this calling
    Was still the best; all your faith was firm in it.
– We'll try to keep that as we grieve and smile.

298   *Temper, Temper*

I chase a bug around a tree,
I'll have his blood, he knows I will!
– And yet the tree forestalls me with
The thought of all the chlorophyll

Flowing into those gentle leaves
That spread themselves above my head;
And so I cease to chase the bug,
And rest my aches and pains instead

Beneath its shade; and pass an hour
Where I can find tranquillity
With ample space for man and beast
– Comprising both the bug and me.

Of course I know that this bug took,
For sustenance, or on a whim,
Some blood from me, five minutes past,
But *need* I take some back from him?

In any case it might be mine,
And I shan't need it anyway:
It's hardly worth expense of spite
On such a genial summer's day.

Instead I'll pluck a shiny leaf,
Which, if he likes, the bug may take,
And thank me, as the equal of
The Buddha, or of William Blake.

299   *The Rassendyll Service*

No longer in the schedules. But you still see it
Through the proper binoculars at the right moment,
Laying down cylinders of steam for the off-sea winds
To disperse when it has passed; lighting tonight
The necklines of bays facing east before it veers
Inland across plains to where cities of porn shops, cathedrals,
Statues and archives solidify others' dreams.
Its passengers are always mysteries (the past
Will have seen to that) with an aura of being claimants
To whatever is impossible elsewhere.

At none of the junctions it stops at does anyone
Leave or join it, it stays proudly self-contained
And amazing to the gaze of excluded travellers
In small-hours stations. At dawn, a railwaywoman
On a country platform whirls on the end of a chain
An irrelevant key, while a young guard makes to wipe
A crumb from her lapel; and see, she smiles
A permissory smile you take in from your corner seat:
A cameo of unrehearsed perfection.
But they do not halt this train, and it moves onwards

Past even smaller halts where they reassure you,
With crimson sleeves horizontal in salute,
That everything in the kingdom is in order.
Then comes the last slowing-up, to the terminus
In the heart of your fantasy: a marvellous mayor,
As archetypal as the bishop with him
– Each renewed in his office for just this occasion –
Is welcoming you on the concourse, to drive you up
To the Metacontinental Hotel on Citadel Hill.
You sign the book with a gold pen you may keep.

At the threshold of the lift you feel the pressure
Of his hand of power on the shoulders of your suit.
He himself now closes the pantographic doors
And smiles you away and up, all gracious
Knowingness . . .
                    Then you're raising your head from where
You lay face downwards with someone on *such* pillows,
And recall that all the foregoing was how you got here,
That cryptic dangers wait outside the door,
That you haven't remembered the code word for going back
– Though meanwhile you look up, and above the bed-board

Is a picture of a great old train coming out of a tunnel.

Close-up: the handling of, the words about
How kites can be handled, practical talk
On when to tug less, or more, the stuff of string
And hooks; also how you need to walk
With good judgement of the breeze, when you turn to bring
A different angle to their flight without
Causing them to swoop down and slap the turf.

With fine eye-glasses you can stand farther off,
Subsume the exercise of skills, and wait
For the chance of any beauty you could remark
In one particular kite: look how it soars
With that red tail rippling figures of eight
To paint the clouds that watch the public park.

Back home, use kites when you want metaphors.

301   *She*

The latest conclusion: *Drink* is rapidly
Acquiring a me problem. The girl I presume
Most of any day to follow, but don't meet at all
– Last thing at night she is actually in the room
As the large hours shift into the small,
Sitting over there and (*Sex* is obsessed with me)
Watching these lines take their particular
Shape as my latest tentative report
On all that she means; laughing too readily
While the halo of my table lamp stops short
Of her hair, which would indisputably
Shine with it, if it could ever reach that far.

Two fifty-year olds, on their own – and a goal each?
I watch them from the stopped train . . . Must be some duel
They are acting out: the big thin bloke, out of reach,
Running hard, and the other chasing; who then, with a cruel
Tackle takes the ball, dribbles fast to the far far end,
All the time pursued by his slow loping scarecrow friend

Who is there first, naturally. His arms, long sticks,
Wave wildly in the goal to reduce its space
As he challenges this side and that; so his partner kicks
Too timidly, and this keeper falls with his face
Pressed hard on the ball, he loves it, he hoists it hard past
The other and gallops to follow it fast

– And so it goes on, and on, in that dusk of the day
Between six thirty-nine and about six fifty-eight,
When you can't really tell if people you're seeing may
Have had their tea, or haven't; and the light
Shining down on this pitch is like their faded
Back kitchen light when only a jaded

Glow stays on, over mangle and draining-board
Where the last groove wet from the stacked-up dinner plates
Has dried, and the air secretes a not-to-be-ignored
Pale radiance, like this courage of two old mates
Regarding life at fifty as much the same
Set of futile chances as their boyhood game.

303   *Sonnet at Sixty-four*

You think of the various things you've never done,
Like going to Greenland, or riding a horse
– Which is unlikely now, though you confess
That if well paid to play Kutuzov . . . And wasn't there one
Great idea you used to have, now of course
Too late to try for: a dignified progress,
Serving an honourable government,
To the House of Lords, relaunched with a different name?

Only yesterday I thought, Come to that, you've never spent
A few measly quid to have an epigram
Or a picture done in the form of a tattoo
On . . . some suitable organ. So I stopped on a yellow line
And scanned the small shop-window. And read this sign
– At last, the AIDS-free needle – here – for *you!*

304   *The Baron's Horse*

So there was I, woken up on the airy height
Of an eighty-foot steeple by my master – the story goes –
Shouting up at me from below, *We must move on!*
It's eight o'clock, and we must be moving on,
And you're stuck up there tied to a past when the snows
Of faith were at the full – ten o'clock last night!

'But I'm happier here,' I neighed back, as my hoofs
Slid, and grappled at the slates, 'I've known far worse
Dilemmas and qualms than this, this feels like comfort
To a horse who has seen and suffered, it's more like
    comfort –'
I have the ultimate shit-scared, fundamental horse,
It seems! he thundered. Drips dropped from all the roofs

As he ranted with no regard for *my* situation,
Some eighty comforting feet above the town,
Still slithering after the thought of the one God,
Or any available prophet of the one God
– Until, with a shot, my master brought me down
To his earth again; and to pure imagination.

305   *Dogs*

She was only a postman's daughter, but . . .
She was only a publican's daughter, but . . .
She was only a tobacconist's daughter, but . . .

She was only a lighthousekeeper's daughter . . .
– They had what it takes, and it seems the world allowed
Them to use it. Were their humble fathers proud?

Did their daughters learn it from them, take after them?
Or were their girls defying them, getting blamed
For leaving those old men bitter and ashamed?

What of their mothers? We are never told
Which way, if any, they wanted their girls to go.
What part *they* played we never get to know.

Their mothers were like dogs that never barked
When footfalls fell during nights as black as ink.
What kept them quiet? Whose daughters were they, do you think?

Only thin planks over the frayed processional
Of white-green waves; and walking, it's possible to prop
One's body up with the wind swaying out-of-season rows
Of unlit, coloured bulbs as if they were skipping ropes,
But made of electric wires.
                            From the vantage-point of the pier,
The town takes up its old Edwardian stand on the cliffs,
Insisting that pleasure and health can still combine here as when,
Before Shangri-La and Atlantis were sold in packages, chartered,
Gentility arrived in the high horseless carriages
They mounted mudguards into, as they had into those pulled by
    horses.
The sea is just as bracing, and even some views of the town
Are what one's grandfather saw . . .
                            But matters like music and crime
Are updated now. The radio, stood on the café shelf
Beyond the 'Home Made Pastries' displayed in plastic foil,
Thunders a cruder love song, then announces that *a man*
Has been found guilty of selling drugs to schoolgirls at a school gate,
And will be sentenced tomorrow.
                            A red-bloused manageress
With shiny stockings walks by, and receives some feedback from
The young boy serving coffee in mugs from a screaming urn,
While the wind that controls our lives clears everything away,
The spume on the beach, the litter, a pedestrian's antique hat
– All of this seen through the swing-door when it opens onto the
    blast
And the vertical lines of the planks all hurl themselves towards
The slopes of the town where the church, with its restored red brick
Crowns the huddle of red bed-and-breakfasts that live on around its
    spire.
Those all match her scarlet blouse as she answers the boy, 'Oh
    ri-i-ght!'
And her walk across the floor is dignified and correct,
While the sea below goes on presenting propositions

Which the beach accepts with patience.
                              All of this, she and I, and the boy,
And a no-doubt familiar man who comes striding into the place
To order 'A flapjack and tea' in a wild falsetto voice,
A daily habit – we are all sentenced, whatever our plans,
Like the criminal peddling drugs to the chattering girls at the gate;
Though the manageress later on, in quite another role,
As lover not manageress, may say, 'You may stroke my thigh
If you promise not to stop there.'
                              The cliffs running out to the west
Dwindle down along the shore, perspective works like that,
Yet increase on the horizon, quite logically because
They are much higher one mile away than they are in front of the
     pier
– And it's this perpetual trick that phenomena seem to achieve
Of being unexpected that makes it hard to bear
The sentence we are under.
                              Because, if everything
Were regular and the same, if routines never changed,
We might bow our heads and say when the time arrived, 'It's enough,
I'll go quietly.' But this is a world that constantly alters and shifts,
The sea casting up other gravel, the mad falsetto man
Going absent for a day, then turning up to demand
'Coffee and baked beans on toast' on Thursday that makes you resent
The fact that it has to go, that the end-of-September blinds
Must finally clatter down and darken the sea's great stage
– And worse, exclude you from it.
                              Yes, deny you your corner seat
On which, a week or so later, the sun could be shining so hard
That your coffee might heat up again, the page after page that you
     write
Make luminous sense after all, and the red-bloused manageress
Stroll across with a different idea, mere stranger though you may be,
Like a cliff increasing again. And not in the distance now.

In the key-cutting shop I thought of the following:
The scream of a key being cut as representing

The pain of opening dangerous doors onto . . . Where?
Then the thought of someone beyond one door, sat there

Expecting my intrusion, it being no shock
As my sudden arrival via a changed lock

Had been anticipated for several years . . .
Next there comes on stream an image of what appears

To be a hand I raise to my lips to kiss,
On the other side of the coffee line; and in this,

As I release the hand, and it falls back
Not-so-slowly to her side, I can see the slack

Downward tilt of the Second World towards
The Third, something surely that accords

With the maxims of Harvard. Thus, obviously,
The ambivalent smiling face the key had brought me

Was proposing a joint venture I should decline,
And the tannoy sound of a conscience I knew was mine

Said: Take the key from the machine, leave it uncut
Leave the door, wherever it might be, silent, shut,

And imagine the ethnic proverb might speak true:
Before bash down brickwork think of polluted view.

The man on the bus to the beach was Chinese.
He was certainly not. He was disguised
As a Chinese. Did you not see how he read
His little Li-Po edition from front to back?

But the only prints on the sand were those
Of a horse. – Or those left by a tall man
Taking careful strides with horseshoes attached
To the soles of cheap wellington boots.

So the third man in the saltmarsh was never
– *There at all?* Quite. Was never there at all.
Because he did not relax his guard and walk
Away. He stood still. He was a scarecrow.

And there was nothing wrong with the old red kiosk
Outside the village store. *But I think there was!*
No! Briggs was standing in it using
His mobile phone to *persuade* us that there was.

All that nodding and shaking of his bald head
At what Carstairs was saying . . . – Yes, messages
To his accomplice on the distant dunes.
He could do nothing when the sun went in.

And the vital missing *element, just*
As important as the rest? – The absence
Of a haystack near the gate. Had one been there,
He would have shoved our needle into it.

Then, you see, those clouds . . . They were *painted* on the sky
In the manner of the artist Magritte.
– *But how could you tell?* – On longer inspection,
I found crucial errors in the forgery.

Bad day, forecast *Sultry*, the flag
On the pole above the Russian
Roulette Club in the High Street limp,
Their bar shut, its blinds drawn, too few
Proven fatalities lately
To attract new members.
                              Try *Life*
Instead? With some rival outfit
Like *Aerobic Death Restriction?*
Well, you could all the same end up
With a craving for risk – years lost
You could have glutted on it.
                              No,
Cross the High Street, and take a look.
On the door of that place it says
Pleasant club requires risk-takers
Less gone on money than seeking
The hazards of high art.
                              The gun,
Primed by Amanda, Natalie,
Cindy (whoever's on duty
On the fateful week-end) has *pen*,
Or *stave, brush* or *chisel* sprayed in
Blood, sperm or tears on its barrel.
On the wall in the corner of
The agonized back saloon where
The baize table stands, among pinned
Banknotes with the price on each face,
You might find Benjamin Franklin
Looking jealous on his greenback:
The frown of power, yes; but scared white.

310 *Facial*

Inaccurate foray, in front of the bathroom mirror,
With blunt scissors angled too awkwardly near the eyes,
That see an infinite snow of hairs spread across
The sheet of white cardboard held widely under my chin . . .

I tap the edge of the card with the closed blades,
And all the hairs shift together like filings pulled
Into sentient activity by a magnet.
Dropped into the bathroom basin they cluster and clog

The outlet like a dampened pubic bush,
A mesh that looks wiry enough to scour the bowl with.
I pick up this excrement, a grey-brown ball
To flush, or dump in a bin, when I have finished;

But I can't say how long that will take, say how much longer
I should spare to go on attempting to reach a state
When I look just trim and suitable; not, as now,
More exposed and less composed than when I started.

311 *Sonnet in Sloppy Joe's*

A red-bead message runs all along the wall:
*For the Best American Breakfast the Flame
-Grilled Burger, This is the PLACE.* Lids of some tall
Coffee-pots with chrome knobs on look much the same
As Kaiser Wilhelm helmets; they don't make sense,
But they've used them by filling them up half-way
With clusters of coffee-bags, like a pretence
Of fungi on trees.

And soon that girl will say,
'Mum, did you see that Tammy Wynette had died?
What will Grandma think? – 'Oh, she knows already,
She heard it on the 6 a.m. news. She cried,
And said, "I think I'll have a glass of sherry."
But six is much too early for sherry, Mum.
"Not for me", she said. "Not for me." And she *had* some.'

312 *Burial of 5-7-5*

He had often said about secrets, 'When you dare
To give one away, the hearer's never grateful, you yourself
Are condemned in the information you devalue.'

But today is the opened umbrella,
Black and dry in the bath above downstairs talk, low-toned,
Concerning a safe route afterwards to lunch.

In both the wing-mirrors in the middle lane
All the cars we see are the same, or compatible, colours; through
The windscreen we only catch the hearse.

At the perilous gates, in the chapel, no one
Admits a personal link with these transactions, we are there
To dissociate ourselves, and respond to music.

We stare out the cemetery wind. Some stumble
Around the wound in the earth, but reach hands to the shoulders
Of others stumbling with mud on their hands.

On the road again: 'Did you pick up a pamphlet?
"Society for the Unexpected Enhancement of Flowers?" Or this:
Sex Now, or in the Hereafter? A Debate?'

411

In the restaurant, pegs for balaclavas, and the lovely
Virgin he discovered on that last night (with her death's-head
   earrings)
      Recurring with an Air Vice-Marshal not her father.

      Then the bill, put down in a leather-cased
Limited edition of the manager's elegies . . . And the waiter's silver
      Bangle sliding down to his knuckle bones.

313   *One Year Today*

Those days in summer when we condescended
To stay at the Summer Palace . . . They didn't turn out
As we assumed they might from the name it had.
Sunshine was rare. We shivered. And there's no doubt

That the days in winter when we reportedly
Enjoyed the Winter Palace, frankly those
Were scarcely frozen enough for the name to apply.
We perspired in humid mists. There were no snows.

As for spring and autumn, they did not require
Their own palaces. They were more ambivalent
Than even the other two seasons. So we swanned through power
With pretend-demarcations. Government

Was in the minds of the governed, made-over faces
And resolute postures suggesting a firm, a nice,
Distinction between right and wrong.
                              And tell me, who raises
Banners when imprecision looks so precise?

In my dream, a new dream, I still have some,
I was in the Apennines – where I haven't been;
I'd in fact been to the cinema and home to sleep
In the Carpathians – in this dream I'd come,
After slogging up some foothills admiring the scene,
To a small mountain hut, no more than a heap
Of stones flung together to keep the winter out . . .
I stood there, and gave a loud unanswered shout.
Inside not, as in the film I'd seen, a wall
With a shepherd's family photograph; instead
A new London tube map pinned up, with a small
Arrow aimed at 'Bank'; and above, in day-glo red,
The words of a less-than-cryptic message: 'All
Your life, wherever you are, YOU WILL BE HERE', it said.

315   *On My 66th Birthday*

The speeding of footsteps, and the shouting
Up an outside stair: the siren race begun
To break down a fire-door and enter. Someone
Locked in to be rescued? Some thing
Occurred there too late to forestall it?
The rumours breed in our block, opposite,
As duty hurries to the place, its hard
Boots and fire-axes and counsellors
Always ready to act on these sudden clamours

... One day it will be there *before* the word
Has formed in the head, and long before the key
Has been clicked in the lock. The emergency
Call will have been, yes, spotted in advance
Pulsating on the screen of the Guaranteed
Death Prevention Unit: *You have all you need*
With your sheet of peel-off stickers. Take no chance,
There are plenty for whenever you want them, to keep
In your wallet, desk diary, car. Awake. Asleep.

316   *Avalanche Dogs*

At a whistling instruction from its trainer,
The little dog leapt at the large bank of snow,
Sniffed and barked and scratched, and its trainer helped it,
And through a hole they made the crowd could see
A face, that soon turned out to be Mrs Sundquist's.

My cat, and all my previous cats, have warned me
Against giving undue respect to any dog
Or credence to its talents. Did I listen too much?
This dog was thrown things for showing off its flair,
Though not many people seemed to value the sacrifice

Donated by Mrs Sundquist, who was covered
With snow again for a second dog to find her
– All this being done to show the ability
Of avalanche dogs to get Mrs Sundquist,
Or you or me perhaps, out of mountain snows,

In this case in the Lappland Arctic region,
Where every husky in the dog-sled teams
Knows left from right . . . And a third dog, and a fourth,
Mrs Sundquist being buried and reburied
Time and time again in the square outside People's House,

And people applauding the dogs, yet not Mrs Sundquist
When she finally came out from her hour-long incarceration
In the twilight drift.
                    I clapped my own soft gloves,
And one or two others took up the applause
– But which of us had brought anything to throw

To Mrs Anna Sundquist, dog's best friend?

317   *Duty Poem*

Avoiding the cluttered table, I pause awkwardly.
It isn't the gift of the image of August snow
Threading through the foreground steam that rises now
From the drink held to my lips. And it's not,
This time, from just a pleasure in pausing. But
Because I have seen one truth concerning Duty

– It need not be an escarpment one has decided
To draw deliberate breaths for, about to see
If muscles and sinews have the energy.
And it isn't so much the case of having to set
Aside some advantage one plotted for months to get.
It's the tiny inertias that ought to be roused and tidied

– And when that's done – Mankind! Such a flat
Smooth, emptied table-top is within one's range . . .
Was ever anything so clean, clear, strange
-ly resolute? Stretching for miles in front of the eyes
Without reproach, or guilt, or compromise?
. . . And you wish, you wish, you wish it would stay like that.

Not the same week every autumn, but the same
Place and surprise: clouds and clouds all day,
At six made over to encroaching dark
– And then this avenue which, for a spell,
We have driven along (planted by Communists
With the decent motive, that time, of providing
A windbreak on a windy plain) suddenly
Lights up our way through the dying afternoon,
As the breeze blows, turns, and flattens the leaves
On their yellow sides, so they provide a wide
Gold illumination, a rush of light.

                                        It gives

A ceremonial radiance to a road
Which once more looks as if it still might offer
A future with possibilities. So does
The instinctive raised thumb of liberal well-wishing
From the shepherd, returning our wave of thanks
When he barred his bleating gang for our car to pass,
Folding down at the end into a fist of hope.

319   *Grain*

Today sun, frost – and restlessness.

                                    Room to room

I walked with my friend and our clinging shadows reached
Right out to the walls. But in the cellar's gloom
They couldn't find us, so we went untouched
Down the steps to look in a sheen of water,,
Seeped in from the lake. At its edge – unsteady –
Shivering – I stopped. I sensed that ice might cover
Even these reflections soon, as the day turned cloudy,
And – *December*, I reflected, *month of my first*
Clear memory of winter . . .

Back then, as well,
Shadows clung to us, boy and friend, dispersed
As we slipped them in the cellar. Skies were set to fall,
Exactly as today. Now too, I'll go
Back up alone to walk the road outside,
Take the touches of the dizzying dots of snow
On my held-out hand, think of loves and dreads and angers
As I did at seven.
                    Frost and snow, unchanged, abide.
All that alters is the grain of my outstretched fingers.

1999, 1939

320   *The Nostalgia Experience*

What a great idea!
                    – Yes, an entire block, shelf on shelf
Of rentable double rooms. And here, the one your
Own card was swiped for, a payment which guarantees
Your admission as a *bona fide* user
Of the past. In those squares you inked in were
Print-outable names and authentic memories
Which someone else would complement on their own sheet
– And already tonight, in Room No. 444,
Is a distant name who filled in for you, *yourself!*

Old newspapers line the drawers, the same harmonics
Of empty hangers are sounding tremblingly,
In tune with the underground trains. All that it needs
Is this feel of candlewick, the nylon pillow,
And one further thing, that lamp outside the window
No curtains ever shut out . . .
                    As each hour leads
Slowly back into the next, there's *your* chance to meet
In a virtual past; and touch where there used to be
Erogenous zones . . . Infallible mnemonics.

321 *Dressing*

The first pit of the day. A moment
When the hole in a much-worn life is like
A hole in the pocket of what I'd intended to wear
To leap over that, a gap down which
Certain things had dropped which I'd stored not
Remembering – pens, peppermints, paper-clips
– Three aspirins put down as deposits on
Anxiety-free hours – my Membership Card –
And look, 50p! With all of these in my hand,
I reviewed the stretch ahead: unpromising,
But coloured with small surprises now, didn't
They shine, too. Were there hopes in the margins
I suddenly could see my existence was framed in?
It would need to be tested.
                                        I set them out,
These reserves, on the table before I open the curtains:
A scarecrow army sentried against daylight.

322 *Antonio: an Epilogue*

The company, I am very pleased to say,
Has survived a troubled year in excellent shape
To face the challenge of the global market.
The rebrand and relaunch under the name
'Sea Pageants plc', with the support
Of capital accruing from court proceedings
(More of which in a moment) has been successful.

Safety checks on all vessels have revealed
No fault in any, though I would accept
That communications technology needs improvement.
(The captain of one ship, the *Enterprise*,
Remains suspended on full pay, pending
The apprehension of the two Moorish sailors
Responsible for its loss on the Goodwin Sands.)

The most serious threat to us during the year
Was, of course, the attempt at a corporate raid
By the Shylock Group, much noted in the media
On the Rialto. Prompt recourse to the law
Fought off that one, and a great deal is owed
To our legal experts that we emerged unscathed,
Also leaner and fitter for the experience.

Now for the future: Our Private Finance Initiative
With the State of Venice and its noble Duke
Is off to an excellent start. We can thus provide
Substantial salary rises, options and bonuses
(Financial and in kind), all well-deserved,
To the directors, whose unswerving loyalty
Has seen us through an uncertain period.

I shall, if I may, end on a more personal note.
This has, for me, been a year of stress and trial.
I have been the unhappy subject of *such* quarrels!
They have taken their toll . . . I have seen the wilderness
And its beasts in another light . . . Am I, are any of us,
Better men (or women)? Will our deeds now shine
More brightly in a naughty world for this?

323   *Microcosms*

The broken tape-end flap-flaps at the place
Where it snapped in mid-bar and left the ear empty.
Lots of days the same: left listening for a conclusion
That doesn't ever come, like this, like this –

Next day I saw, on a pavement alongside the Great
Highway of Life, a tail wagging a dog.
Though the specialty of dog had been neglected,
This hound was terribly proud of the strength of its tail.

My birthday comes round. After a meal, I tear
The dotted-line corner and release a sixteen-fold
Peculiarly cool and clammy refresher pad.
Does this mean I am still on an outgoing flight?

And then this doling-out, to the conscience-fretted,
With people taking and running, in all directions,
Their fists clenched round the coins in their little pockets
To keep them safe from other takers and runners.

I cancel the info-deficit on the screen
And look up at the mock-balustrade on this thirties bank.
So why this embellishment? Well, a balustrade was art,
And a bank was not. So it once thought it needed it.

Avoid smart ripostes on the phone. You can restart letters,
But never recall your phone-call apophthegms.
They will cling to someone else's memory like
A little dog in rhapsodies over an ankle.

No dodging the brutality of associations:
The arcade war-game playing a snatch of Webern,
The boys at the burger counter wearing surgeons' gowns,
My father's dead face driving the tube train home.

Though life still provides little leases: I press,
Then turn, the bulb in the rusty socket – it holds.
I step down, switch on – and it glows. This outcome
Was unforeseen in yesterday's Business Plan.

Or this image from a black-and-white film: a girl
Hears a bell ring and hurries to a bare brick wall
In a darkened garage; stops; lets it ring; saves
Her honour, as we hoped, with the unhooked receiver.

324 *Leaving the World of Pleasure*

I gave up on the Mall of All Desires.
I thought it was pushing too much pleasure at me.

It was also other people's pleasure, thank you,
Not something I'd dreamed and chosen for myself.

They'd like to relaunch it for me, but they can't.
There's no new, lasting desire after twenty-five.

After the Mall, I saw the attraction of sorrow.
There was more scope in it for quenching old desires.

And it seemed to have a border, with happiness
On the unattainable other side of it.

325 *Incident on a Holiday*

The cat between the tables is not worth attention,
But the most of *us* is closed in plastic now,
Magnetic so we stick to their powerful fingers.
I have to swipe to be a citizen.
I have to stand still while they target me.

Though one night on a coast of this vast and
Increasing inattention, a disco selling
Illusions to themselves for a sizeable profit
Goes up in flames in the small hours
– A blaze of interest on the coast opposite.

In this hinterland, however, no one explains it,
Not even the backstreet barber, the big
Conspiracy theorist, who avoids my eyes
In his pocked mirror; or the extrovert licensee
Working faster but very quietly, mopping his bar;

Not even the check-out girl taking one by one
The grapefruit rolled down in a ritual
To break the boredom of her dreadful day
And start her chatting – she doesn't as much as smile
When I ask her, 'Who would trash a lovely disco?'

– And claim the insurance on all the pretty dreams?
What sort of destructive decency? There was
No cc-tv watching, no bar code bleeped
When some unpoliced fingers scratched the match into flame.
And now there is a gap in the esplanade . . .

Though otherwise things go on pretty much the same:
The barber thanks me and tells me to Take Care,
The licensee puts my drink down – 'There you go!' –
The waters eject our pollution onto our shores,
And the cat, without e-mail, susses the customers

In the Sea Café, and refuses their burger bits.

326   *Knock Knock*

Do I need them? The glasses on my face?
The coat snatched to cover me? Not questions that I pose
Warm indoors while thinking *Nude is beautiful*,
But having unlocked the front door onto space,
And stared out into it to discover all
Of nobody there, and no neighbour to tell me whose

Loud knocking that might have been. I feel quite bold,
Because I don't shiver . . . Except I *can't*, my skin
Has suddenly felt content with nothing more
Than taking on, like clothes, the outer cold
– And the notion of re-shutting the opened door
Seems to be receding. With no one to let in,

I could go on standing in the freezing air
While my will to speak or move drained right away,
And the dark fastened hard on my illuminous
Nakedness. And then, if I called, 'Who's there?'
And heard – 'Bonaparte!' I'd say, 'Ridiculous!
Bonaparte *qui?* . . . 'Bon appartement a louer.'

2000s

327   *September 1939*

I walked into the garden afterwards:

Away up there the soft silver elephants

                    hovered   peculiarly

The wireless had gone over to
A band . . . Or a short feature?
Whichever, I didn't listen.

My mother listened on, half-listened on,
And was thinking, as she watched me from the window.
She told me that.

There was no one in the gardens on either side,
And I too thought: *It will be different now.*

The elephants' noses wrinkled in the breeze.

328   *Dialogue of the Believing Gentleman and the Atheist Maid*

The Gentleman:

You crossed your legs and gave no reason why,
A moment ago. We were talking about the high

Implications of great art. I said 'They are religious',
A point of view you called 'preposterous'.

But I love the St Matthew Passion, I love the Mo-
na Lisa, both of which surely show

The power of a Higher Being. Then George Herbert – he
Who chastised wealth and pomp and vanity –

His work, for me, is intrinsic, and surely God
Decreed that it should exist? To me it's odd

To find some – Well, to find a girl like *you*
Who doesn't have any inkling of the true

Religiousness of Great Art. – And one more thought begs
An answer still: Why did you cross your legs?

The Maid:

In bed with you I could cure you of God;
But that wouldn't be to deprive you of Michelangelo's
David, or of the Resurrection
Symphony (so named), or of the Holy Sonnets.
It's 'God' I'm banishing, not the works of man
(Or woman, naturally.) – Including your Gerard Man-
ley Hopkins, great nature poet.
                                    In bed we'd watch
Late dust coming in, as we'd leave a window open
To catch the pollen of the evolving flowers,
The dust from the roadworks, and from the crematoria
Cresting the bland peripheral hills of London
– Particles of our impermanency, but
Shot through with such infamy and pleasure, sent
Up by the tumult of the lovebeds where
Those who love love love Telemann as much.

In a neglected Utopian black-and-white film
Which dates from the nineteen-thirties, a beautiful
Young girl sits in a smart bright restaurant
To which she has been escorted by an old man.
He has a trim white beard and a cunning charm,
And one may assume he planned this carefully.
She had been alone in her cold, bare, silent room.
Here is warmth – and flowers, champagne – and a gypsy band.

Insofar as he is audible above
The deafening silken-shirted Utopian gypsies,
She is listening to him. He is saying, 'Every young woman
As beautiful as you should have three lovers:
A twenty-year-old for passion,
A forty-year-old for passion and experience,
And a sixty-year-old for passion, experience
– And wisdom' (thus the sub-titles render it).

She being a sharp-witted girl, as well
As a beautiful one, she rejoins, 'So which are *you*?'
He smiles, and is about to answer her question
With words of cunning charm that will change her future,
When the waiter interrupts them. He wants their order.
He is not the suave waiter you get in unreal films,
He is slow, and lethargic, and derives *no* interest
From the customers as a salve for his tedious task.

The timing has been ruined, the moment passes
And it can't be recovered. The old man does not seduce her,
She does not marry him and inherit millions
From his trade as an insurer; and launder them
Into a salon for young post-Dadaists.
To attain the ideal, first disperse all crude illusion.
The man who made this bitter-sweet comedy belonged
To the school of directors known as 'Utopian realists'.

330   *Closed Sonnet*

Adequate reasons for the door left open:
The breeze all last night slowly working it open;
The leaving of it by someone – like this – open;
Or 'on the latch', thus intentionally open;
Which would have meant it was certainly open
For someone else to enter or return; though it is an open
Question exactly *when* they fixed it open,
Because no man or woman – or dog with open
Eye pretending sleep – was watching . . . But then – look – OPEN
It says on this side but CLOSED on the other, the open
-ness therefore being relative.
                              So, tell me, did you open
The page at this moment because you wanted some open
Air to enter your head? If so, you may open
At the next page now, describing a window. Open.

331   *Anita 1944*

This refers again to Anita, she
Who was in an earlier poem. We
Never spoke, and I wrote it without praise
Of all her grace among the bygone boys

In those 1940s . . . But to-night I can see her bike,
On the easy pedals of which she mounted high
And rode away from the gang up Shorndean Street.
See it once more, and recall how I dreamed the sleek

Style of her body for a long long while
Before I would think of dreaming it in rhyme.
– Now there revisits, too, her pregnancy
By a legal husband, and the memory

Of her managing a pram with the aid
Of her practical mother as day by day they made
Their way up the same street, the Mum advising,
Anita in the fold, submitting, dying.

Awful to save her as a vision of
Fulfilment that needed nothing approaching love,
Just the dark fumblings of insomnia
When the maths wouldn't come out . . . Then I think of her

As perhaps alive? – Yes. Thankfully unaware
That in these memories she needs to share
Commemoration with the ack-ack sites
That kept me more awake on late June nights.

332　*Thank you Trails*

In the dream, I am heckling – or ignoring
By just talking through them – the commercials.

But what do I do when the 'trails' start advertising
My own future dreams! Coming SOON to all the screens!!?

– Like the one about the waitress in the old café
Where they stopped having waitresses thirty years ago

– She says, 'Come into the bookshop next door
At five thirty-five, I'll wait by the poetry shelf'

– Or the dream which allows me to keep an assignation
I denied myself one Polling Day before that

– When I'm knocking on hundreds of unresponsive doors
And foregoing the one door where I had a chance

– Or the even earlier one where I long to be
Like several envied sixth-form friends from school

– Fifty-five years ago, on the Geography Field Trip,
Described by one of them the following week

– Those dorms at the Centre where the two sexes fought
With pillows well on into the lovely small hours

– And the thought of those bushes he hadn't gone to with girls
But some had, and therein started their adult lives

– Which did not exactly work out like Geography Field Trips
In the wilds of Surrey; this dream was not retrievable

– And hardly produced with the same innocence
In films about later sixth-form generations

– With all the new unrecognised glamour faces
And soft-porn cuts from kissing to bed to clifftop

– And was therefore unique (and if I remembered the title
I'd see it when it came to the Finchley Phoenix)

– Oh thank you cinemas, oh thank you dreams,
Oh thank you trails I never want to talk through.

333   *The Secret Hats*

O dentists, no need for your Santa Hats in August!

If you cannot love me in a corporate hat . . . then I'll remove it

Post coitum no market for hats with feathers

The wedding pics in the locals: the frigid veils, the bridegrooms'
trilbies past lust already

Near her traffic cushion, slow down for Tania raising her champagne –
her paper hat out of the Pisces cracker

Who was it held open the twentieth swing door in succession? It has
to be the gentleman in the black hat

Come out from that wall and put your lid on, post-box. Be a pillar of
real communication

'My apologies!' – Thus the passenger in the hat, as he answers the
mobile lent him against his wish

In fewer memories daily, Mariela's hat. All we ever saw above the wall
as she strode into the Bursary

When he started his new religion what hat did he wear? The one that
still means the worship of Wobbly Hats

The scattered ashes of my deerstalker friend as they plaster the hated
ground elder

With the skewer, make more holes in your belt. Here you need *both*
hands to hold your hat on in the wind

In the windy street, is the vendor's hat really holding down that pile of
papers? Only with a stone inside

So why do they gather in coats and hats at the corner? To rename the
street after a headgear guru

334   *Dynasty*

The small thin ultimate glasses tuned with vermilion,
Or sometimes with ultramarine, trickled in
From the darkest bottles the cellar corners keep

– Our traditional postlude, stored and guarded
By a dynasty of pale and courteous faces
On whom the hereditary rights have been

Exceptionally bestowed; including the right to wield
The duster with the crest to catch away
The cobwebs of the intervening year,

And the ancient worn-out leather that gloves the hand
That twists the cork. *In piam memoriam,*
Or Absent Friends. Whatever. We toast the dead,

We toast the living, we toast each other.
We are nostalgic, so we toast Nostalgia!
It jogs old memories, it warms old spleens,

It outlasts the courteous, pale expressions
Of humble grandfather, father and son
As the dynasty passes the bomb from hand to hand.

335   *Death and Girls*

You reached out a hoping
Hand, articulate in
Every finger, to
Another hand or to
An unpierced ear or to
A navy-blue tight waist.
Then you tried for some skin
Without a crucifix

434

On the white space below
The neck above those, oh
Those . . . And it reached nothing.
And it never did then,
That being in nineteen
Forty-nine.
                    When the brain
No longer moves the hand,
Is it more bearable
When it's past all hope, past
Even the hope of touch?
With all it feels for quite
Incontestably gone
Out of reach? *Out of reach?*

336   *Vocational*

It's black-and-white and jumps, and the sound-track drones
With out-of-date experience. They all speak
In ancient Yorkshire accents, broad flat tones
It took them not much practice to get right.
The band goes slowly through an old-world song.

Later a boy leaves a girl at a garden gate
With a good-night kiss she refuses to prolong.
'Did you see those good-looking chaps in the hall tonight?
One asked me to dance. He asked Jean for a date!
They were from the *colliery*.'
                              This was the idea:

That men were needed to work six days a week
Down the mines, so miners got the girls. But here,
In our new world, girls dance upside down while a guy
In shades raps, growls and smirks, and rests
His hands on a car wheel. Then the girls deny

Gravity no longer, and resume their breasts
The right way up. Some casino you've never found
Is where they'll all finish. Life means: to shirk
Life for its vanities, you have to shave
With a VIREX razor, and not slave underground.

Long before Love and Music came love and work.
The girls can always be got to sing and dance
For the right kind of job, or that is what
The publicity says will happen . . .
                                    Now that he has
(With all the jumping screens turned off) his chance

To address the wordface in the dark, and scrape
At its enduring surface, seriously
Trying to work out how such things take shape,
Will he know why, at the window, all he can see
Is one girl walk past whom he hasn't got?

337   *The Faith Fair*

My Dad was rather short, and he carried me
On his shoulders so I could tell him everything.
'Watch the Bull Courting Europa!' The crowd was dense,

But I did my best to describe things. The second day
Was 'The Gentlemanly Swan Meets the Lovely Leda!'
Same man, same woman, just the costumes different.

I told Dad that, but he wanted to come back
For the third day as well: 'Guaranteed Appearance
Of the Holy Ghost, First Time Here. Feed Him Yourself!'

The crowd was thicker than ever, the man wore
Feathers as for the swan, but fewer now.
I had to tell my Dad that the woman looked

Just as gratified, but that the show lacked spirit.

(for Dennis Saunders)

I am writing this down on a late June evening
In the future we talked about. It's midsummer,
Now as then. The air is still humid, the treetop colours
Are the same as they were at that time, untouched
By any change time might have made. The moment
Feels the same as when we stepped out on the terrace

Fifty years ago, for air, and looked back in from that terrace
At our past, deliberately. For me, the present evening
Has stopped at that sudden recall of the moment:
Saunders closes the glass door on our Midsummer
Party and the dancing, and we both stand there, untouched
By time. I feel it all as I did then, its colours,

Lamps and music – not knowing the colours
Of another world were waiting beyond the terrace
Den and I were standing on, a somewhere untouched
By our youthful energies. That those evening
Sounds of seventy-eights on that midsummer
Night of our last week at school are ending at that moment

We do not understand, it does not seem a moment
For growing that much older in. We look at the colours
Back inside the room, hear the sounds of our midsummer,
And find them sufficient; from that redbrick terrace
They appear to stretch out beyond our evening
And claim all the growing darkness, a place untouched

And ready for their brightness!
                          Our night could not stay untouched
For long. There would come for each of us some moment
To alter everything in less than an evening,
And disclose another future. The dancing colours
Inside the room called us back, but the dusk of the terrace
Predicted (we did not know) a dark to cancel midsummer,

And forestall our inheritance of *any* midsummer.
We could not see, we who were so untouched
By experience, that we stepped away from that terrace
As onto a mountain ledge not long after that moment,
Even though the air felt gentle and the comforting colours
Back there in the room seemed immune to the darkening evening.

Our midsummer became dangerous at that moment.
Such seasons don't stay untouched, and keep the same colours.
Our futures required us on the terrace of that last evening.

339   *Blank Page Between*

Like an unexpected No Man's Time between fear
And some activity dispelling fear

Like a joyful second known on a short walk
To the Post Office or the Co-op, or like a talk

On a telephone suddenly turning
Much happier when a repeated joke is earning

An old friend's laughter, as if he'd never
Heard it before (he being ever-

polite and sensitive, infallibly there
Any day or place, always ready to outstare

The gaze of the passing Princess from her carriage,
Offering death and marketing it as marriage).

Impatient about large things, he loved small,
A tall man who was thought to be easily angered,
But turned out gentle to meet.
                          The pebbles on the beach,
The words on the chimney breast, the hedgerow
Flowers he lived long enough still to find,
He loved those.
                   The vanity, the inflated fame,
The poetry elbowed to the front of the little crowd,
The empty vessel's charisma
                          – He hated them.
What he did all his life was say Look, Look,
When the world was forcing its own pictures on our eyes,
But remember: *Think* while you look.
                                    This was 'serious'
Intelligence (to use a usage he would not
Have liked) . . . But he could also be outrageous.
– Am I right to think:
                      that *in the puritan nineteen-fifties*,
He persuaded a producer to induce an actor
To say it fast, and with no one writing to complain,
The small word 'cunt' was first broadcast? On the Third?

341 *The Alcohol*

The two modes: first the dull and logical
That belongs to morning; and then the second,
The desirable tinted mode of early evening,
Where you smile and you wonder . . . After all,
Was that penny-plain other one really so useful?
Or just a flat version of what has come later on,
A mode that grasps and simplifies whatever
It can touch? And whatever it can't counts as not
Worth touching anyway?
                                    You can walk out on its ice
Forgetting its thinness, and even allow some tears
Of what's called 'generous emotion' to drop
And turn into ice-sculptures. And then there is
A third mode, if or when the ice –

342 *Liaison and Carroll*

I

Here is a corridor cleared to become
A narrowing perspective of doors fixed open
Going forward to a culmination where the sun,
Dropping down through skylights, points to an obvious answer.
– But you know rather well that there is a problem:
There's an apprehension of certain events about
To happen all over again, and it does not please you.

Yet you walk it like a lord of grand indoor distances
Who can conjure up unseen respectful glances
From a hundred fallen-silent side-offices
– Until at the sunlit end, and its special room
With the fruit bowl finely replenished alongside
The Book of Dreams rectangularly open
At Name and Signature and Comments, you turn back.

II

She said, 'Has one as young as me
    Done this with you before?'
He said, 'If you would quietly close
    The estuary door,

'I shall relate a circumstance
    I'd rather not explain
Within two miles of anyone
    Who caught the Oxford train.

'It was an hour of deepest dark
    One sunny afternoon,
I pleaded with her, "No, not yet,"
    But she was saying, "Soon!"

'We lay below the celery hedge,
    She gripped me hard and wept,
"You made a hidden vow to me
    An oyster would have *kept!*"

'I said, "That was not me but you,
    And one vow is absurd,
And are you sure you did not make
    A second and a third?

"We pledged to keep them secret so
    That each might know the facts
Who questions us, infers, or hints
    Or adds up and subtracts?"

'I was her next, she was my last,
    The others said the same,
But others still just looked away
    Or played a safer game.

'And when we stopped, to our relief
    We had not done the worst.
 – It was her fortieth birthday and
    Next day my thirty-first.'

343   *Through Glass*

I have gone by too quickly for only
a second sharply catching the two men
through two walls of glass the bus window's
and the café's where they sit in a fierce crouch
facing each other with strip light falling
across their small glass cups as if there were
still something in them while one of the two
is lifting his own with hope in the silence of
their defeated staring down at a table top
itself made of glass but without a pattern
or anything underneath it to stare out
while outside the feet go patrolling past
at dawn and in twilight perpetually
towards what the two think close in on their short lives
like punctuation marks: satisfactions.

344   *The Ghostly Regions*

There are some left, some ghostly, ghastly regions
    Crossed by stale stopping trains where many seats
Are occupied by pale purposeless poor, and by silent
    Unremembered girls found later dismembered
By Senior Citizens sauntering back from the bingo
    In black bags in alleyways, or shallowly buried
In woodland frequented frequently by rapists
    Descended from decent cheerful chapelgoers.

One such was Melissa, meticulous in arithmetic, always
    Achieving praise for perfection when she presented sums
To the lovely Miss Wolfenden, weary at the teacher's task.
    And she spelt superbly, and her geography projects
Were never less than neat, and chastely coloured.
    She would settle down to be, and be seen to be,
A suitable silent spouse for a friend in her form,
    It being obvious there was no better option.

It was not as if she was utterly unaware
    Of her elder brother's brackish activities.
Insofar as she thought, she thought them unimportant.
    So her parents placed her, they put her down with a frown
As a plain, private girl . . . she'd come to no horrible harm.
    Not for her the coarse canal, near that banal
Locality called 'the Loveys' where local lovers
    Would go and be mocked at by prurient-curious children . . .

– And one day Melissa was found – staying late in the Library
    Rejecting the ruffian who avidly approached her
And rested a rigid hand on her shapely shoulder
    Suggesting a droll little stroll in the brisk bright weather
To the worst of the hairy havens where all hope withered,
    – Found with eyes down on Emily Dickinson, read with dread
For the first timely time – seized and studied,
    To shake herself fatefully free of that breathing shadow.

345 *Sonnet from the Utopian*

The Glitch who live in Paronomasia
Suffer for that. As do the Latitudini
Under the Puritanians, whose Holy Days are
All seven, except for Tuesday.

                  And you should pity
The poor Puritanians in the Glitchian part
Of Latitudinaria, who have to bear
Contempt from both peoples, and practise their art
In secret and in solitude.

             And, oh despair,
Despair, you gentle Arcadians! Loathed by them all
For your emphasis on Mortality, *Et in
Arcadia ego*, etc.

          We Utopians shield
Ourselves from such ridiculous feuds, and shall
Stay safe as chameleons are safe, set in
Strange ways of changing colours and being concealed.

346 *A Day in 1966*

I was ambling up from the Lower Annexe
– As distinct from the 'Upper' or 'First' Annexe built
With the flood of funding that also appointed me –
And along the covered uphill walkway between
The Library and the new Biology Lab
When I saw, as I passed the Senior Kitchen window,
The girl with her hair on fire.

The Principal Lecturer in Cookery, the President
Of the Junior Common Room, the Netball
Vice-Secretary and various beautiful
Young girl – or 'woman' – students (as we were starting
To describe them) were just standing round and looking
– That being the one-tenth second in which
They had heard the howl, and turned, and seen

But hadn't moved. Oh god, Jane's hair,
Is a scream of flame – I have to reach –
Reach her – All they do is stand and watch.
And then I am pushing through the heavy outer door
Of the Senior Kitchen, and through the lobby where
The coats are left, and Jane's howling head
Is being smothered in a coarse white apron

Grabbed from a proximate peg by Victoria
At the Principal Lecturer's shouted instruction.
– Out of which Jane's face comes finally
In a sudden trembling rictus of distress
I have seen before, but might not say when or why,
And with an indrawn Oh of astonishment
Staring at me. And what am I doing there?

347   *Top Down*

Roof Terrace: There are white mountains;
                       And cranes, waiting by the new
                       Cultural Centre.

Ninth Floor: Nominal armchairs . . .
                       Well you could use them of course,
                       If the lift was late.

Eighth Floor: I'm telling my life
                       To last year's blonde chambermaid,
                       In stupid detail.

Seventh Floor: Atmosphere peaceful
                       – Until the lift opens and
                       I get, *Good morning!*

445

Sixth Floor:	I'm a non-smoker In this 'Smoking Zone'. Why should The air be this clear?
Fifth Floor:	In an old armchair An old person sleeps. Well, say An old lady, yes?
Fourth Floor:	(She'd opened her eyes And needed the lift, I had To help her, so make
Fourth Floor:	A second attempt): Red-cloaked cleaners sing, and scour A shining new space.
Third Floor:	I touch a drooping Cactus. It droops farther still. Must I feel guilty?
Second Floor:	My own floor, with three Christian tracts on the table. Not mine. Nobody's.
First Floor:	The lift opens on A depiction of my head, Top half: hair, eyes, nose.
Mezzanine:	These days no chairs. Just An old pool table, ripped at The starting spot. Life.
Ground Floor:	I sink on a couch. Who else would sink on a couch Except haikuphiles?

(for, and about, Peter Porter)

1

It was the thank god not 'youthful' nineteen-fifties,
Before the Teenage Consumer; but even so
It was hard to imagine being thirty. 'This is
My first year of middle age,' a writer I know
Was saying about achieving twenty-nine . . .
One night, as we left the Stockwell basement room
And scanned the next week's songsheets in the shine
From the concrete streetlamps, seven rockers with a zoom
Of gleaming new machines buzzed and bellowed
Past along the dark street; and were younger
Even than we were. 'Thom Gunn's gang
Have followed us here,' you decided.

2

                              Our shared anger
I recall next, some time in (as they now require)
Our 'thirty-somethings'. We were waiting
Nervously, to read at the Royal Court, while a dire
Contemporary went on and on orating,
Overrunning. 'I've got the Christ-shits!' you declared
In the shabby wings darkness; and I heard a liquid noise
Of something hitting the boards, and hardly dared
To think what it was – in fact nothing worse
Than your g and t, spilt from a trembling hand.
But at last the man stopped, and you finally strode out
To the confident footlights and took your stand
On Sydney Cove and Rilke. Without any doubt
Your hilarious, erudite, impeccable
Act was the best that night.

3

Christmas! the very
Word is like a kick in the most vulnerable
Areas of consciousness. And, a scary
Prospect, the TA14 was (I could hear)
Making dangerous noises, an elegant intention
Gone for nothing. I was alone, in a year
All connections seemed in temporary suspension;
So to get invited over to Cleveland Square
Was a better prospect than I could have dreamt.
I drove across there on a crest of rare
Optimism, stressed out and unkempt
But hoping that I could forget it all.
Which I did, with Bruckner's Ninth and what I'd just bought:
Stravinsky's modern take on a Bach chorale:
Von Himmel Hoch, his variations on the same.
I also recall you on the life of the alligator
As 'the new business cosmology, the way the game
Will be played in the seventies'. Two days later
The Alvis finally cracked up on the A4.

4

The nineteen-seventies came. By then, the zeitgeist
Was worse still. When asked – 'I wouldn't open my door
To a knock on a stormy night to: Jesus Christ
As shown in *The Light of the World*, King Lear
Of course, or –' I forget the third. Your terse reply
Helped me slog on through each degrading year
Of the nineteen-eighties, with their vast supply
Of trios on which to slam the door very hard.
Cruel? But not serious; though I learnt to know
That this was the kind of game one always played
With tact and caution – best always not to show
Too much contempt of icons, be too satiric:
Some people think that Elton John is *singing*,
Some can sit straight-faced through a Bob Dylan lyric.

I know I *can* see either of us flinging
Our generous front doors open, unsuspicious,
Kind, and hospitable to literally any
Example of humanity, real or fictitious:
'Come in, Sir David . . . Lisa, I'm honoured! – *Tony!*'

5

And when I am complained at for making light
Of what I maintain isn't worth the sweat –
Costume serials switched off, rock reviews binned on sight –
Sometimes going so far as to say 'Forget
The lower opuses of even the best',
I cite to myself my emphatic conclusion –
'You set your sights higher than practically all the rest' –
On that early-nineties night at the High Commission,
I had sat there looking round without surprise
At an audience with its share of famous faces
Grounded firmly on the shores of compromise
(There I go again!) and had thought, 'The firm traces
Your two feet leave have invariably been
Set in the one camp: with those for whom an art
Mattered more than life, almost, yet are always seen
By those valuing life to have played a large part
In making it more liveable.'
                              Our twenty-first
Century may not be much more improving
Than the one we still inhabit, surely the worst
So far for the wide scope of cold, unloving
Acts done in the name of tribe, or god, or bank
– Or focus group these days – whatever will contribute
Celebrity, power or profit. Listing those I thank
For upsizing art and life, I soon arrive
At your name; and your honest feet now turned
Towards an eighth decade, irrevocably come
Ten months before we all go, praised or spurned,
Up the Shit Creek of the Millennium.

349   *On the Television*

They come at you getting larger all the time,
The vast obscurities; and cloudier, even though
You can tell those are lips and eyes and cease
To look.
        Do we need to live with endless
Coloured grains that won't respond to talk or touch?

Won't respond any more than the eyes and lips of lovers,
With their breathless dotted faces closing in
Wanting love you can't provide?
                     I'm told there is
A handset to switch them off with . . . Can't I tell it
From an electric razor, or a mobile phone?

350   *The Presentation*

She becomes aware of the men around her bed
– The four of them edging up with blue,
Mauve, red and yellow bunches – when one has said,
As she opens her eyes and is plainly seeing them,
'There you go, young woman, all for you
With our love and thanks. Get well, Deb – soon!'
                     The hem

Of the scarlet curtain doesn't keep out the sun
At half-past five; so she wants it pulled, and that
Is done by one. One unwraps the flowers. And one
Goes for scissors to do surgery on the stalks.
Then the cheerfullest, the fourth, in his bobble hat,
Leans down to kiss her, after which he walks

Away up the ward to fetch vases so that each
Can fill and arrange a vase and lodge it there
On her locker, brightly. Then they smile and reach
A hand out, one by one, to her warm long hand,
And stand back to attention, a rigid pair
On either side of her.
                              We can understand

How they all thought this could have been a funeral
They'd come to say goodbye at – but oh, was not –
With the flowers and that; then it sneakily came to all,
And at the same moment, that this was about Life
– Which Deb was for enhancing . . . And so what,
If every man there had a job, and wife?

Hell, for an hour they'd switched their meters off.

351 *Sonnet: Her Husband*

The surgeon spends his weekdays saving bodies.
On some week-ends he climbs into his car
(Leaving his wife behind) and among the trees
Of a particular forest fairly far

From hospital and home, he tracks and shoots
Wild boars. The hunters hire men in black boots
To haul away the bodies, and they expect
To have to bury most of them . . .
                                        Am I correct

To think his colleagues disapprove, concerned –
As he is – with ideas of saving life?
No, I am not. But it's true about his wife.

She can't see how his weekdays should have earned
This kind of leisure, taken with no distress.
– She and I think he is a moral mess.

352 *Trade-in*

I sit in what they call a 'screen' adoring
The colonisation of death by luxury:
The thousand-dollar hair will last for ever,
The stretch limousine drives on even though 'a storm
Of fire engulfs it', as the voice-over says
In the TV report. I survive, and watch
Two rescuers run along a girder, inventions
The world will validate quite soon enough.
The drinks in the cabinet will go on even longer,
They are like the divorces, called on at any time
To renew the life the long-lost marriages
Were once contracted to renew.
                                        But wait – Look – Now –
It's the end at last. Here's the sunset, creeping us out
To darkness over the sea while the credits
For Platonic Productions roll up in pure gold,
An everlasting list of timeless names.
I get up with my own name and feel mortal
Trading all this in for the street outside.

353 *Testamentary*

I

I sit discussing notional death, stared down
By rows of unread tomes and the tall frown
Of the lawyer who owns all those titles in legal gold.
He's just thought to ask: *Now, if I might be so bold*
– If you went under a bus today, seeing that you
Haven't changed this clause, would you want your residue
To go to Flicky? . . . I pause . . . *Well, tell me in due course.*
– And it seems to me that things might get even worse
If more chance deaths came to cancel all this out,
Not just my own, but Flicky's . . . Even, no doubt
My interlocutor's – any of us could meet
Our ultimate bus on the uncongested street

Downstairs; on which, in a dream that very night,
I stand half-dazed in a curious pale light
And gaze across the road at a cemetery
Going on and on from his office right to the sea:
Cross on white cross on unmarked plain white cross,
And none of them due to an accidental bus.
At the seaside, my lawyer and a woman friend
– Christ, it's *Flicky*! – swim towards me from out near the end
Of the pier, transformed and harmless. And I feel fine,
Now I see that none of my residue can be theirs,
Merman and mermaid having no legal heirs.

II

The two sly faces stare across the restaurant
In the direction of a third, thinking they see
Flicky sitting there – what a great coincidence!
The third has no idea why especially she

Is being gazed at, it's one of her paranoid days:
The sun rose late for her alone, lunch is
Served horribly because they knew she was coming.
And then, in the freezing dusk, her toboggan crunches

On a snow-covered rock . . . At Reception, a girl
Who has slept with the casino manager and can map
The unlucky ones a mile off, induces her to
The tables out of loyalty to her chap

– And she goes, and loses.
                              But under the same rock
Is gold, and under the gold a codicil
By some circuitous circumstance providing
For her to *inherit* this land. And so she will

Be wealthy through a careless codicil
When the casino manager dies in the girl's bed:
He has unknowingly willed his residue
To this unknown distant cousin, not having said

Some words to his lawyer to prevent all that.

It would

Be wonderful, the two faces are assuming,
If that *were* Flicky and not just her look-alike.
– They should stop, and remember what's always looming

To alter lives; and not upset with their staring
This one who will board a train of grand events.
She can see them staring, now, so she looks away
And picks at her food with wronged indifference.

354 *Sea-change*

I saw a sea-change that came suddenly,
As they are not supposed to. In the three
Miles or so between Brancaster and where
The North Sea becomes the Wash, the large share
The saltmarsh takes of the landscape finishes
Abruptly in dunes and reeds, diminishes
To mud and sand behind the rising banks
Which keep the ocean back. Beyond them, ranks
Of breakwaters split the waves, cargoes of rocks
Held together by wire meshes. There the sea knocks
And goes away answered and forbidden, sent
Back to the hectares of its own element.
In stretches of this coast it stays like that,
The wind-wrought beach surviving vast and flat,
Not drawn away by ravagements of tide.
This is a place where sour soil has defied
Water – and grown. Because dark grass has spread
Where distant sea has left the beach for dead,
And samphire, growing here in shifting mud,
Not in high cliff-face crevices, can bud
And flourish, threaded with salt but green,
A nominal reclamation; though, where the sea has been
It can come back. Incautious man may find
Sea-change does not exclude a change of mind.

355   *At 5.30*

(for Peter Scupham)

they are leaving
The consultant's recommendations
And the boss's interpretations.

It's all about
The carefreeness of the body having
The evening before it, the day behind,

Though still the consultant's bending
Over his computer, sending
Them off next day like ball-bearings

Up the groove of the machine
To start the helpless casual roll
Down the slope which lights no scores.

There's really a regress in their going
From this hope to home; but they feel,
At evading consultant and boss,

No dread of betraying them, and no vast
Sense of loss, just a sort
Of residual guilt felt faintly.

A sort.

356   *Talking Animals*

Why don't we lie here and make up
New animals, I said to her;

Not thinking that – not consciously –
It was a blatant metaphor.

She left me. And she went and had
Liaison with another chap,

Which in the course of thirteen years
Put various creatures on the map

Who, yes, were new, and animals,
But not the sort *I* would invent . . .

– One's dead, one's rich, and one's still at
The University of Kent.

357   *Heroic Couplets*

On Being About to Commence Reading
Killing Time
by Mr Simon Armitage
(in Transylvania)

I feel compelled to say something in rhyme
Before I start Armitage's *Killing Time*:
Did he *have* to do it, write for t'old folks at t'Dome?
Was it his destiny, fixed in his genome,
That my young Gregory prizewinner should come
To bow down to the New Millennium
Experience Company? Take their Euro-shilling
And spend long starless midnight hours just filling
Screen after screen with longish lines and shorter,
Counting up to a thousand? Intrigued, I bought a
Copy to read it on a Balkan train . . .

I was en route for Târgu Mureş. Not
A bad choice, the book seemed at a first look,
When I found a seat after Miercurea Ciuc.
Yet the reason why much in-your-face poetry
Doesn't appeal to veteran lags like me
Is not its vein of brutal emphasis,
But that its custard pies too often miss
– Unlike the young man in the busy station
At Sfântu Gheorghe where, to the consternation
Of the other passengers he took a leap
At a train as it gathered speed, didn't keep
An eye out for footholds, managed to get
His hands on two bars at shoulder level, set
His left foot to find the carriage step – and failed,
Looked as if he would fall. Gypsy girls wailed
In horror, thinking they'd see him carried
Under the train, and mutilated ('Married,
With two young children, Mr Nagy Bela,
Whose friends said he could be "a daring feller,
But too rash sometimes", died of the injuries
To his back and hips, his ankles and his knees
He suffered trying to jump a moving train,'
The newspaper would say). Then we saw him gain
The merest toe-grip on the metal ledge
Under the carriage door, and on the edge
Of catastrophe drew back, all in a second
Turning away from where his death had beckoned,
Hauling himself to safety.

                              So what's it for,
This long sub-Virgilian metaphor
Derived from what I'd witnessed? Undertaking
To chart a year in verse resembles making
A dash at a moving train to get a hold
On something solid as it speeds up – bold,
But pretty risky. Though the idea appeals,
You could easily get dragged under the wheels
Of the fastest moving century so far,
And one of the most untidy and bizarre.

Nineteen ninety-nine, one of the worst years yet,
Saw Third World nations stuck in deeper debt
To the IMF, who said, please suffer more.
Until you do, we can't be really sure
That you want to 'modernise', 'reform' and be
Part of the great global economy.
Dams must be built, children must die and thank
The WTO and the World Bank
For the opportunity. Drought and flood
Will decimate with wafting sand and mud
The Sudan and Mozambique; although
We'll splash out cash for bombs on Kosovo,
Belgrade and Novi Sad, oh dear, there's no
Way we can, when it's Africa, fly in
Not cluster bombs, but food and medicine.

Well, then – On your marks, Simon . . . Get set . . . *Go!*

'I can say that Darren has been different
Since he started seeing you,' his father says
To Maria, the Andorran meteo-chick.
'You must not be offended that I first thought
You might not be the best sort of influence.
But he has changed, and it must be due to you.'

Maria nods and smiles. 'I come', she replies,
'From a little-known country to a well-known place.
Your Darren has been a firm location for me,
As I, I venture to think, may have been for him'
(Though that line she does only think, doesn't say out loud)
'And he's passed in all his subjects!'
                                        'Seven A's,'

Replies the father, 'and one B which I believe
By rights should have been an A. In geography,
Which is his best subject. We shall appeal,
As you might expect'. And then he leaves
A very slight pause before he says, 'I notice
You are pregnant, by the way. The change of climate?'

359   *Saturday Afternoon*

The helicopter stuck like a trapped fly
In desperate buzzing circles, every eye
In Hampstead High Street wondering exactly
What it was doing. Tersely, matter-of-factly,
A young man I asked said there had just now been
'Two guys raiding the chemist's – they've been seen
And reported via 999. They ran
Into the flats behind the Everyman'
– Where, indeed, five white police cars flashing lights
Are drawn up in the cul-de-sac. Such sights

Seem more connected with a larger sin
Than nicking aspirin or shampoo, and in
Our crazed and fathomless world, who knows
Precisely what transgression meant that those
'Resources were deployed', and at what cost?
What had the chemist actually lost
To justify those forces? What dark potion,
Lethal or psychedelic, caused a commotion
Bringing half Hampstead to a sudden stop
To catch two raiders running from a shop?
Shake the kaleidoscope: all goods mean crime,
And shape a different pattern every time.

360   *Up There*

He could not help seeing their love as like
Two solid-seeming clouds that had blended too suddenly

And left only other people's unsure recall
Of the shapes they had seen in their sky some moments before.

How can two confections of mist unlock themselves
And be distinct again? And live on like that?

And if that is possible, how to require all those others
To see them as separate? As if they had not been one?

361   *Ten Riffs for 2001*

(for John Mole at sixty)

<u>D</u>on't chew it t<u>O</u>o much after dusk, th<u>E</u>n it'<u>S</u> in with a chance

the ambient bedroom: air condi<u>T</u>ioning braces, storage <u>H</u>eating
relaxes. Choose a brand that adapts to eith<u>E</u>r option

but order another as insurance: Sign here, Please tick the box
bElow if you wish your signAture not to be foRged for all purchases
Made In the new millenNium (visit our websiTe)

in the night, dreaming is beLieving! All yOur friendS are flExible

commercial: 'taste ours by e-maLl' . . . (but remember, 'e' sTands for
exceSs)

'your Future without some? Like a tate modern full of bAseball
caps who drink from Vast bOttles of water, and talk Unaware into
mobiles for eveR'

the small hOurs . . . dark Night of the soul in sugar-free withdrawal
. . .

except, well, The tecHnology might be hElpful –

BelievE me, its wonDers surPass belief. You could recOnstitute the
original from Some dna lefT on that brass ball . . .

and on the horizOn at dawn, isn't that a Virtual unchEwed fResh
pastille? An oblong of oNgoing lIfe standinG by to Help if all
opTimism fails?

362   *Found Object*

An unused route back from the beach . . . But there,
A car, stopped; and a dog run over, where
The road curved . . . No – it was a teddy bear!
And we moaned with relief, having assumed
It was a dead, once living, animal, doomed
To die under the wheels of the fast car
Whose driver was hauling it into the verge, not far
From where he had hit it.

461

It had lain splayed out,
With button eyes and open arms, without
Moving, abandoned in some child's small rage,
Throwing it from a car-window . . . Typical gauge,
We thought, of its value: Not a well-loved friend,
Just a dull chattel bought for it; not the end
Of a lifelong devotion, just of a brief phase
As an expensive novelty, a silly craze
Terminated in a moment.
                That was what
We thought as we drew closer to the spot
And saw the creature lying on the verge
Where the motorist had placed it. One feels a surge
At times like this, of various inclinations:
Leave it exposed to the depredations
Of rain and wind? . . . Place a helpful card
In the nearest store window? . . . It was very hard
To decide what was best . . . If it was truly missed,
And grieved for, if it was hugged each night and kissed
Before its owner slept, they would return,
The whole pining family, search hard, and earn
Their reward in finding it safe and sound
On this grass verge of a lane propped on a mound
Of overgrown earth in everybody's view,
So that it would be seen.
                Then there came a new
Slant on the whole thing: what if it had been thrown
Quite deliberately? What if it could be shown
Its owner realised that its striking size
Ensured it would be seen by other eyes
Delighted to adopt it; thus, either way,
This toy would find its old/new home today.
And so on . . . We left it.
                And, as we half-expected,
Within two hours the bear had been collected.

363   *Parole*

(i.m. I. H.)

The lately dead still arrive in the corner of your eye
Past the restaurant window, preparing slow smiles of pride
At achieving their return. They know that without them
You can never be the same, so they cheat for a while.
They keep trying to work a parole to the usual places,
They won't be excluded from them if you are there.

Their fingers have pressed the latch and the door nearly opens,
But then their smile turns embarrassed because they find
It behaves like a turnstile: they think they have admission,
But this door is fixed to prevent them coming back in.
And you just can't help, at all; if you went out to greet them
They would not be there, no one in the street would have seen them.

Then slowly the corner of your eye
Forgets to look.

364   *ANAC 2004*

Suddenly into the hugeness of the Tourist Hotel
Arrive three-hundred-and-twenty archaeologists,
The Annual National Archaeological Congress.

                                        At breakfast,
I ask in faltering parody of their language,
'Why are you here?' 'To excavate an ancient historical site,'
Is the reply of the man whose badge reveals
He is 'Professor Szkrvzc'.

One local paper
Writes with a similar message. The other rag,
The organ of the other ethnicity,
Says, 'That's a lie, faithful readers. They are here
In an arrantly dishonest endeavour to prove
That this terrain was, in the earliest times, the home
Of the ancestors of the present minority,
Who thus can claim it as theirs, old pots and sherds
Will show it beyond doubt, that's what they hope . . .'

I ask no more questions of individuals,
But next day go and stand in unseasonal rain,
And watch the insistent digging going on
In the search for ancient tools and artefacts
Made with much more desire to cultivate, and eat,
Than to validate future boundaries,
And watch their eyes as they prise away hard clay
From potentially momentous bits and pieces,
Or just other hunks of harder ancient clay,
And listen in case there are sudden cheers (which there aren't)
At discovering something wonderful which provides
A much-desired political revelation

– And recall the words Albert Camus used in
A story I used to read to grammar school boys
Fifty years ago, before the latest troubles,
Though long after Hamlet's father and the Polacks
Went out on the frozen wastes to smite each other,
With many articulate sons dead because of that:
Camus on the 'rotten spite, the tireless hates,
The blood lust of all men'.

365   *At Natalie's*

An arm reached round a shoulder and not removed,
A long kiss taken freely on closed lips
– She knew they meant much more than two feet spread
Three feet apart at the end of a kitchen roll.

So this was the convention enforced at Natalie's:
All tenderness was forbidden, act or word.
It couldn't be listed, priced, or done with screams
For extra payment, topless or quite stark.

It meant real names, and meetings out of bounds.
It did not go with her pictures, rugs, or lamps . . .
It was such innocence, such wasted energy . . .
She required it to be as rare there as anywhere.

366   *Entertainments*

Here's the TV and here's the handset lying
Alongside . . . After half-an-hour defying
My techno-incapacity, I can show
Anyone how to work this, how to go
Through the different recondite symbols on
The buttons, and get it working. – And there's one
Hell of a girl on! Stripping to next-to-nothing
As a band plays a tripping little theme. In a sing-

song voice she says Thank you, *thank you*, for the applause.
Then a boy brings a basket, there's a short pause
While she takes the lid off and dips a hand inside
To produce her accomplice, which has tried
Not to get involved, but . . . This big tabby cat
She sets on a step-ladder, gives a gentle pat
To its furry finale – And look! It doesn't stop
Until it's climbed up to the very top,

Where it perches – and leaps safely into her arms.
None of this folly actually harms
The cat, its owner, the manager, or the audience
– Which then claps again – but the whole experience
Leaves me concerned about the small extra ozone gap
It tears out of the already mottled map
Of the atmosphere of consciousness . . .

How I feel the lack

Of old maypoles, just to dance round. Bring them back.

367   *Brazier*

We have brought out the brazier because the brute
   Heads are hectoring again,
And the rat-eyes in the heads are re-checking old reels
   For invidious information.

Small brains behind the eyes are trying to find
   Grey traces of the faces
In the crowd that created confusion during that last
   – Inconclusive – confrontation.

The money behind the memory tracking the moment
   Recorded on audio
When conniving voices were caught in the corridor after
   That 'deplorable demonstration'

Has paid for the dismal devices designed
   To nest in walls neatly,
And listen, and for the CC equipment eyeing
   Long delays over defecation

In the interim. Touch these inserted instruments
   If you could, they would be cold.
Touch the brazier with brute money, take your hand
   Back in consternation.

A tannoy is bellowing bald and brutal advice:
    'Damp the brazier down,
Save your jobs, save your families, save the nation.
    Stay in negotiation.'

– 'What? Get ripped off, and hassled and harried?
    Left stranded, and empty-handed,
And nearly run down on the line? That's fine!
    That's some salvation!'

'Our brazier settles and glows as the drear day darkens.
    Come over and open your own
Empty hands, warm them, feel the strength of fire
    In its proper station.'

368   *Ending my Seventy-third Year*

The urbanity of these fine foreign waiters,
The daunting deferential speech and stance:

They will cap your Tibullus tags, guess your Florence churches,
Complete your hummings of twelve-tone string quintets.

In my nineteen-ninety-six new suit, giving now
At sundry seams, I aspire to their faultless mien…

Or such is the last deep personal emotion
I remember two hours later in the night air

Stumbling off the final escalator home.
Very deep. Very personal. Except the deference.

369   *Overlaps*

For twenty-two years it was the Old Dog Restaurant.
For twenty-two years Karl stood at the door by the dog

To welcome you in and show you to Lula's tables.
Young impressionists crowded into the Old Dog.

One day without notice it was the New Dog Bistro,
With new, smiling dog, no welcome and different decor;
But Lula still worked there so I stayed with it.
Old Karl was in the background and I was happy.

New people sat at the beautiful Loramine's tables,
They were post-impressionists.
                              Then after sixteen years
It refurbished as the Brand New Hound Attitude:
No dog, no service, fast food through a hatch;

Though Loramine, in charge, kept Lula who remembered Karl
And didn't get on with the neo-Brit nihilists
Who more or less carved up the place for about four years.
Until – Well then I myself stopped going back…

Some managing hand had managed to hand it on
To a lifestyle beyond description or definition,
A dysfunctional game-plan that linked with nothing before
And wanted nothing after, an anti-dog mode.

I had spent three adolescences in thrall
To those three regimes, no wish for a fourth
Without Karl, without Lula, without even Loramine
And the dogbite scar on her left leg, above the knee.

The place is still part of me, as 'my spiritual home'.
Though the food when you ate it was lousy, it did become
More edible with nostalgia.
                              I see old Loramine
And she often recalls 'dear Lula, dear old Karl.' I say,

'Like me, you need overlaps to go on living.'

(for John Cooney and Catherine Sutton)

1.   Sure there is music even in the beauty, and the silent note which Cupid strikes, far sweeter than the sound of an instrument. For there is music where ever there is a harmony, order or proportion and thus far we may maintain the music of the spheres. – Sir Thomas Browne, *Religio Medici*, 9.

2.   The music of beauty, of silence, of Cupid, is finer
        Than when castanets are snapped or marimbas tapped,
        There is music in all things harmonised or ordered,
        There is music in proportion, and in the spheres
        – Are we speaking of music – or analogies music provides?

3.   There is sure music even in
                The music of the spheres thus far
                – Far sweeter than the silent note
                For which an instrument (we may
                Maintain) strikes a proportion. And
                Where ever order is there is
                The beauty or the sound of – *there*:
                Music and Cupid! Harmony!

4.   How to 'maintain' the music of the spheres?
        Support the silence ringing in our ears?
        – Block all intrusive sound that interferes?
        Nod our assent while that far screaming sears
        Our consciousness?
                        The stern old doctor went
        To no small trouble striving to invent
        Reasons for thinking music best when sent
        Down from the spheres . . . Surely it's evident
        Music requires a *human* instrument?

5.   a an and and
       beauty
       Cupid

       even ever
       far far for

       harmony
       in instrument is is is

       music music music
       note
       of of or order
       proportion

       silent sound spheres strikes sweeter sure
       than the the the the the there thus

       we where which

6.   spheres the of music the maintain may we far thus and pro-
portion or order harmony a is there ever where music is there for
instrument an of sound the than sweeter far strikes Cupid which
note silent the and beauty the in even music is there sure

7.

sure	for	spheres
there	there	music
is	is	even
in	where	beauty
the	there	silent
and	is	Cupid
the	a	sweeter
note	or	music
which	and	ever
strikes	thus	order
far	far	maintain
than	we	music

470

the	may	instrument
sound	the	harmony
of	of	proportion
an	the	

8.   And there, where ever Cupid strikes, we may maintain the sound of a far instrument – or music! Thus even the note of the spheres is music for which, in the silent and the sure harmony, there is proportion sweeter than order. The far music there is beauty.

9.   The serenades relayed by antique clocks,
The slowing tinkle of a music box,
The shaken handbell of the muffin man,
The childhood chiming of the ice cream van
– These seem nostalgic and acceptable.
Problems began when it became the rule
To follow us with jingling everywhere,
When, day and night, in buses, boats or trains
You have to hear some bland melodious strains,
Endure the comfort of a background drone
To reassure you you are not alone . . .
It's such a pleasure to have mus*a*c dropping
Into your ears wherever you are shopping
So nice to hear – five times – Vivaldi's Spring
While waiting for some 'direct line' to ring
– Hullo – you've reached Amanda – bear with me
While I play you the Haffner symphony . . .

10.   If the power fails, don't worry
– We use the spheres as a generator.
We also rent out music for the tannoys of Hell
If you don't believe us and think there *is* no Hell,
Click on us and we'll install one.

11.   'At last we might get some decent music,'
The poet is said to have said; not speaking of Cupid,
But of the Prussian armies striking at Paris.

12. [silent]

13.   But is beauty only to be praised with silence?
    This sounds like someone who prefers love to music,
    Whereas Signor Puccini – or his librettist –
    Was in favour of both and preferably together.
    And there's something contradictory in the way
    He assigns to the harmony, order and proportion of the world
    The properties of music, as if music existed before *they* did.
    He almost concedes that art is what gives the world structure.

14.   And where was the *voice* in all this?
        The voice is missing from his reasoning.
        The bow itself may be silent, but surely after
        The arrow strikes the beauty wakes up
        And is vocal in delight? So isn't
        The voice also an instrument, most pure,
        Most delicate, most intimate, most sure
        – Sure – Sure – Sure –

15.   Sure there is music even in the beauty, and the silent note which Cupid strikes, far sweeter than the sound of an instrument. For there is music where ever there is a harmony, order or proportion: and thus far we may maintain the music of the spheres.

371   *Marechiare,*

By Tosti. Lousiest of love songs, and on Radio Three
At that! But my finger pauses an inch
Away from the button because I've remembered something.
I've remembered my daily journey to that school
In the late nineteen-fifties, with that colleague

In the same eight-seat compartment, smog-stained windows,
Soiled upholstery, seaside pictures, Elmers End,
Eden Park, West Wickham, Hayes. All the time,

My companion, the cynical music master,
Would drone and hum and smile and apologise

– Lesson preparation. The suburban landscape
Would modulate through Macmillan's constituency
From inner to outer, and 'You could call that *countryside*,
For a yard or two,' he'd say. And throughout one week,
When we had the Parents' Evening on the Friday,

Having sung at Glyndebourne, and being capable
Of presenting himself as a decent *tenore robusto*,
He practised Tosti's ballad for the Parents,
Its fustian intro, its maudlin vocal acrobatics . . .
The windows rattled on their leather straps.

Scrubland with never-inhabited workshop ruins.
Golf-course with flags in holes on pallid greens.
– He practised for the Parents as it all went by,
'And who *cares*! Honestly, Brownjohn, who fucking *cares*!'
He would say, with the formality of the age.

At Elmers End, if I'm right, on the Friday morning,
With 'another day opening its squalid legs
For us to squander ourselves in', he got out,
And 'not to ruin your entire bloody journey', he
Climbed into the next compartment, which was empty.

– But now I'm back in the present, my pausing finger
Still allowing the song to go on to its awful end
On the radio fifty years later; and I believe
I can still hear him singing over the slow wheels
That carried us on to a place he said 'didn't deserve us',

His howling impassioned tenor heard through a wall
On which they'd put, as in most of those compartments,
A mirror, a small clear mirror, for combing
Your hair in or pulling your face into shapes
Better suited to facing interviews or girlfriends

473

Or just teaching spelling . . . Which I see myself in today,
As I was at twenty-six and am no longer;
And I find I'm crying at these two swooping voices,
Jim Farr's and Tito Schipa's, reminding me
That like Tosti's fishes I go on 'gasping for love.'

372   *A Scream in 1890*

A scream in the room that goes on for ever, long
Tidy table after table into the distance, my grandmother
Pedals harder suddenly, and stops.
Any time you stopped, you looked at the clock and wondered
Can I rest for a moment and still catch up with the work?
This is five-and-twenty to nine, she remembers
Fifty-two years on.
                    The scream has come
From a girl a long way behind her, a needle
Has gone through somebody's thumb several tables back.
– First, a second so quiet that you could have heard a –

Then other screams, like late echoes. The girl looks at
The thumb pinned down as if it wasn't hers.
Girls from elsewhere crowd round her, they always
Said it would happen, most girls knew someone who'd done it,
It was when you were tired – but then you were always tired.
Why should careful Flora have done it?
                          The overseer
(She thinks it was the word) shoves them all aside –
'Get back to work. No talking!' And takes a look
At the girl, at the thumb, at the blood
Spreading under the nail in the nineteenth-century sunlight.

Obediently no one talks, but they seize
Sidelong glances at each other and sit still.
They can hear his words in the silence before resuming,
Their eyes all going back to their own thumbs.

They can hear what he says, and will always remember the tone
Mr Podmore the overseer uses, applying
The discipline of his own overseers, telling Flora:
Move the wheel *listen* to me move it *yourself*
Move it very slowly slowly as slowly
As you can that's it that's it Are you all right?

373 *Latest*

(for F. N.)

More and more, because they are 'no longer with us',
You catch yourself speaking of 'the late' someone or other.
It distances the young, who often won't
Have heard of the names you proclaim to be unpunctual.
It doesn't help to say 'These "late" were my friends.'
The distance just widens. 'So he has friends who died,
I don't have those, I'm too young', thinks someone or other;
Whom you hope, one day soon, will change it to 'Let's be early.'

374 *Ludbrooke His 1-4-7-1*

No one has phoned him for what seems several days.
Ludbrooke tries one-four-seven-one, the lonely man's friend,
And confirms it, his last call was on the ninth.
'The caller withheld "their" number.' The adjective 'their'
Annoys the pedantic Ludbrooke, who detects yet another
Example of political correctness. If only
A plural of persons *were* phoning Ludbrooke.
The message suggests it was a commercial call.
The commercial callers hate people to phone back,
People might ring back who hate being targeted.
Sometimes Ludbrooke would love to be targeted.
He imagines the short skirt of the targeter walking
Home from the call centre with her mobile off.

to where the last door is held open for her alone
Atalanta is running all the length of the train along
the emptied platform while whistles shriek warnings and
I don't recall forgetfulness ever being
named as the virtue of any classical someone
so believe overlooking the bag containing items
she must have valued more than the train already
missed through stopping to buy them was untypical the truth
is she felt it worth risking the loss of another train
racing back to recover them from the chair next
the one where she sat fifteen minutes before
with her coat draped over it plenty of time
for coffee or so she thought until she turned
looked up at the digital clock and gasping saw
it was late again grabbed her coat failed to pick up
the bag she has just retrieved having had
to leap out of Coach E tear back to the upstairs café
with hardly a minute left find it still there
and clutch it preciously close to her now as I
slam the door shut with the train edging away into
a sunlight we hope will last take her seat again
where she empties the bag arranges them in a row
on the table in front of her like a fruit machine
arbitrarily choosing to be generous picks up
the middle one of these three lemons peels it
with intricate smiling attention and eats it
segment by
segment

List of Subscribers

Dannie Abse
Anna Adams
Fleur Adcock
Kjell Åkerlund & Margareta
  Hansell*
Leo Aylen
Michael Baldwin
Susan Barker
Nina Bawden
Martin & Judy Bax
Stuart & Ann Bayley*
Bernard Bergonzi*
Sonja & John Besford*
John Birtwhistle
David L. Bisset
Sheila Brooks*
Penny Brownjohn*
Nadine Brummer*
Sharon Brunsden (née) Loveday
David Burnett*
Sir Robin & Lady Chichester-
  Clark
David Cooke
John Cooney & Catherine
  Sutton*
Nigel Cragg*
The Revd.Wendy A. Cranidge*
Alison Reeves Cresswell
Kevin Crossley-Holland

Martyn Crucefix
Tim Cunningham
Neil Curry
Peter Dale
Gerald Dawe
Dennis Detweiler
Tom Deveson
Hugh Dickson
Martin Dodsworth
Bernard Donoughue*
Margaret Drabble & Michael
  Holroyd
Dr Alex Drace-Francis
Jane Duran
Alistair & Barbara Elliot
Tony Ellis, Kings Lynn Poetry
  Festival*
Charles Evans
Elisabeth Eyers
U.A. Fanthorpe & Dr R.V.
  Bailey
Peter Faulkner
James Fenton
Eva Figes
Vic & Jean Finlayson*
Kieran Finnegan*
Michael Finnissy*
Duncan Forbes*
Rosie Ford

Stephen & Margaret Freeth*
Jean Overton Fuller
John Fuller*
Richard Furniss*
Carlo Gébler
Bertie Gilbert
Jane Gregg (née Wilson)
Dr F. John Gregory*
Anne Harvey
Jeremy Hawthorn*
Dr David Hay*
Peter C. Hecker
Sonja Henrici
Cicely Herbert
Charles Higgins*
Hannah Hobsbaum-Kelly
Richard Holmes
Jeremy Hooker
Peter Isacké*
Catriona Jarvis*
Claire Jordan*
John R. Kaiser*
Michael & Dorothy Kauffmann
Judith Kazantzis
Sezgin Kemal
Miss M. Kennedy
Patricia Kennedy*
Rosalind Kent
Anne Khazam
Dewi Lewis & Caroline
    Warhurst*
Lilly Library, Indiana University*
Michael Longley
John Loveday
Bill Mason
Donna Maxam
Hank & Barbara McCloughan

J.W. McCormick*
Ian McKelvie*
Stanley Middleton
David James Miles*
Adrian & Celia Mitchell
John & Mary Mole
C. Morey de Morand
Madeline Munro
Alastair Niven*
Paddy Nolan
Betty O'Callaghan*
Sean O'Connor*
Bernard O'Donoghue
Dennis O'Driscoll
Masa Ohtake*
Michael O'Sullivan*
Patricia & William Oxley
Palmers Green Bookshop
Terry P. Pearson
David Pease*
Pennsylvania State University*
Christopher Pilling
Peter Porter
Isobel Primrose
Keith Redman*
Alan Rosenberg*
Tom Rosenthal*
Jon Rosser & Carol Jennings*
Anthony Rudolf, Menard Press
Lawrence Sail
Dennis Saunders
Vernon Scannell
Cecilia Scurfield
Fred Sedgwick*
G.G.T. Stanton*
George Szirtes & Clarissa
    Upchurch

D.M. Thomas

Ann & Anthony Thwaite

A. Trevor Tolley

Shirley Toulson

Don Underwood

Edward Upward

Brenda Walker*

Michelene Wandor

Len Webster*

Sue West

David Whiting

G.B.H. Wightman

Peter Wilkinson

University of Wisconsin,
Madison

Antony Wood

Malcolm Woolgar

Peter Wybrew*